Praise for *The New Rules of Marketing and PR*

"This excellent look at the basics of new-millennial marketing should find use in the hands of any serious PR professional making the transition."

—*Publishers Weekly* (starred review)

"Most professional marketers—and the groups in which they work—are on the edge of becoming obsolete, so they'd better learn how marketing is really going to work in the future."

—BNET, "The Best & Worst Business Books"

"*The New Rules of Marketing and PR* has inspired me to do what I have coached so many young artists to do, 'Find your authentic voice, become vulnerable, and then put yourself out there.' David Meerman Scott expertly and clearly lays out how to use many great new tools to help accomplish this. Since reading this book, I have been excited about truly connecting with people without the filter of all the 'old PR' hype. It has been really energizing for me to speak about things that I really care about, using my real voice."

—Meredith Brooks, Multi-Platinum Recording Artist,
Writer and Producer, and Founder of record label
Kissing Booth Music

"I've relied on *The New Rules of Marketing & PR* as a core text for my New Media and Public Relations course at Boston University for the past six semesters. David's book is a bold, crystal clear, and practical guide toward a new (and better) future for the profession."

—Stephen Quigley, Boston University

"What a wake-up call! By embracing the strategies in this book, you will totally transform your business. David Meerman Scott shows you a multitude of ways to propel your company to a thought leadership position in your market and drive sales—all without a huge budget. I am a huge fan and practitioner of his advice."

—Jill Konrath, Author of *Selling to Big Companies*,
Chief Sales Officer, SellingtoBigCompanies.com

"The Internet is not so much about technology as it is about people. David Meerman Scott, in his remarkable *The New Rules of Marketing and PR*, goes far beyond technology and explores the ramifications of the Web as it pertains to people. He sets down a body of rules that show you how to negotiate those ramifications with maximum effectiveness. And he does it with real-life case histories and an engaging style."

—Jay Conrad Levinson, Father of Guerrilla Marketing
and Author, *Guerrilla Marketing* series of books

"*The New Rules of Marketing and PR* teaches readers how to launch a thought leadership campaign by using the far-reaching, long-lasting tools of social media. It is an invaluable guide for anyone who wants to make a name for themselves, their ideas, and their organization."

—Mark Levy, Co-Author, *How to Persuade People Who Don't Want to Be Persuaded*, and Founder of Levy Innovation: A Marketing Strategy Firm

"*Revolution* may be an overused word in describing what the Internet has wrought, but revolution is exactly what David Meerman Scott embraces and propels forward in this book. He exposes the futility of the old media rules and opens to all of us an insiders' game, previously played by a few well-connected specialists. With this rule book to the online revolution, you can learn how to win minds and markets, playing by the new rules of new media."

—Don Dunnington, President, International Association of Online Communicators (IAOC); Director of Business Communications, K-Tron International; and Graduate Instructor in Online Communication, Rowan University, Glassboro, New Jersey

"The history of marketing communications—about 60 years or so—has been about pushing messages to convince prospects to take some action we need. Now marketing communications, largely because of the overwhelming power and influence of the Web and other electronic communications, is about engaging in conversation with prospects and leading/persuading them to take action. David Meerman Scott shows how marketing is now about participation and connection, and no longer about strong-arm force."

—Roy Young, Chief Revenue Officer, MarketingProfs.com, and Co-Author, *Marketing Champions: Practical Strategies for Improving Marketing's Power, Influence, and Business Impact*

"As someone who has come up through the marketing ranks to run several companies, I've come to realize that the rules I lived by to manage the marketing mix have become obsolete. What David Meerman Scott shows that is so fascinating is that the new rules are actually better than the old rules because they cut through all the communications clutter and myths about big-budget advertising. This book is a must-read for any executive looking to gain a cost-effective edge in marketing operations and to reach buyers directly in ways they'll appreciate."

—Phil Myers, President, Pragmatic Marketing

"David Meerman Scott not only offers good descriptions of digital tools available for public relations professionals, but also explains strategy, especially the importance of thinking about PR from the public's perspectives, and provides lots of helpful examples. My students loved this book."

—Karen Miller Russell, Associate Professor,
Grady College of Journalism and Mass Communication,
University of Georgia

"This is a must-read book if you don't want to waste time and resources on the old methods of Internet marketing and PR. David Meerman Scott reviews the old rules for old times' sake while bridging into the new rules for Internet marketing and PR for your cause. He doesn't leave us with only theories, but offers practical and results-oriented how-tos."

—Ron Peck, Executive Director,
Neurological Disease Foundation

"*The New Rules of Marketing and PR* is all about breaking the rules and creating new roles in traditional functional areas. Using maverick, non-traditional approaches to access and engaging a multiplicity of audiences, communities, and thought leaders online, PR people are realizing new value, influence, and outcomes. We're now in a content-rich, Internet-driven world, and David Meerman Scott has written a valuable treatise on how marketing-minded PR professionals can leverage new media channels and forums to take their stories to market. No longer are PR practitioners limited in where and how they direct their knowledge, penmanship, and perception management skills. The Internet has multiplied and segmented a wealth of new avenues for directly reaching and activating key constituencies and stakeholders. A good book well worth the read by all marketing mavens and aging PR flacks."

—Donovan Neale-May, Executive Director, CMO Council

"*The New Rules of Marketing and PR* provides a concise action plan for success. Rather than focusing on a single solution, Scott shows how to use multiple online tools, all directed toward increasing your firm's visibility and word-of-mouth awareness."

—Roger C. Parker, Author, *The Streetwise Guide to Relationship Marketing on the Internet* and *Design to Sell*

"Once again we are at a critical inflection point on our society's evolutionary path, with individuals wrestling away power and control from institutions and traditional gatekeepers who control the flow of knowledge and maintain the silo walls. As communications professionals, there is little time to figure out what has changed, why it changed, and what we should be doing about it. If you don't start doing things differently and start right now, you may as well start looking for your next career path. In a world where disruption is commonplace and new ways of communicating and collaborating are invented every day, what does it take for a hardworking, ethical communications professional to be successful? David Meerman Scott's book, *The New Rules of Marketing and PR*, is an insightful look at how the game is changing as we play it and some of the key tactics you need to succeed in the knowledge economy."

—Chris Heuer, Co-Founder, Social Media Club

Also by David Meerman Scott

World Wide Rave: Creating Triggers that Get Millions of People to Spread Your Ideas and Share Your Stories

Tuned In: Uncover the Extraordinary Opportunities that Lead to Business Breakthroughs (with Craig Stull and Phil Myers)

Cashing in with Content: How Innovative Marketers Use Digital Information to Turn Browsers into Buyers

Eyeball Wars: A Novel of Dot-Com Intrigue

The New Rules of Marketing and PR

How to Use Social Media, Blogs, News Releases, Online Video, & Viral Marketing to Reach Buyers Directly

Second Edition

David Meerman Scott

WILEY

John Wiley & Sons, Inc.

Published by John Wiley & Sons, Inc., Hoboken, New Jersey.
Published simultaneously in Canada.

For general information on our other products and services please contact our Customer Care Department within the United States at (800) 762-2974, outside the United States at (317) 572-3993 or fax (317) 572-4002.

Wiley also publishes its books in a variety of electronic formats. Some content that appears in print may not be available in electronic books. For more information about Wiley products, visit our web site at www.wiley.com.

Library of Congress Cataloging-in-Publication Data:
Scott, David Meerman.
    The new rules of marketing and PR : how to use social media, blogs, news releases, online video, and viral marketing to reach buyers directly / David Meerman Scott.—2nd ed.
        p. cm.
    Rev. ed. of: The new rules of marketing and PR : how to use news releases, blogs, podcasting, viral marketing, and online media to reach your buyers directly. 2007.
    Includes index.
    ISBN 978-0-470-54781-6 (pbk.)
    1. Internet marketing. 2. Public relations.   I. Title.
    HF5415.1265.S393 2010
    658.8'72—dc22

                                                          2009051245

Printed in the United States of America.

10 9 8 7 6 5

For the Scott women

My mother, Carolyn J. Scott;
my wife, Yukari Watanabe Scott;
and my daughter, Allison C.R. Scott

Contents

Foreword

You're not supposed to be able to do what David Meerman Scott is about to tell you in this book. You're not supposed to be able to carry around a $250 video camera, record what employees are working on and what they think of the products they are building, and publish those videos on the Internet. But that's what I did at Microsoft, building an audience of more than four million unique visitors a month.

You're not supposed to be able to do what Stormhoek did. A winery in South Africa, it doubled sales in a year using the principles discussed here.

You're not supposed to be able to run a presidential campaign with just a blogger, a videographer, and a Flickr photographer. But that's what John Edwards did in December 2006 as he announced he was running for President.

Something has changed in the past 10 years. Well, for one, we have Google now, but that's only a part of the puzzle.

What really has happened is that the word-of-mouth network has gotten more efficient—much, much more efficient.

Word of mouth has always been important to business. When I helped run a Silicon Valley camera store in the 1980s, about 80 percent of our sales came from it. "Where should I buy a camera this weekend?" you might have heard in a lunchroom back then. Today that conversation is happening online. But, instead of only two people talking about your business, now thousands and sometimes millions (Engadget had 10 million page views in a single day during the Consumer Electronics and MacWorld shows in January 2006) are either participating or listening in.

What does this mean? Well, now there's a new medium to deal with. Your PR teams had better understand what drives this new medium (it's as influential as the *New York Times* or CNN now), and if you understand how to use it you can drive buzz, new product feedback, sales, and more.

But first you'll have to learn to break the rules.

Is your marketing department saying you need to spend $80,000 to do a single video? (That's not unusual, even in today's world. I just participated in such a video for a sponsor of mine.) If so, tell that department "Thanks, but no thanks." Or, even better, search Google for "Will it blend?" You'll find a Utah blender company that got six million downloads in less than 10 days. Oh, and 10,000 comments in the same period of time. All by spending a few hundred bucks, recording a one-minute video, and uploading that to YouTube.

Or, study what I did at Microsoft with a blog and a video camera. *Economist* magazine said I put a human face on Microsoft. Imagine that. A 60,000-employee organization and I changed its image with very little expense and hardly a committee in sight.

This advice isn't for everyone, though. Most people don't like running fast in business. They feel more comfortable if there are lots of checks and balances or committees to cover their asses. Or, they don't want to destroy the morale of PR and marketing departments due to the disintermediating effects of the Internet.

After all, you can type "OneNote Blog" into Google, Live.com, or Yahoo!, and you'll find Chris Pratley. He runs the OneNote team at Microsoft. Or, search for "Sun CEO." You'll find Jonathan Schwartz and his blog.

You can leave either one a comment and tell them their product sucks and see what they do in response. Or, even better, tell them how to earn your sale. Do they snap into place?

It's a new world you're about to enter, one where relationships with influentials *and* search engine optimization strategy are equally important, and one where your news will be passed around the world very quickly. You don't believe me?

Look at how the world found out I was leaving Microsoft for a Silicon Valley startup (PodTech.net).

I told 15 people at a videoblogging conference—not A-listers either, just everyday videobloggers. I asked them not to tell anyone until Tuesday—this was on a Saturday afternoon and I still hadn't told my boss.

Well, of course someone leaked that information. But, it didn't pop up in the *New York Times*. It wasn't discussed on CNN. No, it was a blogger I had never even heard of that posted the info first.

Within hours it was on hundreds of other blogs. Within two days it was in the *Wall Street Journal*, in the *New York Times*, on the front page of the BBC

Web site, in *BusinessWeek*, *Economist*, in more than 140 newspapers around the world (friends called me from Australia, Germany, Israel, and England, among other countries) and other places. Waggener Edstrom, Microsoft's PR agency, was keeping track and said that about 50 million media impressions occurred on my name in the first week.

All due to 15 conversations.

Whoa, what's up here? Well, if you have a story worth repeating, bloggers, podcasters, and videobloggers (among other influentials) will repeat your story all over the world, potentially bringing hundreds of thousands or millions of people your way. One link on a site like Digg alone could bring tens of thousands of visitors.

How did that happen?

Well, for one, lots of people knew me, knew my phone number, knew what kind of car I drove, knew my wife and son, knew my best friends, knew where I worked, and had heard me in about 700 videos that I posted at http://channel9.msdn.com on behalf of Microsoft.

They also knew where I went to college (and high school and middle school), and countless other details about me. How do you know they know all this? Well, they wrote a page on Wikipedia about me at http://en.wikipedia.org/wiki/Robert_Scoble—not a single thing on that page was written by me.

What did all that knowledge of me turn into? Credibility and authority. Translation: People knew me, knew where I was coming from, knew I was passionate and authoritative about technology, and came to trust me where they wouldn't trust most corporate authorities.

By reading this book you'll understand how to gain the credibility you need to build your business. Enjoy!

ROBERT SCOBLE
Co-author, *Naked Conversations*
Scobleizer.com

Welcome to the Second Edition of the New Rules

The two and a half years since the first edition of *The New Rules of Marketing and PR* was published have been an absolute blast. I spend my time traveling all over the world speaking to groups about the new rules, spreading the word, opening people's eyes to the possibilities, and motivating them to change the ways they do marketing and public relations.

We've been liberated!

Before the Web came along, there were only three ways to get noticed: buy expensive advertising, beg the mainstream media to tell your story for you, or hire a huge sales staff to bug people one at a time about your products. Now we have a better option: publishing interesting content on the Web that your buyers *want* to consume. The tools of the marketing and PR trade have changed. The skills that worked offline to help you buy or beg or bug your way in are the skills of interruption and coercion. Online success comes from thinking like a journalist and a thought leader.

The first edition of this book has sold remarkably well since its release in June 2007, remaining a top title for more than two years among thousands of books about marketing and public relations, and even making the *Business-Week* bestseller list multiple months. But wanna know the amazing thing? I didn't spend a single penny advertising or promoting it. Here's what I did do: I offered advance copies to approximately 130 important bloggers, I sent out nearly 20 news releases (you'll read later in the book about news releases as a tool to reach buyers directly), and my publisher alerted contacts in the media. That's it. Thousands of bloggers have written about the book (thank you!), significantly driving its sales. And the mainstream media have found me as a result of this blogger interest. the *Wall Street Journal* called twice for interviews that landed me quotes in the paper because they read about my ideas online first. I've appeared on national and local television and radio including

MSNBC, Fox Business, and NPR. I've been interviewed on dozens of podcasts. Magazines and newspaper reporters email me all the time to get quotes for their stories. How do they find me? Online, of course! And it doesn't cost me a single penny. I'm not telling you all this to brag about my book sales or my media appearances. I'm telling you to show you how well these ideas work.

But the coolest part of my life since the book was published isn't that I took advantage of the new rules of marketing and PR, nor is it that this book has been selling like hotcakes as a result. No, the coolest part of my life right now is that people contact me every day to say that the ideas in these pages have transformed their businesses and changed their lives. Really! That's the sort of language people use. They write just to thank me for putting the ideas into a book so that they could be enlightened to the new realities of marketing and PR.

Every day I get exciting feedback from people who are charged up about the new rules. Take Jody. He sent me an email to tell me the book had an unexpected effect on him and his wife. Jody explains that, to them, the really exciting and hopeful idea is that they can actually use their genuine voices online; they've left behind the hype-inflated PR-speak their agencies had used so tediously.

Or Andrew. He left a comment on my blog: "David, your book so inspired me, I decided to start a brand-new business (launching shortly) based around the principles you espouse. You cogently expressed many of the things that I'd been grappling with myself. So your book has certainly changed one life."

Mike wrote to say that his company's software, which helps small- and medium-sized businesses get found by the right prospects and capture more leads, takes advantage of all the trends and techniques described in the book. He purchased a bunch of copies to share with everyone in his organization. Larry bought copies for all the members of his professional association. Richard did, too. Robin, who works for a company that offers public relations services, purchased 300 copies for clients. Len, who runs a strategic marketing agency, sent copies to his clients, too. Julie, who is a senior executive at a PR firm, handed out copies to all 75 of her staff members. People approach me at conferences asking me to sign wonderfully dog-eared, coffee-stained, Post-it-noted copies of the book. Sometimes they tell me some funny secrets too. Kathy, who works in PR, said that if everyone read it, she'd be out of a job! David told me he used what he learned to find a new job.

While all this incredible feedback is personally flattering, I am most grateful that my ideas have empowered people to find their own voices and tell their own stories online. How cool is that?

Now let me disclose a secret of my own. As I was writing the book, I was a bit unsure of the global applicability of the new rules. Sure, I'd found a number of anecdotal stories about online marketing, blogging, and social networking outside of North America (you will read about some later in the book). But I couldn't help but wonder: Are organizations of all kinds reaching their buyers directly, with Web content written in languages other than English and for cultures other than my own? The answer is a resounding yes! About 25 percent of the book's English language sales have come from outside the United States. As I write this, the book has been or is being translated into 24 other languages including Bulgarian, Finnish, Korean, Vietnamese, Serbian, and Turkish. I'm also receiving invitations from all over the world to speak about the new rules. In the past year, I've traveled to nearly a dozen countries, including Saudi Arabia, the UK, Estonia, Latvia, Turkey, Croatia, the Netherlands, Australia, New Zealand, and the Dominican Republic. So I can say with certainty that the ideas in these pages do resonate worldwide. We are indeed witnessing a global phenomenon.

Second Edition

This second edition of the book has gone through an extensive rewrite. Of course, I have checked every fact, figure, and URL. But I've also listened. In the past two years, I've met thousands of people like you who have shared their stories with me, so I have drawn from those experiences and included in these pages many new examples of success. While including so many new stories and examples has resulted in my removing many of the less interesting originals, I'm convinced that these exciting replacements are even more valuable. And for those of you who have read the first edition, you'll still find many fresh ideas in these pages.

I've made some major additions as well. When I wrote the first edition of the book, Facebook was only available to those with a *.edu* email address (students and educators), so I didn't feature Facebook. And Twitter didn't even exist at the time I was researching the first edition. So I have added extensive new information and examples on Facebook, Twitter, and other social media sites. In fact, the rise of the term *social media* has been so strong in the past few years that I've even changed the subtitle of the book to include it.

Finally, I must give credit to the thousands of smart people who found success with the new rules before I ever put the ideas into print. The marketers these pages profile—and many others like them—deserve the credit for pioneering the ideas I've chronicled.

Thank you for your interest in the new rules. I hope that you too will be successful in implementing these strategies and that your life will be made better as a result.

DAVID MEERMAN SCOTT
David@DavidMeermanScott.com
www.WebInkNow.com
twitter.com/dmscott
facebook.com/dmscott

Introduction

At the height of the dot-com boom, I was vice president of marketing at NewsEdge Corporation, a NASDAQ-traded online news distributor with more than $70 million in annual revenue. My multimillion-dollar marketing budget included tens of thousands of dollars per month for a public relations agency, hundreds of thousands per year for print advertising and glossy collateral materials, and expensive participation at a dozen trade shows a year. My team put these things on our marketing to-do list, worked like hell to execute, and paid the big bucks because that's what marketing and PR people did. These efforts made us feel good because we were *doing something*, but the programs were not producing significant, measurable results.

At the same time, drawing on experience I had gained in my previous position as Asia marketing director for the online division of Knight-Ridder, then one of the largest newspaper companies in the world, my team and I quietly created content-based, "thought leadership" marketing and PR programs on the Web. Against the advice of the PR agency professionals we had on retainer (who insisted that press releases were only for the press), we wrote and sent dozens of releases ourselves. Each time we sent a release, it appeared on online services such as Yahoo!, *resulting in sales leads*. Even though our advertising agency told us not to put the valuable information "somewhere where competitors could steal it," we created a monthly newsletter called *TheEdge* about the exploding world of digital news and made it freely available on the homepage of our Web site *because it generated interest from buyers, the media, and analysts*. Way back in the 1990s, when Web marketing and PR was in its infancy, my team and I ignored the old rules, drawing instead on my experience working at an online publisher, and created a marketing strategy using online content to reach buyers directly on the Web. The homegrown, do-it-yourself programs we created at virtually no cost consistently generated more interest from qualified buyers, the media, and analysts—and resulted in more sales—than the big-bucks programs that the "professionals" were running for us. People we never heard of were finding us through search engines. I had stumbled on a better way to reach buyers.

In 2002, after NewsEdge was sold to The Thomson Corporation, I started my own business to refine my ideas, work with select clients, and teach others through writing, speaking at conferences, and conducting seminars for corporate groups. The object of all this work was reaching buyers directly with Web content. Since then, many new forms of social media have burst onto the scene, including blogs, podcasts, video, and virtual communities. But what all the new Web tools and techniques have in common is that together they are the best way to communicate *directly* with your marketplace.

This book actually started as a Web marketing and PR program on my blog. In January 2006, I published an e-book called *The New Rules of PR*,[1] immediately generating remarkable enthusiasm (and much controversy) from marketers and businesspeople around the world. Since the e-book was published, it has been downloaded more than 250,000 times and commented on by thousands of readers on my blog and those of many other bloggers. To those of you who have read and shared the e-book, thank you. But this book is much more than just an expansion of that work, because I have made its subject marketing *and* PR instead of just PR and because I've included many different forms of online media and conducted years of additional research.

This book contains much more than just my own ideas, because I have blogged the book, section by section, as I have written it. Thousands of you have followed along, and many have contributed to the writing process by offering suggestions via comments on my blog and e-mail. Thank you for contributing your ideas. And thank you for arguing with me when I got off track. Your enthusiasm has made the book much better than if I had written in isolation.

The Web has changed not only the rules of marketing and PR, but also the business-book model, and *The New Rules of Marketing and PR* is an interesting example. My online content (the e-book and my blog) led me directly to a print book deal. I published early drafts of sections of the book on my blog and used the blog to test ideas for inclusion into this, the second edition.

---

[1] http://www.webinknow.com/2006/01/new_complimenta.html

Other publishers would have freaked out if an author wanted to put parts of his book online (for free!) to solicit ideas. John Wiley & Sons encouraged it. In fact, some of my favorite books evolved on blogs, including *Naked Conversations* by Robert Scoble[2] and Shel Israel,[3] *The Long Tail* by Chris Anderson,[4] and *Small Is the New Big* by Seth Godin[5]—great company indeed. Thanks for leading the way, guys.

The New Rules

One of the more interesting debates about this book has been over its title. Many people have told me they like the title because they know what they will be getting. It's descriptive. But others have fought me, saying that there are all kinds of new rules being touted in books and elsewhere but that rarely deliver. "New rules" are just hype, they say. While it's true that a search on Amazon for "new rules" brings up thousands of book titles, the Web truly does offer marketers a new way of doing things. I am confident in my choice of title, because before the Web the only way you could get your organization noticed was to buy advertising of some kind or convince a journalist to write about you. Telling your organization's story directly (via the Web) *is* new, because, until now, you've never been able to reach a potential audience in the millions without buying expensive advertising or getting media coverage.

Here's the problem, though: There are many people who *still* apply the old rules of advertising and media relations to the new medium of the Web, and fail miserably as a result. I am firmly convinced that we're now in an environment governed by new rules, and this book is your guide to that (online) world.

Trying to Write Like a Blog, But in a Book

As the lines between marketing and PR on the Web have blurred so much as to be virtually unrecognizable, the best media choice is often not as obvious as in the old days. But I had to organize the book somehow, and I chose to

---

[2] http://scobleizer.com/
[3] http://redcouch.typepad.com/
[4] http://thelongtail.com/
[5] http://sethgodin.typepad.com/

create chapters for the various online media, including blogs, podcasts, online forums, social networking, and so on. But the truth is that all these tools and techniques intersect and complement one another. Some things were difficult to place into a particular chapter, such as the discussion on RSS (Really Simple Syndication). I moved that section four times before settling on Chapter 13.

These online media are evolving very rapidly, and by the time you read these words, I'll no doubt come across new techniques that I'll wish I could have put in this second edition of the book. At the same time, I agree that the fundamentals are important, which is why Chapter 10—where you'll start to develop your own online marketing and PR plan—is steeped in practical, commonsense thinking.

The book is organized into three parts. Part I is a rigorous overview of how the Web has changed the rules of marketing and PR. Part II introduces and provides details about each of the various media, and Part III contains detailed "how-to" information and an action plan to help you put the new rules to work for your organization.

While I think this sequence is the most logical way to present these ideas, there's no reason why you shouldn't flip from chapter to chapter in any order that you please. Unlike a mystery novel, you won't get lost in the story if you skip around. And I certainly don't want to waste your time. As I was writing, I was wishing that I could link you (like in a blog) from one chapter to a part of another chapter. Alas, a printed book doesn't allow that, so instead I have included suggestions where you might skip ahead or go back for review on specific topics. Similarly, I have included hundreds of URLs as footnotes so you can choose to visit the blogs, Web sites, and other online media that I discuss that interest you. You'll notice that I write in a familiar and casual tone, rather than the formal and stilted way of many business books, because I'm using my "blog voice" to share the new rules with you—I just think it works better for you, the reader.

When I use the words *company* and *organization* throughout this book, I'm including all types of organizations and individuals. Feel free to insert *nonprofit, government agency, political candidate, church, school, sports team, professional service person,* or other entity in place of *company* and *organization* in your mind. Similarly, when I use the word *buyers,* I also mean subscribers, voters, volunteers, applicants, and donors, because the new rules work for reaching all these groups. Are you a nonprofit organization that needs to increase donations? The new rules apply to you as much as to a corporation. Ditto for political campaigns looking for votes, schools that want to increase applicants, consultants searching for business, and churches hunting for new members.

This book will show you the new rules and how to apply them. For people all over the world interacting on the Web, the old rules of marketing and PR just don't work. Today, all kinds of organizations communicate directly with their buyers online. According to the Pew Internet and American Life Project, the Internet is now used by 1.6 billion people worldwide, with another billion expected to be added soon.[6] In order to reach the individuals online who would be interested in their organization, smart marketers everywhere have altered the way they think about marketing and PR.

Showcasing Innovative Marketers

The most exciting aspect of the book is that, throughout these pages, I have the honor of showcasing some of the best examples of innovative marketers building successful marketing and PR programs on the Web. One of the most remarkable is that of Robert Scoble, who kindly shared his story about Microsoft in the Foreword to the book. Thank you, Robert. There are nearly 50 other profiles throughout the book, much of them in the marketers' own words drawn from my interviews with them that bring the concepts to life. You'll learn from people at Fortune 500 companies and at businesses with just a handful of employees. These companies make products ranging from racing bicycles to jet helicopters and from computer software to hamburgers. Some of the organizations are well-known to the public, while others are famous only in their market niche. I profile nonprofit organizations, political advocacy groups, and citizens supporting potential candidates for political office. I tell the stories of independent consultants, churches, rock bands, and lawyers, all of whom successfully use the Web to reach their target audiences. I can't thank enough the people who shared their time with me on the phone and in person. I'm sure you'll agree that they are the stars of the book.

As you read the stories of successful marketers, remember that you will learn from them even if they come from a very different market, industry, or type of organization than your own. Nonprofits can learn from the

[6] http://www.pewinternet.org/

experiences of corporations. Consultants will gain insight from the success of rock bands. In fact, I'm absolutely convinced that you will learn more by emulating successful ideas from outside your industry than by copying what your nearest competitor is doing. Remember, the best thing about new rules is that your competitors probably don't know about them yet.

DAVID MEERMAN SCOTT
David@DavidMeermanScott.com
www.WebInkNow.com
twitter.com/dmscott
facebook.com/dmscott

How the Web Has Changed the Rules of Marketing and PR

1

The Old Rules of Marketing and PR Are Ineffective in an Online World

Several times in the past few years, I have thought about buying a new car. As with hundreds of millions of other consumers, the Web is my primary source of information when considering a purchase, so I sat down at the computer and began poking around. Figuring they were the natural place to begin my research, I started with the big three automaker sites. That was a big mistake. At all three, I was assaulted on the home page with a barrage of TV-style broadcast *advertising*. And all the one-way messages focused on price. At Ford,[1] the headlines screamed, "Model Year Clearance! 0% financing! 0 for gas!" Chrysler[2] announced a similar offer: "Get employee pricing plus 0% financing!" And over at GM,[3] they were having a "72-hour sale!" I'm not planning to buy a car within 72 hours, thank you. I may not even buy one within 72 days! I'm just kicking the virtual tires. All three of these sites assume that I'm ready to buy a car *right now*. But I actually just wanted to learn something.

Although I didn't know exactly what I wanted, I was sort of thinking about a compact SUV. Only GM offered a way to check out all of the company's SUV models in one place. To learn about all the Ford products, I had to go to the Ford, Mercury, and other brand sites separately, even though each brand is owned by Ford. These individual sites were no better help to me, a person who was considering a new car purchase possibly many months in the future.

---

[1] www.fordvehicles.com/
[2] www.chrysler.com/
[3] www.gm.com/vehicles/

Sure, I got flash-video TV commercials, pretty pictures, and low financing offers on these sites, but little else.

I looked around for some personality on these sites and didn't find much, because the automaker web sites portray their organizations as nameless, faceless corporations. In fact, the three sites are so similar that they're effectively interchangeable. I want to know about the people behind the cars! I'd love to meet the designers and maybe find out how they chose that weird shade of purple for my latest GM rental car. What I *really* wanted to ask is this: "Are there any real people at these auto companies?"

At each site, I felt as if I was being marketed to with a string of messages that had been developed in a lab or via focus groups. It just didn't feel authentic. If I wanted to see TV car ads, I would have flipped on the TV. I was struck with the odd feeling that all of the big three automakers' sites were designed and built by the same Madison Avenue ad guy. These sites were advertising *to* me, not building a relationship *with* me. They were luring me in with one-way messages, not educating me about the companies' products. Guess what? When I arrive at a site, you don't need to grab my attention; you already have it!

Automakers have become addicted to the crack cocaine of marketing: big budget TV commercials and other offline advertising. Everywhere I turn, I see an automobile ad that makes me think "This has got to be really freakin' expensive." The television commercials, the "sponsored by" stuff, and other high-ticket Madison Avenue marketing might make you feel good, but is it effective? These days, when people are thinking of buying a car (or any other product or service), they usually go to the Web first! Hey, even my mother does it! When people come to you online, they are not looking for TV commercials. They are looking for information to help them make a decision.

Here's the good news: I did find some terrific places on the Web to learn about compact SUVs. Unfortunately, the places where I got authentic content and where I became educated and where I interacted with humans just aren't part of the big three automakers' sites. Edmunds's cool Car Space,[4] a free consumer-driven social networking and personal page site with features such as photo albums, user groups based on make and model of car, and favorite links, was excellent in helping me narrow down choices. For example, in the forums, I could read more than 2,000 messages just on the

---

[4] www.carspace.com/

Toyota FJ Cruiser. I could see pages where owners showed off their vehicles. This is where I was making my decision, *dozens of clicks removed from the big automaker sites.*

Since I first wrote about automaker sites on my blog, hundreds of people jumped in to comment or email me with their similar car shopping experiences and frustrations with automaker web sites. Something is seriously broken in the automobile business if so many people are unable to find, directly on a company site, the information they need to make a purchase decision. And it's not just automakers.

> Prior to the Web, organizations had only two significant choices to attract attention: Buy expensive advertising or get third-party ink from the media. But the Web has changed the rules. The Web is not TV. Organizations that understand the New Rules of Marketing and PR develop relationships directly with consumers like you and me.

I'd like to pause here a moment for a clarification. When I talk about the new rules and compare them to the old rules, I don't mean to suggest that all organizations immediately drop their existing marketing and PR programs and use this book's ideas exclusively. Moreover, I'm not of the belief that the only marketing worth doing is on the Web. If your newspaper advertisements, Yellow Page listings, media outreach programs, and other programs are working for you, that's great! Please keep going! There is room in many marketing and PR programs for traditional techniques.

That being said, there's no doubt that, today, people solve problems by turning to the Web. (Just consider your own habits. How do *you* research products and services?) If your organization isn't present and engaged in the places and at the times that your buyers are, then you're losing out on potential business—no matter how successful your offline marketing program is. Worse, if you are trying to apply the game plan that works in your mainstream-media-based advertising and PR programs to your online ones, you will not be successful.

Ask yourself this simple question: How are my existing advertising and media relations programs working?

Advertising: A Money Pit of Wasted Resources

In the old days, traditional, nontargeted advertising via newspapers, magazines, radio, television, and direct mail were the only ways to go. But these media make targeting specific buyers with individualized messages very difficult. Yes, advertising is still used for megabrands with broad reach and probably still works for some organizations and products (though not as well as before). Guys watching football on TV drink a lot of beer, so perhaps it makes sense for mass-marketer Budweiser to advertise on NFL broadcasts (but not for small microbrews that appeal to a small niche audience). Advertising also works in many trade publications. If your company makes deck sealant, then you probably want to advertise in *Professional Deck Builder Magazine* to reach your professional buyers (but that won't allow you to reach the do-it-yourself market). If you run a local real estate agency in a smaller community, it might make sense to do a direct mailing to all of the homeowners there (but that won't let you reach people who might be planning to move to your community from another location).

However, for millions of other organizations, for the rest of us who are professionals, musicians, artists, nonprofit organizations, churches, and niche product companies, traditional advertising is generally so wide and broad that it is ineffective. Big media advertising buys may work for products with mass appeal and wide distribution. Famous brands carried in national chain stores come to mind as examples, as do blockbuster movies shown on thousands of screens. But a great strategy for Procter & Gamble, Paramount Pictures, and the Republican U.S. presidential candidate—reaching large numbers of people with a message of broad national appeal—just doesn't work for niche products, local services, and specialized nonprofit organizations.

> The Web has opened a tremendous opportunity to reach niche buyers directly with targeted messages that cost a fraction of what big-budget advertising costs.

One-Way Interruption Marketing Is Yesterday's Message

A primary technique of what Seth Godin calls the TV-industrial complex[5] is interruption. Under this system, advertising agency creative people sit in hip offices dreaming up ways to interrupt people so that they pay attention to a one-way message. Think about it: You're watching your favorite TV show, so the advertiser's job is to craft a commercial to get you to pay attention, when you'd really rather be doing something else, like quickly grabbing some ice cream before the show resumes. You're reading an interesting article in a magazine, so the ads need to jolt you into reading the ad instead of the article. Or, you're flying on U.S. Airways from Boston to Philadelphia (which I frequently do), and 20 minutes or so after takeoff, the airline deems it important to interrupt your nap with a loud advertisement announcing vacation destinations in the Caribbean. The idea in all of these examples is that advertising, in all forms, has traditionally relied on getting prospects to stop what they are doing and pay attention to a message.

Moreover, the messages in advertising are product-focused one-way spin. Forced to compete with new marketing on the Web that is centered on interaction, information, education, and choice, advertisers can no longer break through with dumbed-down broadcasts about their wonderful products. With the average person now seeing hundreds of seller-spun commercial messages per day, people just don't trust advertising. We turn it off in our minds, if we notice it at all.

> The Web is different. Instead of one-way interruption, Web marketing is about delivering useful content at just the precise moment that a buyer needs it.

Before the Web, good advertising people were well versed in the tools and techniques of reaching broad markets with lowest-common denominator messages via interruption techniques. Advertising was about great "creative

---

[5] http://sethgodin.typepad.com/seths_blog/2006/01/nonlinear_media.html

work." Unfortunately, many companies rooted in these old ways desperately want the Web to be like TV, because they understand how TV advertising works. Advertising agencies that excel in creative TV ads simply believe they can transfer their skills to the Web.

They are wrong. They are following outdated rules.

The Old Rules of Marketing

- Marketing simply meant advertising (and branding).
- Advertising needed to appeal to the masses.
- Advertising relied on interrupting people to get them to pay attention to a message.
- Advertising was one-way: company-to-consumer.
- Advertising was exclusively about selling products.
- Advertising was based on campaigns that had a limited life.
- Creativity was deemed the most important component of advertising.
- It was more important for the ad agency to win advertising awards than for the client to win new customers.
- Advertising and PR were separate disciplines run by different people with separate goals, strategies, and measurement criteria.

> None of this is true anymore. The Web has transformed the rules, and you must transform your marketing to make the most of the Web-enabled marketplace of ideas.

Public Relations Used to Be Exclusively about the Media

I'm a contributing editor at *EContent* magazine, as a result of which I receive hundreds of broadcast e-mail press releases per month from well-meaning PR people who want me to write about their widgets. Guess what? In five years, I have *never* written about a company because of a nontargeted broadcast press release that somebody sent me. Something like 25,000 press releases have been sent to me, resulting in no stories. Discussions I've had with journalists in other industries confirm that I'm not the only one who doesn't use unsolicited press releases. Instead, I think about a subject that I want to cover in a column or an article, and I check out what I can find on blogs and through search engines. If I find a press release on the subject through Google News or a company's online media room, great! But I don't wait for press releases to come to me. Rather, I go looking for interesting topics, products, people, and companies. And when I do feel ready to write a story, I might try out a concept on my blog first, to see how it flies. Does anyone comment on it? Do any PR people jump in and e-mail me?

There's another amazing thing: In five years, only a tiny number of PR people have commented on my blog or reached out to me as a result of a blog post or story I've written in a magazine. How difficult can it be to read the blogs of the reporters you're trying to pitch? It teaches you precisely what interests them. And then you can e-mail them with something interesting that they are likely to write about rather than spamming them with unsolicited press releases. When I don't want to be bothered, I get hundreds of press releases a week. But when I do want feedback and conversation, I get silence.

Something's very wrong in PR land.

> Reporters and editors use the Web to seek out interesting stories, people, and companies. Will they find you?

Public Relations and Third-Party Ink

Public relations was once an exclusive club. PR people used lots of jargon and followed strict rules. If you weren't part of the in crowd, PR seemed like an esoteric and mysterious job that required lots of training, sort of like being a space shuttle astronaut or court stenographer. PR people occupied their time by writing press releases targeted exclusively to reporters and editors and by schmoozing with those same reporters and editors. And then they crossed their fingers and hoped ("Oh, please write about me . . . ") that the media would give them some ink or some airtime. The end result of their efforts—the ultimate goal of PR in the old days—was the clip that proved they had done their job. Only the best PR people had personal relationships with the media and could pick up the phone and pitch a story to the reporter for whom they had bought lunch the month before. Prior to 1995, outside of paying big bucks for advertising or working with the media, there just weren't any significant options for a company to tell its story to the world.

> This is not true anymore. The Web has changed the rules. Today, organizations are communicating directly with buyers.

Yes, the Media Are Still Important

Allow me to pause for a moment to say that the mainstream and trade media are still important components of a great public relations program. On my blog and on the speaking circuit, I've sometimes been accused of suggesting that the media are no longer relevant. That is not my position. The media are critically important for many organizations. A positive story in *Rolling Stone* propels a rock band to fame. An article in the *Wall Street Journal* brands a company as a player. A consumer product talked about on the *Today Show* gets noticed. In many niche markets and vertical industries, trade magazines and journals help decide which companies are important. However, I do believe that, while these outlets are all vital aspects of an overall PR program, there are easier and more efficient ways to reach your buyers. And here's something really neat: If you do a good job telling your story directly, the media will find out. And then they will write about you!

Public relations work has changed. PR is no longer just an esoteric discipline where great efforts are spent by companies to communicate exclusively to a handful of reporters who then tell the company's story, generating a clip for the PR people to show their bosses. Now, great PR includes programs to reach buyers directly. The Web allows direct access to information about your products, and smart companies understand and use this phenomenal resource to great advantage.

> The Internet has made public relations public again, after years of almost exclusive focus on media. Blogs, online video, news releases, and other forms of Web content let organizations communicate directly with buyers.

Press Releases and the Journalistic Black Hole

In the old days, a press release was actually a release to the press, so these documents evolved as an esoteric and stylized way for companies to issue "news" to reporters and editors. Because it was assumed that nobody saw the actual press release except a handful of reporters and editors, these documents were written with the media's existing understanding in mind.

In a typical case, a tiny audience of several dozen media people got a steady stream of product releases from a company. The reporters and editors were already well versed on the niche market, so the company supplied very little background information. Jargon was rampant. *What's the news?*, journalists would think as they perused the release. *Oh, here it is—the company just announced the Super Techno Widget Plus with a New Scalable and Robust Architecture.* But while this might mean something to a trade magazine journalist, it is just plain gobbledygook to the rest of the world. Since press releases are now seen by millions of people who are searching the Web for solutions to their problems, these old rules are obsolete.

The Old Rules of PR

- The only way to get ink and airtime was through the media.
- Companies communicated to journalists via press releases.
- Nobody saw the actual press release except a handful of reporters and editors.
- Companies had to have significant news before they were allowed to write a press release.
- Jargon was okay because the journalists all understood it.

- You weren't supposed to send a release unless it included quotes from third parties, such as customers, analysts, and experts.
- The only way buyers would learn about the press release's content was if the media wrote a story about it.
- The only way to measure the effectiveness of press releases was through "clip books," which noted each time the media deigned to pick up a company's release.
- PR and marketing were separate disciplines run by different people with separate goals, strategies, and measurement techniques.

> None of this is true anymore. The Web has transformed the rules, and you must transform your PR strategies to make the most of the Web-enabled marketplace of ideas.

The vast majority of organizations don't have instant access to mainstream media for coverage of their products. People like you and me need to work hard to be noticed in the online marketplace of ideas. By understanding how the role of PR and the press release has changed, we can get our stories known in that marketplace.

There are some exceptions. Very large companies, very famous people, and governments might all still be able to get away with using the media exclusively, but even that is doubtful. These name-brand people and companies may be big enough, and their news just so compelling, that no effort is required of them. For these lucky few, the media may still be the primary mouthpiece.

- If you are J.K. Rowling and you issued a press release about, say, a new Harry Potter book, the news will be picked up by the media.
- If Apple Computer CEO Steve Jobs announces the company's new iPhone at a trade show, the news will be picked up by the media.
- If Brad Pitt and Angelina Jolie issue a press release about adopting another baby, the news will be picked up by the media.
- If President Obama announces his pick to fill a vacancy on the U.S. Supreme Court, the news will be picked up by the media.

> If you are smaller and less famous but have an interesting story to tell, you need to tell it yourself. Fortunately, the Web is a terrific place to do so.

Learn to Ignore the Old Rules

To harness the power of the Web to reach buyers directly, you must ignore the old rules. Public relations is not just about speaking through the media, although the media remain an important component. Marketing is not just about one-way broadcast advertising, although advertising can be part of an overall strategy.

I've noticed that some marketing and PR professionals have a very difficult time changing old habits. These new ideas make people uncomfortable. When I speak at conferences, people sometimes fold their arms in a defensive posture and look down at their shoes. Naturally, marketing and PR people who learned the old rules resist the new world of direct access. But I've also noticed that many marketing executives, CEOs, entrepreneurs, enlightened nonprofit executives, and professionals jump at the chance to tell stories directly. These people love the new way of communicating to buyers. Smart marketers are bringing success to their organizations each and every day by communicating through the Web.

Here's how to tell if the new rules are right for you. Consider your goals for communicating via marketing and public relations. Are you buying that Super Bowl ad to score great tickets to the game? Are you designing a creative magazine ad to win an award for your agency? Do you hope to create a book of press clips from mainstream media outlets to show to your bosses? Does your CEO want to be on TV? Are you doing PR to meet Oprah? If the answers to these questions are "yes," then the new rules (and this book) are not for you.

However, if you're like millions of smart marketers whose goal is to communicate with buyers directly, then read on. If you're working to make your organization more visible online, then read on. If you want to drive people into your company's sales process so they actually buy something (or apply, or donate, or join, or submit their name as a lead), then read on. I wrote this book especially for you.

2

The New Rules of Marketing and PR

Gerard Vroomen will tell you that he is an engineer, not a marketer. He will tell you that the company he co-founded, Cervélo Cycles,[1] does not have any marketing experts. But Vroomen is wrong. Why? Because he is obsessed with the buyers of his competition bikes and with the engineering-driven product he offers them. He's focused his company to help his customers win races—and they do. In the 2005 Tour de France, David Zabriskie rode the fastest time trial in the race's history on a Cervélo P3C at an average speed of 54.676 kph (33.954 mph). As I write this, the Cervélo Pro Cycling Test-Team is ranked the top team in the world. Vroomen also excels at using the Web to tell cycling enthusiasts compelling stories, to educate them, to engage them in conversation, and to entertain them. Because he uses Web content in interesting ways and sells a bunch of bikes in the process, Vroomen is a terrific marketer.

The Cervélo site works extremely well because it includes perfect content for visitors who are ready to buy a bike and also for people who are just browsing. The content is valuable and authentic compared to the marketing messages that appear on so many other sites. On the Cervélo site, enthusiasts find detailed information about each model, bikes that can cost $3,000–$5,000 or more. An online museum showcases production models dating from the early days of the company and some interesting past prototypes. Competitive cycling enthusiasts can sign up for an email newsletter, download audio such as interviews with professional riders from the Cervélo Pro

[1] www.cervelo.com/

Cycling TestTeam, or check out the company blog. Cervélo Pro Cycling TestTeam wins races, and you can follow the action on Cervélo's Team pages, which include news and bike race photos. Most recently, Cervélo launched Cervélo.tv, an online channel with product features, race reports, and cycling celebrity interviews.

"Our goal is education," Vroomen says. "We have a technical product, and we're the most engineering-driven company in the industry. Most bike companies don't employ a single engineer, and we have eight. So we want to have that engineering focus stand out with the content on the site. We don't sell on the newest paint job. So on the site, we're not spending our time creating fluff. Instead, we have a good set of content."

Ryan Patch is the sort of customer Cervélo wants to reach. An amateur triathlon competitor on the Vortex Racing team, Patch says, "On the Cervélo site I learned that Bobby Julich rides the same bike that is available to me. And it's not just that they are riding, but they are doing really well. I can see how someone won the Giro de Italia on a Cervélo. That's mind-blowing, that I can get the same bike that the pros are riding. I can ride the same gear. Cervélo has as much street cred as you can have with shaved legs."

Patch says that if you're looking to buy a new bike, if you are a hard-core consumer, then there is a great deal of detailed information on the Cervélo site about the bikes' technology, construction, and specs. "What I really like about this web site is how it gives off the aura of legitimacy, being based in fact, not fluff," he says.

Vroomen writes all of the content for the Cervélo site himself, and the design work has been done by a moonlighting chiropractor. There's a content management tool built in, so Vroomen can update the site himself. You wouldn't call it a fancy site, but it works. "We get negative feedback from Web designers about our site," Vroomen says. "But we have great comments from customers."

Search Engine Marketing is important for Cervélo. Because of the keyword-rich cycling content available on the site, Vroomen says, Cervélo gets the same amount of search engine traffic as many sites for bike companies that are 10 times larger. Cervélo is growing very rapidly, but Vroomen is quick to note that growth is not the result of any one thing. "We take as gospel that people have to see the product five different ways [for us] to really get the credibility." Vroomen makes certain that his bikes are in front of people many different ways, starting with search engines, so that they get those five exposures. "For example, they may see the bike on the site, on TV in a pro race, at the dealer, and on a blog," He says.

Vroomen says building out the Web marketing at Cervélo takes a lot of time, but it is simple and cost effective. "This is the future for companies like us," he says. "You can be very small and occupy a niche and still sell your products all over the world. It's amazing when we go into a new country the amount of name recognition we have. The Internet gives you opportunities you never had before. And its not rocket science. It's pretty easy to figure out."

The Long Tail of Marketing

I'm a fan of Chris Anderson and his book, *The Long Tail*, and I followed, via his blog, Anderson's groundbreaking ideas about the Web's economic shift away from mainstream markets toward smaller niche products and services well before his book was published in July 2006. There is no doubt that Anderson's thesis in *The Long Tail* is critically important for marketers:

> The theory of the Long Tail is that our culture and economy is increasingly shifting away from a focus on a relatively small number of "hits" (mainstream products and markets) at the head of the demand curve and toward a huge number of niches in the tail. As the costs of production and distribution fall, especially online, there is now less need to lump products and consumers into one-size-fits-all containers. In an era without the constraints of physical shelf space and other bottlenecks of distribution, narrowly targeted goods and services can be as economically attractive as mainstream fare.[2]

Some of today's most successful Internet businesses leverage the long tail to reach underserved customers and satisfy demand for products not found in traditional physical stores. Examples include Amazon, which makes available at the click of a mouse hundreds of thousands of books not stocked in local chain stores; iTunes, a service that legally brings niche music not found in record stores to people who crave artists outside the mainstream; and Netflix, which exploited the long tail of demand for movie rentals beyond the blockbuster hits found at the local DVD rental shop. Anderson shows that

[2] www.thelongtail.com/about.html

the business implications of the long tail are profound and illustrates that there's much money to be made by creating and distributing at the long end of the tail. Yes, hits are still important. But as the above businesses have shown, there's money to be made beyond *Harry Potter*, U2, and *Pirates of the Caribbean*.

So, what about marketing? While Anderson's book focuses on product availability and selling models on the Web, the concepts apply equally well to marketing. There's no doubt that there is a long-tail market for Web content created by organizations of all kinds—corporations, nonprofits, churches, schools, individuals, rock bands—and used for reaching buyers—those who buy, donate, join, apply—directly. As consumers search the Internet for answers to their problems, as they browse blogs and chat rooms and web sites for ideas, they are searching for what organizations like yours have to offer. Unlike in the days of the old rules of interruption marketing with a mainstream message, today's consumers are looking for just the right product or service to satisfy their unique desires at the precise moment they are online. People are looking for what you have to offer right now.

> Marketers must shift their thinking from the short head of mainstream marketing to the masses to a strategy of targeting vast numbers of underserved audiences via the Web.

As marketers understand the Web as a place to reach millions of micro-markets with precise messages just at the point of consumption, the way they create Web content changes dramatically. Instead of a one-size-fits-all web site with a mass-market message, we need to create many different microsites—with purpose-built landing pages and just-right content—each aimed at a narrow target constituency. As *marketing* case studies, the examples of Netflix, Amazon, and iTunes are also fascinating. The techniques pioneered by the leaders of long-tail retail for reaching customers with niche interests are examples of marketing genius.

Tell Me Something I Don't Know, Please

Amazon.com has been optimized for browsing. At a broad level, there are just two ways that people interact with Web content: They search and they browse. Most organizations optimize sites for searching, which helps people answer their questions but doesn't encourage them to browse. But people also want a site to tell them something they didn't think to ask. The marketers at Amazon understand that when people browse the site, they may have a general idea of what they want (in my case, perhaps a book for my daughter about surfing), but not the particular title. So if I start with a search on Amazon for the phrase "surfing for beginners," I get 99 titles in the search results. With this list as a starting point, I shift into browse mode, which is where Amazon excels. Each title has a customer ranking where I instantly see how other customers rated each book. I see reader-generated reviews together with reviews from other media. I can see "Customers who bought this item also bought" lists and also rankings of "What do customers ultimately buy after viewing items like this?" I can check out customer tags (a way for consumers to categorize a book to purchase later or to aid other consumers) on the item or I can tag it myself. And I can poke around the contents of the book itself. After I purchase the perfect book for my daughter (*The Girl's Guide to Surfing*), I might get an e-mail from Amazon weeks or months later suggesting, based on this purchase, another book that I might find useful. This is brilliant stuff.

The site is designed to work for a major and often-ignored audience: people who do their own research and consider a decision over a period of time before making a commitment. Smart marketers, like the folks at Amazon and Cervélo, unlike those at the big three automakers we saw in Chapter 1, know that the most effective Web strategies anticipate needs and provide content to meet them, even before people know to ask.

Marketing on the Web is not about generic banner ads designed to trick people with neon color or wacky movement. It is about understanding the keywords and phrases that our buyers are using and then deploying micro-campaigns to drive buyers to pages replete with the content that they seek.

Bricks-and-Mortar News

The new rules are just as important for public relations. In fact, I think that online content in all of its forms is causing a convergence of marketing and PR that does not really exist offline. When your buyer is on the Web browsing for something, content is content in all of its manifestations. And in an interconnected Web world, content drives action.

On the speaking circuit, I often hear people claim that online content such as blogs and news releases is really good only for technology companies. They believe that traditional bricks-and-mortar industries can't make the strategy work. But I've always disagreed. Great content brands an organization as a trusted resource and calls people to action—to buy, subscribe, apply, or donate. And great content means that interested people return again and again. As a result, the organization succeeds, achieving goals such as adding revenue, building traffic, gaining donations, or generating sales leads.

For instance, The Concrete Network[3] provides information about residential concrete products and services and helps buyers and sellers connect with each other. The company targets consumers and builders who might want to plan and build a concrete patio, pool deck, or driveway—this audience makes up the business-to-consumer (B2C) component of The Concrete Network—as well as the concrete contractors who comprise the business-to-business (B2B) component. The Concrete Network's Find-A-Contractor[4] service links homeowners and builders who need a project done with contractors who specialize in 22 different services located in 221 metropolitan areas in both the United States and Canada. The company's Web content, combined with a comprehensive direct-to-consumer news release strategy, drives business for The Concrete Network. Yes, ladies and gentlemen, Web content sells concrete! (You can't get any more bricks-and-mortar than, well, mortar.)

"The new rules of PR are that anybody who wants to be the leader has to have news coming out," says Jim Peterson, president of The Concrete Network. The company's ongoing PR program includes two direct-to-consumer news releases per week; a series of articles on the site; free online catalogs for categories such as countertops, pool decks, patios, and driveways; and photo galleries for potential customers to check out what is available. As a result of all of the terrific content, The Concrete Network gets more than ten times the traffic of any other site in the concrete industry, according to Peterson. He says that releases with headlines that are tied to holidays and educational releases work best. If is for the Fourth of July holiday, it's going to be about pool decks, patios, or outdoor fireplaces or fire pits. News releases designed specifically to sell haven't done as well. "We ran a concrete furniture release on April Fool's Day that did really well," Peterson says. The headline, *Concrete*

---

[3] www.concretenetwork.com/

[4] www.concretenetwork.com/contractors/

Furniture? No April Fools with Concrete Tables, Benches, Bookcases and Even Chairs, was written in news-story format. Peterson is very conscious of the words and phrases that he uses in news releases and crafts them to reach specific niche targets. For example, "contemporary fireplace," "fireplace mantel," and "fireplace design" are important phrases to reach people who are in the market for a fireplace. The news releases are all sent with beautiful news photos drawn from "Earth's largest collection of decorative concrete photos" on The Concrete Network. For example, Peterson can choose from dozens of photos just of concrete patios.[5]

"We know how many visitors reach us via the news releases, and it is similar to paid search engine marketing," Peterson says, but at a lower cost. "We're also generating links from other sites that index the news releases, and there is a media bonus, too, when we get mentioned in a story." He adds that the site averaged 550,000 visitors per month in 2005 and 850,000 in 2006. In 2009, against a backdrop of an economic crisis and a dramatically slower construction market and 40 percent less searches in the concrete category, the site is garnering over 1,000,000 visitors per month. Peterson expects traffic to explode as the economy starts to improve. "Direct-to-consumer news releases are a big part of the increased traffic. When you break it down, we're spending about twenty thousand dollars per year on news release distribution . . . . We see it as another component of our marketing. Some businesses won't want to spend that, but they probably won't be the leader in their marketplace."

Advice from the Company President

As president of The Concrete Network, Peterson is that rare executive who understands the power of content marketing, search engine optimization, and direct-to-consumer news releases to reach buyers directly and drive business. What is his advice to other company presidents and CEOs? "Every business has information that can contribute to the education of the marketplace. You need to ask yourself, 'How can I get that information out there?' You have to have a bit longer view and have a sense of how your business will be better down the line. For example, we created an entire series of buyer guides, because we knew that they would be valuable to the market. You need to think about how a series of one hundred news releases over two years will

---

[5] www.concretenetwork.com/photo_library/patios.htm

benefit your business and then commit to it, understanding that nothing is an overnight thing."

Peterson also suggests getting help from an expert to get started with a program. "Don't sit there and leave this [as] just a part of your list of good intentions," he says. "Businesses will live or die on original content. If you are creating truly useful content for customers, you're going to be seen in a great light and with a great spirit—you're setting the table for new business. But the vast majority of businesses don't seem to care. At The Concrete Network, we're on a mission. Get down to the essence of what your product solves and write good stories about that and publish them online."

You've got to love it. If content sells concrete, content can sell what you have to offer, too!

The Long Tail of PR

In PR, it's not about clip books. It's about reaching our buyers.

I was vice president of marketing and PR for two publicly traded companies and I've done it the old way. It doesn't work anymore. But the new rules do work—really well.

Instead of spending tens of thousands of dollars per month on a media relations program that tries to convince a handful of reporters at select magazines, newspapers, and TV stations to cover us, we should be targeting the plugged-in bloggers, online news sites, micro-publications, public speakers, analysts, and consultants that reach the targeted audiences that are looking for what we have to offer. Better yet, we no longer even need to wait for someone with a media voice to write about us at all. With social media, we communicate directly with our audience, bypassing the media filter completely. We have the power to create our own media brand in the niche of our own choosing. It's about being found on Google and Yahoo! and vertical sites and RSS (Really Simple Syndication) feeds. Instead of writing press releases only when we have "big news"—releases that reach only a handful of journalists—we should be writing releases that highlight our expert ideas and stories, and we should be distributing them so that our buyers can find them on the news search engines and vertical content sites.

To succeed in long-tail marketing and PR, we need to adopt different criteria for success. In the book world, everyone says, "If I can only get on Oprah, I'll be a success." Sure, I'd like to be on Oprah too. But instead of focusing countless (and probably fruitless) hours on a potential blockbuster of a TV appearance, wouldn't it be a better strategy to have lots of people reviewing your book in smaller publications that reach the specific audiences that buy books like yours? Oprah is a longshot, but right now bloggers would love to hear from you. Oprah must ignore 100 books a day, but bloggers run to their mailbox to see what interesting things might be in there (trust me, I know from experience). Sure, it would be great to have our businesses profiled in *Fortune* or *BusinessWeek*. But instead of putting all of our public relations efforts into that one potential PR blockbuster (a mention in the major business press), wouldn't it be better to get dozens of the most influential bloggers and analysts to tell our story directly to the niche markets that are looking for what we have to offer?

The New Rules of Marketing and PR

If you've been nodding your head excitedly while reading about what some of these companies are up to, then the new rules are for you. In the next chapter, I offer interesting case studies of companies that have been successful with the new rules. In each case example, I've interviewed a particular person from that organization so we can learn directly from them. Following are chapters on specific areas of online content (such as blogging, online video, news releases) and then more detailed how-to chapters. But before we move on, let me explicitly state the *New Rules of Marketing and PR* that we'll discuss throughout the rest of the book:

- Marketing is more than just advertising.
- PR is for more than just a mainstream media audience.
- You are what you publish.
- People want authenticity, not spin.
- People want participation, not propaganda.
- Instead of causing one-way interruption, marketing is about delivering content at just the precise moment your audience needs it.
- Marketers must shift their thinking from mainstream marketing to the masses to a strategy of reaching vast numbers of underserved audiences via the Web.
- PR is not about your boss seeing your company on TV. It's about your buyers seeing your company on the Web.

- Marketing is not about your agency winning awards. It's about your organization winning business.
- The Internet has made public relations public again, after years of almost exclusive focus on media.
- Companies must drive people into the purchasing process with great online content.
- Blogs, online video, e-books, news releases, and other forms of online content let organizations communicate directly with buyers in a form they appreciate.
- On the Web, the lines between marketing and PR have blurred.

The Convergence of Marketing and PR on the Web

As I originally wrote this list and edited it down, I was struck by how important one particular concept was to any successful online strategy to reach buyers directly: this concept is the convergence of marketing and PR. In an offline world, marketing and PR are separate departments with different people and different skill sets, but this is not the case on the Web. What's the difference between what Amazon, iTunes, and Netflix are doing to reach customers via online marketing and what The Concrete Network does with direct-to-consumer news releases? There's not much difference. How is the news that Cervélo Cycles creates itself and posts on the site different from a story on *Bicycling* magazine's web site? It isn't. And when a buyer is researching your product category by using a search engine, does it really matter if the first exposure is a hit on your web site, or a news release your organization sent, or a magazine article, or a post on your blog? I'd argue that it doesn't matter. Whereas I presented two separate lists for The Old Rules of Marketing and The Old Rules of PR, now there is just one set of rules: *The New Rules of Marketing and PR*. Great content in all forms helps buyers see that you and your organization "get it." Content drives action.

3 Reaching Your Buyers Directly

The frustration of relying exclusively on the media and expensive advertising to deliver your organization's messages is long gone. Yes, mainstream media is still important, but today smart marketers craft compelling information and tell the world directly via the Web. The tremendous expense of relying on advertising to convince buyers to pay attention to your organization, ideas, products, and services is yesterday's headache.

Chip McDermott founded ZeroTrash Laguna[1] as a nonprofit organization to rid the streets and beaches of Laguna Beach, CA, of trash. Population and tourism had exploded, and the city had not kept up in providing a sufficient infrastructure for public trash and recycling. McDermott used the Web to rally the community with a grassroots movement.

"The spark of the idea in 2007 was that trash was becoming commonplace on the streets and the sidewalks of Laguna Beach," McDermott says. "We started to tackle the problem with a Facebook[2] fan page for ZeroTrash Laguna and quickly built it to hundreds of members."

People use the ZeroTrash Facebook page to organize events and to connect local storeowners with residents. Facebook was instrumental in launching the ZeroTrash "First Saturday" movement, where storeowners and volunteers walk the city and pick up trash on the first Saturday of each month. The storeowners love it because people support local stores and keep the shopping areas clean. In turn, McDermott has tapped storeowners as sponsors

---

[1] www.zerotrashlaguna.org/

[2] www.facebook.com/pages/ZeroTrash/71671924615

who fund the purchase of supplies and tools like trash pickers, T-shirts, trash bags, and gloves.

McDermott also started the ZeroTrash blog[3], and he's on Twitter[4] as well. The social media sites serve to keep people updated about what ZeroTrash is up to. For example, on a recent First Saturday, the Laguna Beach community helped to remove another 590 pounds of trash and 375 pounds of recyclables from the streets; McDermott used the social media sites to report these totals to interested people.

He has high hopes for the organization, including ambitions to spread the movement beyond Laguna Beach. "We want people to take individual ownership of each new local ZeroTrash community," he says. "How can they get people with a passion to take control and start in their own communities? The obvious answer is to use social media to influence people."

There's no doubt that getting the word out about an idea, a product, or a service is much simpler when you can rely on social media sites like blogs, Facebook, and Twitter. The Web allows any organization—including nonprofits like ZeroTrash Laguna as well as companies large and small, candidates for public office, government agencies, schools, artists and even job seekers—to reach buyers directly. This power is clear to nearly everyone these days, but many executives and entrepreneurs still struggle to find the right mix of traditional advertising and direct communication with buyers.

The Right Marketing in a Wired World

Century 21 Real Estate LLC[5] is the franchisor of the world's largest residential real estate sales organization, an industry giant comprising approximately 8,000 offices in 45 countries. The company had been spending on television advertising for years but, in a significant strategy change, pulled its national television advertising in 2009 and invested those resources into online marketing.

Wow! I've seen Century 21 TV ads for years. We're talking millions of dollars shifting from TV to the Web. This is a big deal.

---

[3] http://zerotrash.wordpress.com/

[4] http://twitter.com/ZeroTrash

[5] www.century21.com/

"We are moving our advertising investments to the mediums that have the greatest relevance to our target buyers and sellers, and to where the return on our investment is most significant," says Bev Thorne, chief marketing officer at Century 21. "In 2008, we found that our online investments provided a return that was substantively higher than our more traditional TV media investments."

Thorne and her team learned that people who are in the market to buy or sell a home rely heavily on the Web and that the closer they get to a real estate transaction, the more they use online resources. "We are beginning to embrace LinkedIn, Facebook, Twitter, Active Rain, and others," Thorne says. "YouTube is already a central component of our activities, and we seek to utilize it even more."

Many companies spending large amounts of money on television advertising (and other offline marketing such as direct mail, magazine and newspaper advertising, and Yellow Page listings) are afraid to make even partial moves away from their comfort zones and into online marketing and social media. But the evidence describing how people actually research products overwhelmingly suggests that companies must tell their stories and spread their ideas online, at the precise moment that potential buyers are searching for answers.

It's an exciting time to be a marketer no matter what business you're in. We have been liberated from relying exclusively on buying access through advertising or convincing mainstream media to talk us up. Now we can publish information on the Web that people are eager to pay attention to.

Let the World Know about Your Expertise

All people and organizations possess the power to elevate themselves on the Web to a position of importance. In the new e-marketplace of ideas, organizations highlight their expertise in various forms such as great web sites, podcasts, blogs, e-books, and online news releases that focus on buyers' needs. All these media allow organizations to deliver the right information to buyers, right at the point when they are most receptive to the information. The tools at our disposal as marketers are Web-based media to deliver our own thoughtful and informative content via web sites, blogs, e-books, white papers, images, photos, audio content, and video, and even things like product placement, games, and virtual reality. We also have the ability to interact and participate in conversations that other people begin on social media sites like Twitter, blogs, chat rooms, and forums. What links all of these techniques together is that organizations of all types behave like *publishers*, creating content that people are eager to consume. Organizations gain credibility and loyalty with buyers through content, and smart marketers now think and act like publishers in order to create and deliver content targeted directly at their audience.

Jeff Ernst, vice president of marketing at Kadient, helps sell a complex business-to-business product that is not easy to explain but provides tremendous value to the sales teams that use it. The company develops software that gives salespeople important information and guidance, specific to the sales opportunities they are managing and the people they are selling to. Ernst shared his expertise with the world by publishing an e-book called *The New Rules of Sales Enablement: How to Stop Sabotaging Your Sales Teams and Start Empowering Them for Success*.[6] In it, he articulates how the old model of a salesperson as a lone cowboy gunning for deals just isn't as successful these days; instead, he argues, sales teams must work together to share knowledge of what works. Of course, it just so happens that Kadient's tool is one that can help, but it's important to note that Ernst's e-book was more than just a sales pitch. By thinking like a publisher and creating valuable information to reach his buyers (sales managers in large organizations), Ernst has reached tens of thousands of people with his e-book. The result has been many engaged readers who want to learn more about Kadient. And—best of all—except for some outside help to design the e-book, this kind of online publishing is free.

Develop Information Your Buyers *Want* to Consume

Companies with large budgets can't wait to spend the big bucks on slick TV advertisements. It's like commissioning artwork. TV ads make marketing people at larger companies feel good. But broadcast advertisements dating from the time of the TV-industrial complex don't work so well anymore. When we had three networks and no cable, it was different. In the time-shifted, multichannel, Webcentric world of the long tail, YouTube, TiVo, and blogs, spending big bucks on TV ads is like commissioning a portrait back in

---

[6] www.kadient.com/sales_enablement_ebook.aspx

the nineteenth century: It might make you feel good, but does it bring in any money?

Instead of deploying huge budgets for dumbed-down TV commercials that purport to speak to the masses and therefore appeal to nobody, we need to think about the information that our niche audiences want to hear. Why not build content specifically for these niche audiences and tell them an online story about your product, a story that is created especially for them? Once marketers and PR people tune their brains to think about niches, they begin to see opportunities for being more effective at delivering their organization's message.

Buyer Personas: The Basics

Smart marketers understand buyers, and many build formal "buyer personas" for their target demographics. (I discuss buyer personas in detail in Chapter 10.) It can be daunting for many of us to consider who, exactly, is visiting our site. But if we break the buyers into distinct groups and then catalog everything we know about each one, we make it easier to create content targeted to each important demographic. For example, a college web site usually has the goal of keeping alumni happy so that they donate money to their alma mater on a regular basis. A college might have two buyer personas for alumni: young (those who graduated within the past 10 or 15 years) and older alumni. Universities also have a goal of recruiting students by driving them into the application process. The effective college site might have a buyer persona for the high school student who is considering college. But since the parents of the prospective student have very different information needs, the site designers might build another buyer persona for parents. A college also has to keep its existing customers (current students) happy. In sum, that means a well-executed college site might target five distinct buyer personas, with the goal of getting alumni to donate money, high school students to complete the application process, and parents to make certain their kids complete it. The goals for the current student aspects of the site might be making certain they come back for another year, plus answering routine questions so that staff time is not wasted.

By truly understanding the needs and the mindset of the five buyer personas, the college will be able to create appropriate content. Once you understand the audience very well, then (and only then) you should set out to satisfy their informational needs by focusing on your buyers' problems and creating and delivering content accordingly. As mentioned earlier, web site content too often simply describes what an organization or a product does from an egotistical perspective. While information about your organization and products is certainly valuable on the inner pages of your site, what visitors really want is content that first describes the issues and problems they face and then provides details on how to solve those problems. Once you've built an online relationship, you can begin to offer potential solutions that have been defined for each audience. After you've identified target audiences and articulated their problems, content is your tool to show off your expertise. Well organized Web content will lead your visitors through the sales cycle all the way to the point when they are ready to make a purchase or other commitment to your organization.

Understanding buyers and building an effective content strategy to reach them is critical for success. And providing clear links from the content to the place where action occurs is critical. Consider Mike Pedersen, who is widely acknowledged as one of the leading golf fitness training experts in the United States, having taught thousands of golfers the fitness approach to playing a consistently great game of golf. Pedersen runs an online business providing products to help golfers improve their game by getting in better shape. Pedersen's site[7] and his Perform Better Golf blog[8] are chock full of content created specifically for a narrow target market (buyer persona). "I write for the sixty-year-old golfer who has rapidly declining physical capabilities," says Pedersen. "I like to call it targeted content. When I write an article, I'm targeting a very specific element of golf for my readers. The article might be targeted to a small aspect of the golf swing, for example, and the guys I write for know how it can help them."

Pedersen offers hundreds of free articles and tips on his site and blog, such as "Golf-Specific Warm-ups" and "Golf Muscles Need to Be Strong and Flexible to Produce More Power in Your Golf Swing." "Most golfers don't prepare their bodies before they play golf, and they aren't able to play a good game," he says. "I write to be easy to understand and offer exercises that help people to prepare quickly and efficiently." Each article includes multiple photos of Pedersen illustrating how the exercises should be performed.

---

[7] www.golf-trainer.com/

[8] www.performbettergolf.com/blog/

Pedersen relies on search engines to drive much of his traffic, and his site is number one on search engines for important phrases like "golf training." He also works with partners and affiliates, and he has been the featured fitness expert for *Golf* magazine's web site, generating even more traffic for his own site. Pedersen says that the key to everything about his business is targeting his buyers directly with content specifically for them. His focus on his buyer persona of the older man who loves golf but is physically able to do less in his declining years is relentless. "I rely on getting into the consumers' mind and feeling their pain and their frustration," he says. "It is easy to write what I think, but much more difficult to write about what my buyers are thinking. With these guys, my target market, if they don't do anything now, they physically can't play the game that they love in future years. But I'm a forty-year-old, really fit, healthy guy. If I just wrote for myself, I'd be shooting myself in the foot because I'm not the target market."

Pedersen makes his money by selling products such as his Golf Fitness Training System for $150 (the system includes DVDs, books, and manuals) and membership in his online Golf Training Program. He also offers individual-topic DVDs and exercise supplies such as weighted golf clubs. At the bottom of each article on the site, there is a clear path and a call to action. "I'm diligent about links from every page both to something free and to the products page," he says. For example, a recent offer read, "Do you want to learn how your body is keeping you from a near perfect golf swing? Get my Free Golf Fitness Ebook and find out!"

When people register on the site for a free offer, they are added to Pedersen's 40,000-person e-mail list to get alerts on significant new content added to the site and blog, as well as special offers. The majority of e-mail messages he sends are alerts about new content and contain no sales pitch at all. "I know that if I provide valuable content, then I'll get more sales," Pedersen says.

Think Like a Publisher

The new publishing model on the Web is not about hype and spin and messages. It is about delivering content when and where it is needed and, in the process, branding you or your organization as a leader. When you understand your audience, those people who will become your buyers (or those who will join, donate, subscribe, apply, volunteer, or vote), you can craft an editorial and content strategy just for them. What works is a focus on your buyers and their problems. What fails is an egocentric display of your products and services.

In order to implement a successful strategy, think like a publisher. Marketers at the organizations successfully using the new rules recognize the fact that they are now purveyors of information, and they manage content as a valuable asset with the same care that a publishing company does. One of the most important things that publishers do is start with a content strategy and *then* focus on the mechanics and design of delivering that content. Publishers carefully identify and define target audiences and consider what content is required in order to meet their needs. Publishers consider all of the following questions: Who are my readers? How do I reach them? What are their motivations? What are the problems I can help them solve? How can I entertain them and inform them at the same time? What content will compel them to purchase what I have to offer?

Tell Your Organization's Story Directly

Victor Konshin, the author of the top book on gout, *Beating Gout: A Sufferer's Guide to Living Pain Free*, provides valuable information for gout sufferers on his Beating Gout site.[9] He provides what he says is the most accurate information about gout available anywhere on the Internet, all of it focused on solving the problems of his buyers: gout patients and and their families.

Unlike so many other web sites, Beating Gout is not just a big online brochure. The people who create product-centric, brochure-like sites really miss out on an opportunity to educate and inform their potential customers. When visitors receive something of value, as they do on Beating Gout, they become eager to do business with the company that helped and educated them.

Prior to creating his content-centric site, Konshin had a basic site to promote his book. "I had been disappointed with the lack of attention that my site was getting both from customers and the media," he says.

The new site delivers information with headlines such as "Gout, the forgotten disease"; "The Impact of Gout on Your Quality-of-Life, Finances, and Family"; and "Kidney Stones, a Gout Early Warning?" Each of the

---

[9] www.beatinggout.com/

information-packed posts is ranked highly by search engines such as Google, greatly increasing the traffic to his site while decreasing the bounce rate (frequency of one page views) by about 60 percent.

"My site has been coming up in much higher position in search results," Konshin says. "For example, my site used to come up on the third or fourth search page for the phrase 'gout myths,' but it is now at the top of the first page. In the past I was afraid to give away content; now I realize customers reward you for it."

Another measure that Konshin monitors is his book's Amazon ranking. Since he launched his new site, *Beating Gout* has consistently been the top book on gout. The bottom line is that Konshin is selling a lot more books as a result of his creation of an information-rich resource for buyers. What about you? If you have a product-centric site, can you transform it into a buyer-centric one?

Know the Goals and Let Content Drive Action

On the speaking circuit and via my blog, I am often asked to critique marketing programs, web sites, and blogs. My typical responses, "What's the goal?" and "What problems do you solve for your buyers?" often throw people off. It is amazing that so many marketers don't have established goals for their marketing programs and for web sites and blogs in particular. And they often cannot articulate who their buyers are and what problems they solve for them.

An effective Web marketing and PR strategy that delivers compelling content to buyers gets them to take action. (You will learn more about developing your own marketing and PR strategy in Chapter 10.)

Companies that understand the new rules of marketing and PR have a clearly defined *business* goal—to sell products, to generate contributions, or to get people to vote or join. These successful organizations aren't focused on the wrong goals, things like press clips and advertising awards. At successful organizations, news releases, blogs, web sites, video, and other content draw visitors into the sales-consideration cycle, then funnel them toward the place where action occurs. The goal is not hidden, and it is easy for buyers to find the way to take the next step. When content effectively drives action, the next step of the sales process—an e-commerce company's "products" button, the

B2B corporation's "white paper download" form, or a nonprofit's "donate" link— are easy to find.

Working from the perspective of the company's desire for revenue growth and customer retention (the goals), rather than focusing on made-up metrics for things like leads and web site traffic, yields surprising changes in the typical marketing plan and in the organization of Web content. Web site traffic doesn't matter if your goal is revenue (however, the traffic may *lead to* the goal). Similarly, being ranked number one on Google for a phrase isn't important (although, if your buyers care about that phrase, it can lead to the goal).

Ultimately, when marketers focus on the same goals as the rest of the organization, we develop marketing programs that really deliver action and begin to contribute to the bottom line and command respect. Rather than meeting rolled eyes and snide comments about marketing as simply the "T-shirt department," we're seen as part of a strategic unit that contributes to reaching the organization's goals.

Content and Thought Leadership

For many companies and individuals, reaching customers with Web content has a powerful, less obvious effect. Content brands an organization as a thought leader. Indeed, many organizations create content especially to position them as thought leaders in their market. Instead of just directly selling something, a great site, blog, or podcast series tells the world that you are smart, that you understand the market very well, and that you might be a person or organization that would be valuable to do business with. Web content directly contributes to an organization's online reputation by showing thought leadership in the marketplace of ideas. See Chapter 11 for more on thought leadership.

In the following chapters that make up Part II of the book, I introduce blogs, news releases, podcasting, online video, viral marketing, and social media. Then in Part III, I present a guide to creating your marketing and PR plan (Chapter 10), followed by detailed chapters with how-to information on each technique. Content turns browsers into buyers. It doesn't matter whether you're selling premium wine cabinets or a new music CD, or advocating to stop sonar harm to whales; Web content sells any product or service and advocates any philosophy or image.

Web-Based Communications to Reach Buyers Directly

4

Social Media and Your Targeted Audience

A s millions of people use the Web for conducting detailed research on products and services, getting involved in political campaigns, joining music and film fan clubs, reviewing products, and discussing hobbies and passions, they congregate in all kinds of online places. The technologies and tools, which many people now refer to collectively as "social media," all include ways for users to express their opinions online:

- **Social Networking** sites like Facebook, Twitter, LinkedIn, and MySpace help people cultivate a community of friends and share information.
- **Blogs**, personal web sites written by somebody who is passionate about a topic, provide a means to share that passion with the world and to foster an active community of readers who provide comments on the author's posts.
- **Video and photo sharing** sites like YouTube, Flickr, and Vimeo greatly simplify the process of sharing and commenting on photos and videos.
- **Chat rooms and message boards** serve as online meeting places where people meet and discuss topics of interest, with the main feature being that anyone can start a discussion thread.
- **Listservs**, similar to chat rooms, send messages out by email to a collection of registered members.
- **Wikis** are web sites that anybody can edit and update.
- **Social bookmarking** sites like Digg and Delicious allow users to suggest content to others and "vote" on what is interesting.

What Is Social Media, Anyway?

Since "social media" is such an important concept (and is so often misunderstood) I'll define it:

> Social media provides the way people share ideas, content, thoughts, and relationships online. Social media differ from so-called "mainstream media" in that anyone can create, comment on, and add to social media content. Social media can take the form of text, audio, video, images, and communities.

The best way to think about social media is not in terms of the different technologies and tools but, rather, how those technologies and tools allow you to communicate directly with your buyers in places they are congregating right now.

Just as a point of clarification, note that there are two terms that sound similar here: "social media" and "social networking." *Social media* is the superset and is how we refer to the various media that people use to communicate online in a social way. Social media include blogs, wikis, video and photo sharing, and much more. A subset of social media is *social networking*, a term I use to refer to how people interact on sites like Facebook, Twitter, LinkedIn, MySpace, and other similar sites. Social networking occurs when people create a personal profile and interact to become part of a community of friends and like-minded people and to share information. You'll notice throughout the book that I use both terms. This chapter is about the larger concept of social media, while in Chapter 14 we dive into detail about social networking.

I'm fond of thinking of the Web as a city—it helps make sense of each aspect of online life and how we create and interact. Corporate sites are the storefronts on Main Street peddling wares. Craigslist is like the bulletin board at the entrance of the corner store; eBay, a garage sale; Amazon, a bookstore replete with patrons anxious to give you their two cents. Mainstream media sites like the *New York Times* online are the newspapers of the city. Chat rooms and forums are the pubs and saloons of the online world. You've even got the proverbial wrong-side-of-the-tracks spots: the Web's adult-entertainment and spam underbelly.

Social Media Is a Cocktail Party

If you follow my metaphor of the Web as a city, then think of social media and the ways that people interact on blogs, forums, and social networking sites as the bars, private clubs, and cocktail parties of the city. To extend the (increasingly tortured) analogy even further, Twitter can be compared to the interlude when the girls go to the ladies' room and talk about the guys, and the guys are discussing the girls while they wait.

Viewing the Web as a sprawling city where social media are the places people congregate to have fun helps us make sense of how marketers can best use the tools of social media. How do you act in a cocktail party situation?

- Do you go into a large gathering filled with a few acquaintances and tons of people you do not know and shout "BUY MY PRODUCT!"?
- Do you go into a cocktail party and ask every single person you meet for a business card before you agree to speak with them?
- Do you listen more than you speak?
- Are you helpful, providing valuable information to people with no expectation of getting something tangible in return?
- Do you try to meet every single person, or do you have a few great conversations?
- Or do you avoid the social interaction of cocktail parties altogether because you are uncomfortable in such situations?

I find these questions are helpful to people who are new to social media. This analogy is also a good one to discuss with social media cynics and those who cannot see the value of this important form of communication.

The Web-as-a-city approach is especially important when dealing with people who have been steeped in the traditions of advertising-based marketing, those skilled at interrupting people to talk up products and using coercion techniques to make a sale. Sure, you can go to a cocktail party and treat everyone as a sales lead while blabbing on about what your company does. But that approach is unlikely to make you popular.

Guess what? The popular people on the cocktail circuit make friends. People like to do business with people they like. And they are eager to introduce their friends to each other. The same trends hold true in social media. So go ahead and join the party. But think of it as just that—a fun place where you give more than you get. Of course, you can also do business there, but the kind you do at a cocktail party and not at the general store. What you get in return for your valuable interactions are lasting friendships, many of which lead to business opportunities.

This chapter is an introduction to the concepts of social media. In subsequent chapters, I go into much greater detail about blogs (Chapters 5 and 15), video (Chapters 6 and 16), and social networking (Chapter 14).

Facebook Group Drives 15,000 People to Singapore Tattoo Show

I speak at dozens of conferences a year all over the world. Since organizers usually book me many months in advance, I gain a great deal of insight into how they promote the events. It tends to be the same old methods: Send an email and a postal direct mail to everyone who attended last year, buy some mailing lists, and send some more promotions. Most shows build good web sites and most have decent search engine optimization. But that's usually it.

What if you're charged with promoting a brand-new show? Because there are no previous attendees to draw from, the work is much more difficult. Or is it? When a show is new, the "old rules" of promotion don't apply. You can do something new and untested.

The 1st Annual Singapore Tattoo Show,[1] held in January 2009, was endorsed and supported by the Singapore Tourism Board and included Chris Garver of Miami Ink as the show's embassador. The goal of the show's first year was to get 5,000 visitors to one place where more than 120 artists from around the globe, representing all the various traditional and modern tattoo styles, ticked away with their machines. All sorts of fun and funky exhibitors were there, and emcee and official DJ Shawn Lee kept awesome sounds pumping throughout the hall.

Andrew Peters,[2] Asia Pacific regional director of The Pacific West Communications, is the brains behind the social media promotions leading up to the Singapore Tattoo Show, working on both traditional and social media publicity. "The show was launched via social media, including Facebook, my blog, and other social networking platforms because of my

---

[1] www.tattoo.com.sg/

[2] http://aplink.wordpress.com

belief in how social media could make a far-reaching impact," Peters says. "This ultimately becomes a collective of voices that cannot be ignored, and it becomes contagious as others want to be a part of the collective."

Peters used Facebook as a way for people to connect well before the physical event. He established a Facebook group called Tattoo Artistry[3] three months prior to the show. The group grew very quickly, securing a place as the center of tatoo artistry for the region. In a sense, the physical show started with a virtual group. Note that Peters' brilliant choice of the Facebook Group name (Tattoo Artistry) was not the name of the event (The Singapore Tattoo Show). That way, the group could build momentum independently of the show and live on beyond the first year.

The passion of the Tattoo Artistry Facebook group members meant they would help promote the group to their friends, so the online community eventually included many people eager to attend the live event. Instead of relying on expensive advertising, Peters built a community of passionate fans who built anticipation and buzz for the event. "Quite simply, I was amazed at the result," he says. "One morning I checked into Facebook to see if a few people had joined the Tattoo Artistry group. Not only had people joined, they had added photos, were leaving messages, and chatting to each other. The group had come to life."

The Tattoo Artistry Facebook group quickly reached 3,000 members and was an important reason that more than 15,000 people attended the first Singapore Tattoo Show—that's three times the expected number of attendees.

The Tattoo Artistry Facebook group is now Asia's largest social network for the tattoo industry, tattoo enthusiasts, and fans. The group will continue to grow as an online destination to connect with about additional Singapore Tattoo Shows, which will be held annually. "Engaging community involvement is not so easily achieved in more traditional marketing methods," Peters says. "Social media like Facebook offer immediacy, freedom to be who you are, the opportunity to meet others who are similar, and to have a place to fit in. Event organizers must see beyond their immediate need to put 'bums on seats' for the next event and instead engage people to build support and loyalty over many years."

---

[3] www.facebook.com/group.php?gid=32140274011

The New Rules of Job Search

Company lost its funding. Outsourced. Caught in a merger. Downsized. Fired. It seems like every day I learn of another person who is in the job market. Usually that's because when they need a job, all of a sudden people jump into networking mode, and I hear from them after years of silence. Hey, I'm okay with that; it's always good to hear from old friends. And I've been fired three times, so I certainly know what it's like to be in the job market.

Since looking for a job is all about marketing a product (you), I wanted to include a section in the book for those of you who are currently in the job market, those soon to graduate from college or university, or otherwise looking for a career opportunity.

If you're like the vast majority of job seekers, you'd do what "everyone knows" is the way to find a job: You prepare a resume, obsessing over every entry to make sure it paints your background in the best possible light. You'd also begin a networking campaign, emailing and phoning your contacts and using networking tools like LinkedIn, hoping that someone in your extended network knows of a suitable job opportunity.

While many people find jobs the traditional way, social media allow a new way to interact and meet potential employers. The old rules of job searchers required advertising a product (you) with direct mail (your resume that you send to potential employers). The old rules of job searches required you to interrupt people (friends and colleagues) to tell them that you were on the market and to ask them to help you.

As people engage with each other on social media sites, there are plenty of opportunities to network. Just like a physical cocktail party, if you are unemployed and looking for work, the people you meet may be in a position to introduce you to that perfect employer. Of course, the opposite is also true: Smart employers look to social networking sites to find the sort of plugged-in people that would fit in at their company or in a certain job.

So you want to find a new job via social media? You have to stop thinking like an advertiser of a product and start thinking like a publisher of information. Create information that people want. Create an online presence that people are eager to consume. Establish a virtual front door that people will happily link to—one that employers will find. The new rules of finding a job require you to share your knowledge and expertise with a world that is looking for what you have to offer.

How David Murray Found a New Job via Twitter

David Murray[4] says that after being laid off, he immediately did the traditional things, completing his resume and calling a bunch of contacts. But he eventually realized that he would also have to change gears and pay attention to blogs, social networks, and online communities. Murray already had a Twitter account, so he reached out to his Twitter followers and publicly announced that he was looking for work.

"I guess you could say I used a new tool for old-school networking," Murray says. "The response was overwhelming, and I received several leads and opportunities that were far more fruitful than my previous attempts."

Murray then hit on a creative way to use Twitter Search[5] in his job search. "I came across a comment from Chris Brogan[6] on how he used Twitter Search to keep track of his tens of thousands of followers using RSS feeds," Murray says. "So I simply began entering keywords in Twitter Search like 'Hiring Social Media,' 'Social Media Jobs,' 'Online Community Manager,' 'Blogging Jobs,' and so on. I then pulled the RSS feeds of these keyword conversations into Google Reader[7] and made it a habit to check these first thing in the morning every day."

Bingo. Murray came across conversations related to his keywords and if something sounded like a good fit for him, he took the liberty of introducing himself via Twitter. "Many times when inquiring about the open positions, the jobs had not been officially posted," Murray says.

How cool is it that on Twitter you can express interest in a job opportunity that hasn't even been announced yet? It's like getting inside information!

Hired. It didn't take long for Murray to land the ideal job as assistant Webmaster of client services for The Bivings Group.[8] Several months later he was promoted to director of Social Web Communications.

[4] http://twitter.com/DaveMurr
[5] http://search.twitter.com/
[6] http://twitter.com/chrisbrogan
[7] www.google.com/reader
[8] www.bivings.com/

As Heather Huhman, who writes the Entry Level Careers pages for Examiner.com,[9] says: "The Internet is changing just about everything—the internship/entry-level job search included. Gone are the days of printing out your cover letter and resume on 'special' paper, sticking both in an envelope and mailing the application package off. We are officially in the Job Search 2.0 era."

Some people might argue that this technique only works to find jobs related to social media and online marketing (like Murray did). While it's true that social-media-savvy people like Murray are first to use these techniques, I'm convinced that they'd work for many other kinds of roles too. These days Twitter is used by all kinds of people and a tweet like: "I'm looking for an accountant to join my London office" appears frequently. You should be monitoring what people are saying. And here's an added benefit. If you're an accountant, or salesperson, or production manager looking for work, then you're really going to stand out from the crowd of 1,000 resumes if you use social media to find a job.

As long as we're discussing social media and job searches, here's an important consideration: *What comes up when you Google your name with the name of your most recent employer?* Potential employers do that all the time. And you can influence what they see! Remember, on the Web, you are what you publish.

Insignificant Backwaters or Valuable Places to Connect?

At specialty sites of all kinds, like-minded hobbyists, professionals, fans, and supporters meet and discuss the intricate nuances of subjects that interest them. Interactive forums were once seen as insignificant backwaters by PR and marketing people—not worth the time to even monitor, let alone participate in. I've heard many marketers dismiss online forums with disdain, saying things like, "Why should I worry about a bunch of geeks obsessively typing away in the dead of night?" However, as many marketers have learned, ignoring forums can be hazardous to your brand, while participating as a member allows you to reap rewards.

---

[9] www.examiner.com/x-828-Entry-Level-Careers-Examiner

In a post on his blog called "Sony, Rootkits and Digital Rights Management [DRM] Gone Too Far,"[10] Mark Russinovich presented his detailed analysis on characteristics of the software used on Sony BMG[11] music CDs to manage permissions for the purchased music. Russinovich argued that shortcomings in the software design create security issues that might be exploited by malicious software such as worms or viruses. He also showed that both the way the software is installed and its lack of an uninstaller utility were troublesome.

"The entire experience was frustrating and irritating," Russinovich wrote on his blog. "Not only had Sony put software on my system that uses techniques commonly used by malware [malicious software] to mask its presence, the software is poorly written and provides no means for uninstall. Worse, most users that stumble across the cloaked files with an RKR scan will cripple their computer if they attempt the obvious step of deleting the cloaked files. While I believe in the media industry's right to use copy protection mechanisms to prevent illegal copying, I don't think that we've found the right balance of fair use and copy protection, yet. This is a clear case of Sony taking DRM too far."

The reaction to Russinovich's post was immediate and dramatic. In the next several days, hundreds of comments, many harshly critical of Sony BMG Music, were posted on his blog. "Thank you very much for bringing to light what Sony is doing. I have purchased many thousands of dollars of their products over the years. Next year's purchases will be zero," said User101. "I SAY BOYCOTT THE BASTARDS!!" said Jack3617. "If you plan on boycotting, let the offending company know. They need to know that they are losing customers and WHY. Perhaps others companies will get the message as well," said Kolby. "Great article by Mark and scandalous behavior by Sony," said Petter Lindgren.

Hundreds of other bloggers jumped in with their own take on the issue, and chat rooms and forums such as Slashdot[12] were abuzz. Many people expressed frustration that the music industry disapproves of music piracy and sues music downloaders, yet it treats its customers poorly (which

---

[10] http://blogs.technet.com/markrussinovich/archive/2005/10/31/Sony-rootkits-and-digital-rights-management-gone-too-far.aspx

[11] www.sonybmg.com/

[12] http://it.slashdot.org/article.pl?sid=05/10/31/2016223tid=172tid=1584

reflected negatively on the entire industry, not just Sony BMG). Soon, reporters from online news sites such as ZDNet and InformationWeek wrote their own analyses, and the issue became international news.

So where was Sony BMG during the online hullabaloo? Not on the blogs. Not on the message boards. Nobody from Sony BMG participated in the online discussions. Nobody spoke with online media. Sony BMG was dark (not participating in the communities at all), which added to the frustrations of those who were concerned about the issues. Finally, five days later, Sony BMG's global digital business president Thomas Hesse went on NPR's *Morning Edition*[13] to defend the company. The choice of radio as a forum to react to a storm of protest on the Web was a poor one. Had Hesse immediately commented on Russinovich's blog or agreed to speak with a technology reporter for an online publication, he could have gotten his take on the issue onto the screens of concerned people early in the crisis, helping to diffuse their anger. But instead of understanding customer concerns, Hesse downplayed the issue on *Morning Edition*, saying he objected to terms such as malware, spyware, and rootkit. "Most people, I think, don't even know what a rootkit is, so why should they care about it?" he said in the interview.

Online debate intensified. Sony BMG reacted with the announcement of an exchange program. "To Our Valued Customers," the announcement read. "You may be aware of the recent attention given to the XCP content protection software included on some SONY BMG CDs. This software was provided to us by a third-party vendor, First4Internet. Discussion has centered on security concerns raised about the use of CDs containing this software. We share the concerns of consumers regarding these discs, and we are instituting a mail-in program that will allow consumers to exchange any CD with XCP software for the same CD without copy protection and receive MP3 files of the same title . . . ."

Unfortunately for Sony BMG, the exchange program didn't end the issue. Texas Attorney General Greg Abbott sued Sony BMG under the state's 2005 spyware law. California and New York followed with class-action lawsuits. Soon after, law student Mark Lyon started a blog[14] to track Sony BMG XCP rootkit lawsuits. "I trusted Sony BMG when they asked to install a 'small program' on my computer," Lyon wrote on his blog. "Instead, they infected my

---

[13] www.npr.org/templates/story/story.php?storyId=49892605
[14] www.sonysuit.com/

computer with poorly written code, which even if it wasn't designed for a malicious purpose (like reporting my activities—something they expressly promised they were not going to do), opened me up to a number of computer viruses and security problems. This site exists to help others who have been harmed by Sony BMG and their XCP Content Protection." As of this writing, Sony has settled with 40 states and Lyon has continued to cover all the action on his Sony Suit blog.

Of course, we will never know what would have happened if someone from Sony BMG had quickly jumped into the blogstorm, apologized, stated Sony's plan of action, and offered the exchange program immediately. Yes, I'm sure it would still have been a crisis situation for the music publisher, but I'm also certain that the negative effects would have been substantially reduced.

What's important for all organizations to take away from this incident is that it is critical to respond quickly to situations as they unfold on the Web. Reacting quickly and honestly in the same forums where the discussions are taking place is essential. You may not be able to completely turn a negative situation around, but you will instantly be seen as a real person who gives a name and a personality to a large, seemingly uncaring organization. Just by participating you will contribute to making the situation right. The Web's power of linking should ensure that participants who see your posts on one forum or blog will link to them from other forums and blogs, so you don't have to worry about contributing to multiple places. What's important is first getting out there; after that, remember that authenticity and honesty are always paramount.

Your Best Customers Participate in Online Forums—So Should You

On the Web, customers, stakeholders, and the media can immediately see what's on people's minds. There's never been so good an opportunity to monitor what's being said about you and your products than the one we have now. The Internet is like a massive focus group with uninhibited customers offering up their thoughts for free!

Tapping this resource is simple: You've got to monitor what's being said. And when an organization is the subject of heated discussions, particularly negative ones, it just feels weird if a representative of that organization doesn't jump in with a response. If the company is dark, not saying a thing online, participants start wondering, "What are they hiding?" Just having a presence on the blogs, forums, and chat rooms that your customers frequent shows that you care about the people who spend money with your organization. It is best not to wait for a crisis. You should participate as appropriate all the time. How can you afford not to become closer to your most vocal constituents?

Let's look at another example, but one with a much different outcome. It happened when Nikon introduced a new "prosumer" digital camera, the D200 model, which appeals to very advanced amateur photographers and professionals alike. Nikon launched the new model globally through specialty distributors and high-end camera stores frequented by these target buyers. But Nikon also offered the D200 outside of the normal distribution channels by selling the model in big-box stores such as Circuit City and Best Buy. The camera was a hot commodity when launched just prior to the holidays, and supply was constrained when it first hit the stores.

"The places where camera guys like me normally get Nikon gear were caught out because of a lack of supply," says Alan Scott, an experienced photographer and long-time Nikon customer. "People who preordered the D200 or who were waiting for camera retailer sites to go live with an announcement of availability were gnashing their teeth wanting to get the camera."

Like many other photographers, Scott frequents popular online digital photography forums, including Nikonians: The Nikon User Community and DPR: Digital Photography Review. "The forums were active with lots of people complaining that they couldn't get the camera from their normal long-term suppliers but that the big box stores had them," Scott says. "Then a thread was started on Nikonians[15] and later picked up on DPR[16] that discussed how popular New York City photography supplier B&H Photo-Video, a trusted source with a knowledgeable staff that many professionals and high-end hobbyists go to, had taken orders but then were canceling them."

The first post, from ceo1939, said, "I ordered a D200 from B&H this afternoon about 4:30 mountain time. The charge was made against my credit card. An hour later I got an email that said they had a technical problem and the camera was actually not in stock, but they would hold my order and charge

---

[15] www.nikonians.org/

[16] http://forums.dpreview.com/forums/

for it when they actually get in stock. I tried cancelling the charge, and got an email back on how to handle a disputed charge. I will see what happens when I call them in the morning."

Many camera enthusiasts and customers of B&H were monitoring the thread at this point. "Within a few hours, several dozen posts appeared on the thread, and the tone had become critical of B&H, with people complaining that the company was purposely screwing them," Scott says. "Forum participants said that email notifications from B&H did not work and people who called in were getting cameras in front of those who had signed up for an alert system."

The B&H situation sounds a bit like the Sony BMG incident, doesn't it? In both cases, avid participants in specialty online forums sounded off about a company, its products, and its business practices. Both sets of threads occurred in little-known nooks of the Web, far outside mainstream media channels and other typical places that PR people monitor for what's being said about their company and its products. But the B&H case is very different because a B&H employee was an active participant on the boards.

"Unfortunately as everyone who frequents this site knows, Nikon USA has been remarkably reluctant (diplomatic, eh?) to put this camera in retailers' hands," wrote Henry Posner of B&H Photo-Video, Inc. on the DPR thread. "The result in this particular case is that had we left the order open, we'd still be sitting on your money and would have been unable to fulfill the D200 order and it's reasonable to presume you'd be chafing to get your camera, which we'd have been (and are) unable to supply due to circumstances beyond our control . . . . We regret and apologize for having vexed you."

Unlike in the Sony BMG example, people at B&H had been monitoring the messages and were prepared to participate. "So in steps Henry Posner, who is with B&H," Scott says. "He came into the forum and said, basically, 'you're right, we screwed you,' but then explained what happened, apologized, and said that B&H will make it right. By acknowledging the issue, one guy with one post changed the whole tone of the thread and the reputation of B&H. After that, the posts changed to become incredibly positive."

Indeed, they were. "Henry's participation in various Web forums is something I respect greatly," wrote BJNicholls on one thread. "I can't think of someone of power with any other business who engages in public discussion of store issues and products."

"I also admire his forthrightness," added N80. "He admits there have been some mistakes and that the situation has been hard to handle. However, he firmly denies the charges of lying and deceitfulness that have been flying around. And I absolutely believe him."

What happened at B&H was not a coincidence or a one-time situation. The message boards and online forums are a critical component of the company's marketing and communications strategy.

"I spend a great deal of time poking around in the forums," says Henry Posner, director of corporate communications for B&H Photo-Video Inc. "Being a part of the forums is really important and is actually in my job description. Because my background is in professional photography, as a person who has actually used the equipment we sell I have legitimacy in the forums." Before joining B&H in the mid-1990s, Posner worked for a company that provided photography services for colleges and high schools; he covered events such as basketball and football games.

Posner monitors about a dozen message boards and forums on a daily basis. "I try to find things about photography equipment or technique where I can make a meaningful contribution," he says. "We want to make certain that my credibility is maintained—that's the most important thing—so I don't go in and say something like 'that's right' just to get my name and the B&H name into a conversation. But if I see that there is a discussion that I can add value to, about equipment or a technique that I am familiar with, I will jump in."

B&H has a mail-order catalog, an e-commerce web site, and a 35,000-square-foot retail store in Manhattan. "Our customer is anyone from the amateur up to the professional photographer working in Beirut who is running around with cameras bouncing on his hips while looking for a Wi-Fi connection to send images back to the bureau," he says. "I contribute to the forums when it is appropriate, but if anyone ever asks about where to buy something being discussed, I immediately take the conversation offline via email. I don't want to promote my company directly. The other conversations I look for are when people are talking about B&H itself. I often hold back and let others speak for me. Other people will often say positive things about B&H because I am so active in the forums. So if someone does jump in about B&H, I will thank them, and then I will address the issue directly."

Don't you wish your customers had been as understanding as the photography enthusiasts on these forums the last time your company screwed up? Well, as Henry Posner shows, if you actively participate in the online communities that your customers frequent, you will earn their sympathy and patience when things go wrong.

Your Space in the Forums

The last two examples were of companies that had discussions started about them on online forums. But how should a marketer interact? "Participation in forums is a must," says Robert Pearlman, editor of collectSPACE: The Source for Space History & Artifacts.[17] Pearlman started collectSPACE in 1999 because there wasn't a single site to serve collectors of space memorabilia and to preserve space history. "Before the Internet, there were space memorabilia collectors, but they were in pockets of communities in Germany and Japan, in Houston, and near the Kennedy Space Center in Florida," he says. "But there was no way for them to communicate with each other. The biggest impact is that collectSPACE has educated the market. We've brought the various pockets of collectors into one place."

The collectSPACE community has grown into a network of collectors around the world who share their knowledge of the pieces that they own. The site counts 25,000 registered users (about 5,000 actively post on the site) and about 250,000 unique readers each month. Interestingly, collectSPACE also includes many people who worked in the early space program; they participate in the forums and talk about the history of the artifacts that they had a hand in building. Pearlman says many astronauts read the forums because they are able to get a sense of the market for the memorabilia that they may have amassed over the years and to find out what fellow astronauts are up to on the lectures and appearances front. Astronauts also use the forums to monitor the history of the space program and protect their legacy.

"In other areas of collecting, collectors and museums have been at odds," says Pearlman. "Museums looked at collectors as hoarders storing stuff in the basement, while their own mission was more altruistic: sharing with the public. And collectors looked at museums and said that they did a good job with major items like spacesuits and spacecraft but did a lousy job with literally the nuts and bolts except put them away in the archive. What collectSPACE does is allow museums to read what their 'competition' is doing and interact with collectors and ask their advice. Collectors have helped to plan exhibits

[17] www.collectspace.com/

and loaned items to the museums, and at the same time, museums were able to sell surplus items to collectors."

Pearlman sees a huge benefit for dealers, manufacturers, and auction houses that specialize in space items to participate in the collectSPACE forums. "By participating in the forums, dealers and manufacturers now know what collectors are interested in," he says. "Products can be developed based on what the current trends are in the market. Auction houses and dealers have been able to preview items to the market before a sale to gauge interest. In the case of unique items, you get instant feedback through a mini-market study."

As moderator of the collectSPACE forums, Pearlman has personally followed hundreds of thousands of posts and seen the good and the bad from space memorabilia dealers. "If there is a post that is not flattering to a business, someone from that business needs to have been monitoring the posts and respond as required," he says. "In discussion forums where people have a common bond, people feel that the forum is theirs. We see people who have 1,000 or even 5,000 posts, and they treat that as a badge of honor. People who represent businesses need to let the collectors know that you care enough about them to go to [their] turf instead of expecting them to come to yours."

As Pearlman advises and the Sony BMG and B&H Photo-Video examples show, marketers must take active participation in the communities that matter for their markets. But you can't just stand on the virtual sidelines and post only when you have something for sale or a comment about your products or services. The most successful companies come in and provide ideas and advice on a wide variety of subjects and topics in their field. They are full and active participants in the community. Then, when people complain or want specific product advice from a company, they trust the community member more. Active participation can pay off exponentially for companies who are treated as members of the community.

Wikis, Listservs, and Your Audience

Close cousins to the forums like Nikonians and collectSPACE include group email lists (often called listservs) and wikis. Just like forums, a listserv is a way that groups of like-minded people stay connected to one another. Typically, any member can post to the list, but instead of requiring that people go to a central place to read messages, a listserv sends messages out to the members of the group via email.

Lisa Solomon, Esq.[18] provides legal research and writing services to other attorneys on an outsourced basis. Solomon has been extremely involved in participating in listservs such as the Solosez[19] discussion list for solo attorneys, which is run by the American Bar Association. "The listserv has been important in the way that I develop my law practice. I am an active participant and try to always add value to the subjects that are being discussed. In my listserv signature is my Web address. That is the place that I send people to show them what I do. I have writing samples on the site, and that's how they can check out what I do at their convenience. The participation has been great for meeting contacts and building business."

Wikis are web sites that permit users to update, delete, or edit the content on the site. The most famous wiki is Wikipedia,[20] the free encyclopedia that anyone can edit, which has more than 13 million articles in over 260 languages, all contributed by people like you and me. If you haven't done so already, you should hightail it over to Wikipedia and conduct some searches on your organization name, important brand names, your CEO, and other notable executives and board members. The fact is that Wikipedia entries loom large in search engine rankings, and Wikipedia is in the top 10 most visited sites on the Web.

When you find an entry about your company or brand, you should check it for accuracy. It's fair game to correct any inaccuracies (such as the number of employees in your company). But don't try to manipulate the entry. The Wikipedia community is quick to react when articles are edited to present a certain point of view. It is not uncommon to see an entry updated several times per day and with larger organizations the updates can be much more frequent. In fact, one of the pillars of the community is: "All Wikipedia articles must be written from a neutral point of view, representing views fairly and without bias." So, if your organization was party to a lawsuit that makes you look bad in some way and it's in Wikipedia, don't try to remove the reference.

Sometimes, it might be best to create a new article on Wikipedia. For some organizations, authoring something on a particular niche where you have

---

[18] www.questionoflaw.net/

[19] www.abanet.org/soloseznet/

[20] www.wikipedia.org/

expertise may have tremendous value. Make sure that you aren't promoting your company and its products or services, though; it needs to be an article of value to people researching the topic you know well. As a starting point, you might notice that there are articles in the area you have knowledge in and that those articles link to an empty Wikipedia page. Blue (or purple, if you have already visited them) links represent pages that do exist. Red links point to pages that don't yet have any content. If you see a bunch of red links indicating that an author expects new content to be added, and you have knowledge and expertise in that area, maybe it's time for you to create a page to fulfill a need. For example, a technology company might provide details on patents it holds that relate to products that already have Wikipedia entries.

Creating Your Own Wiki

It's entirely possible that for your organization's area of expertise, no appropriate forum, listserv, or wiki has been established. Just like Robert Pearlman of collectSPACE, you may find an unfulfilled need in your marketplace to organize people and ideas into a single resource. A wiki could be just what the doctor ordered—and you can start it, gaining tremendous value for your organization as a result.

Consider Alacra, a company that creates online technology and services for financial institutions and professional service firms to find, package, and present business information. In the crowded field of professional information services, Alacra, a company of about 60 people, competes with much bigger players such as Thomson Reuters (50,000 employees) and Reed Elsevier (32,000 employees). An important part of Alacra's marketing and communications strategy has been its early forays into corporate blogs and corporate wikis.

In September 2005, Alacra and its CEO, Steve Goldstein, unveiled Alacra-Wiki,[21] an open and collaborative resource for producers and consumers of business information. AlacraWiki brings together in-depth profiles of information sources, companies, and important people in the industry (and much more). The front page, which populates via RSS feeds, is filled with information and industry news from the premier analysts and trade publications. "We had amassed a tremendous amount of valuable information on publishers and

---

[21] www.alacrawiki.com/

databases through our content licensing efforts," Goldstein says. "We thought it would be useful to make this information available on the Web, and a wiki was clearly the best format."

Goldstein was surprised that at the time AlacraWiki was launched, there was no directory of business information in the market. "We included reference data for the industry in a wiki form as a service to industry," he says. The wiki is a collaborative effort where anybody can create and update listings. To start the project, Goldstein hired a summer MBA student intern, who built the initial infrastructure and initial listings in just eight weeks. Although many people have contributed, some don't update their personal or company profiles. "It's strange that people don't go in and change it, because it's so easy," he says.

As someone who has created both a blog and a wiki, how would Goldstein compare the skill sets to create them? "To be successful at blogging, you need to have something to say," Goldstein says. "You need to have some communications skills to be successful. Over on the wiki side, you need to be an expert in something to get it populated to begin with, and then you need the resources to keep it up."

Social media sites are places that people congregate to discuss things that are important to them. Where are people discussing your industry, and the products and services you offer? If that place already exists, you should monitor it and participate as appropriate. If it doesn't yet exist, consider starting a place for colleagues and customers to meet and revel in "information central" for your market. Now let's turn to blogs, another form of social media.

5

Blogs: Tapping Millions of Evangelists to Tell Your Story

Blogging is my front door. Since 2004, my blog[1] has been where I post my ideas, both big and small. There's no doubt that my blog is the most important marketing and PR tool I have as a marketing and PR speaker, writer, and consultant. Even after five years and hundreds of blog posts, I'm always surprised at how effectively this tool helps me accomplish my goals.

My blog allows me to push ideas into the marketplace as I think of them, generating instant feedback. Sure, many blog posts just sit there with little feedback, few comments, and no results. But I learn from these "failures," too; when my audience doesn't get excited about something, it's probably either a dumb idea or poorly explained. On the other hand, some posts have had truly phenomenal results, quite literally changing my business in the process. I'll admit that my ravings about the importance of my blog may sound over the top. But the truth is that blogging really has changed my life.

The first time I shared my ideas about the new rules of PR, in a post on my blog that included a link to an e-book I had written, the reaction was dramatic and swift. In the first week, thousands of people viewed the post. To date, over 250,000 people have seen the ideas, over a hundred bloggers have linked to them, and thousands of people have commented on them, on my blog and others'. That one blog post—and the resulting refinement of my ideas after receiving so much feedback, both positive and negative—created the opportunity to write the book you are now reading. As I was writing the first edition of the book during much of 2006 and this edition in 2009,

[1] www.webinknow.com/

I continually posted parts of it, which generated even more critical feedback—hundreds of comments—that made the book much better. And suggestions were followed in this new revised second edition of the book that you're reading now.

Thanks to the power of search engines, my blog is also the most vital and effective way for people to find me. Every word of every post is indexed by Google, Yahoo!, and the other search engines, so when people look for information on the topics I write about, they find me. Journalists find me through my blog and quote me in newspaper and magazine articles *without me having to pitch them*. Conference organizers book me to speak at events as a result of reading my ideas on my blog. I've met many new virtual friends and created a powerful network of colleagues.

As I write and talk to these corporate audiences and other professionals about the power of blogging, many people want to know about the return on investment (ROI) of blogging. In particular, executives want to know, in dollars and cents, what the results will be. The bad news is that this information is difficult to quantify with any degree of certainty. For my small business, I determine ROI by asking everyone who contacts me for the first time, "How did you learn about me?" That approach will be difficult for larger organizations with integrated marketing programs including blogs. The good news is that blogging most certainly generates returns for anyone who creates an interesting blog and posts regularly to it. So what about me? My blog has gotten my ideas out to thousands of people who have never heard of me before. It has helped me get booked for many important speaking gigs around the world. I've determined that about 25 percent of the new consulting business I've brought in during the past five years has been either through the blog directly or from purchasers who cited the blog as important to their decision to hire me. Consider this: If I didn't have a blog, you literally wouldn't be reading these words, because I couldn't have been writing this book without it.

Will writing a blog change your life, too? I can't guarantee that. Blogging is not for everyone. But if you're like countless others, your blog will reap tremendous rewards, both for you personally and for your organization. Yes, the rewards may be financial. But your blog will most certainly serve you as a valuable creative outlet, perhaps a more important reward for you and your business.

The rest of this chapter describes more about blogs and blogging. You will meet other successful bloggers who have added value to their organizations and benefited themselves by blogging. I'll describe the basics of getting started with blogs, including what you should do first—monitor the blogosphere and comment on other people's blogs—before even beginning to write your own. The nittygritty stuff of starting a blog, what to write about, the technology you will need, and other details are found in Chapter 15.

Blogs, Blogging, and Bloggers

Weblogs (blogs) have burst onto the content scene because the technology is such an easy and efficient way to get personal (or organizational) viewpoints out into the market. With easy-to-use blog software, anyone can create a professional-looking blog in just minutes. Most marketing and PR people know about blogs, and many are monitoring what's being said about their company, products, and executives on this new medium. A significant number of people are also blogging for marketing purposes, some with amazing success.

I have found writing this chapter to be a challenge because there is great variance in people's knowledge of blogs and blogging. I always ask the audiences I present to, via a show of hands, "How many people read blogs?" I'm continually surprised that only about 20 to 30 percent of marketing and PR people read blogs. That's a ridiculously low percentage. There's never been an easier way to find out what the marketplace is thinking about you, your company, and your products! When I ask how many people are writing their own blogs, the number is always less than 10 percent. While even the people who are currently reading and writing blogs have varying expertise in the blogosphere, there are significant misconceptions about blogs and blogging among those who don't read them at all. So with apologies in advance to readers who already understand them, I'd like to start with some basics.

A blog is just a web site. But it's a special kind of site that is created and maintained by a person who is passionate about a subject and wants to tell the world about his or her area of expertise. A blog is almost always written by one person who has a fire in the belly and wants to communicate with the world. There are also group blogs (written by several people) and even corporate blogs produced by a department or entire company (without individual personalities at all), but these are less common. The most popular form by far is the individual blog.

A blog is written using software that puts the most recent update, or post, at the top of the site (reverse chronological order). Posts are tagged to appear in selected information categories on the blog and often include identifiers about the content of the post to make it easy for people to find what they want on the blog and via search engines. Software for creating a blog functions essentially as an easy-to-use, personal *content management system* that allows bloggers to become authors without any HTML experience. If you can use Microsoft Word or successfully buy a product online from Amazon, you have enough technical skills to blog! In fact, I often suggest that small companies and individual entrepreneurs create a blog rather than a standard web site because a blog is easier to create for someone who lacks technical skills. Today there are thousands of smaller companies, consultants, and professionals who have a blog but no regular web site.

Many blogs allow readers to leave comments. But bloggers often reserve the right to remove inappropriate comments (spam or profanity, for example). Most bloggers tolerate negative comments on their blogs and don't remove them. I actually like some controversy on my blog because it can spark debate. Opinions that are different from mine on my blog are just fine! This might take some getting used to, especially for a traditional PR department that likes to control messaging. However, I strongly believe that comments from readers offering different viewpoints from the original post are actually a good thing on a blog, because they add credibility to your viewpoint by showing two sides of an issue and by highlighting that your readership is passionate enough to want to contribute to a debate on *your blog*. How cool is that?

Understanding Blogs in the World of the Web

Blogs are independent, Web-based journals containing opinions about anything and everything. *However, blogs are often misperceived by people who don't read them.* Journalists as well as public relations and marketing professionals are quick to dismiss the importance of blogs because they often insist on comparing blogs to magazines and newspapers, with which they are comfortable. But the blogger's usual focus of promoting a single point of view is dramatically different from the journalist's goal of providing a balanced perspective. In my experience, blogs are deemed "bad" or "wrong" only by people who do not read them regularly. In journalism school and on their first-beat assignments when they begin their career, aspiring reporters and editors are taught that stories are developed through research and interviews with knowledgeable sources. Journalists are told that they can't express their own opinions directly, but instead need to find experts and data to support their views. The journalist's craft demands fairness and balance.

Blogs are very different. Blogging provides experts and wannabes with an easy way to make their voices heard in the Web-based marketplace of ideas. Companies that ignore independent product reviews and blog discussions about service quality are living dangerously. Organizations that don't have their own authentic and human blog voices are increasingly seen as suspect by many people who pay attention to what's being said on blogs. But as millions of independent voices shout and whisper all over the Internet, certain mainstream media and PR people still maintain rigid defensive postures, dismissing the diverse opinions emerging from the Web's main streets and roads less traveled.

Many people prefer to box blogs into their existing world view rather than to understand blogs' and bloggers' unique roles on the Web. Often people who don't understand these roles simply react with a cry of "Not real journalism!" But bloggers never claimed to be real journalists; unfortunately, many people continue to think of the Web as a sprawling online newspaper, and this mentality justifies their need to (negatively) compare blogging to what journalists and PR people do. But the metaphor of the Web as a newspaper is inaccurate on many levels, particularly when trying to understand blogs. It is better to think of the Web as a huge city teeming with individuals, and blogs as the sounds of independent voices, just like those of the street-corner soapbox preacher or that friend of yours who always recommends the best books.

Consider the now well-known September 2004 example of how blogs exerted tremendous influence on an issue but were dismissed by people who didn't understand bloggers' role in information dissemination. The controversy, dubbed the "memogate" or "Rathergate" case, involved documents critical of President George W. Bush's service in the United States National Guard. In a *60 Minutes Wednesday* broadcast aired by CBS on September 8, 2004, the documents were presented as authentic, but had not been properly authenticated by CBS. The situation unfolded just hours later on the Free Republic news forum site, where a message was posted by a person called "Buckhead," who said the memos Dan Rather used as the basis of his story appeared typographically impossible.[2] Buckhead's post was followed the next morning by entries to blogs including Little Green Footballs[3] and PowerLine[4] that raised questions about the documents' authenticity. For days, Rather dug in while CBS dismissed the bloggers as a bunch of geeks in pajamas typing away in the dead of night. Of course as we know now, ignoring bloggers cost Rather his job. Had he taken the bloggers seriously and immediately investigated the documents, perhaps he, too, would have very quickly concluded that they were fake. In that case, an explanation and apology might have resulted in the affair blowing over. But dismissing bloggers and their opinions was clearly a mistake. That was years ago. Although bloggers have become more influential since then, there is still a great deal of similarly dismissive behavior going on inside media companies and corporate PR departments.

Okay, so bloggers aren't journalists. Many people in traditional media companies and corporate communications positions trip up because they misunderstand bloggers' actual role in information dissemination. Consider it from the Web-as-a-city perspective: The woman next to you at the bar may not be a journalist, but she sure knows something, and you can choose to believe her or not. Incidentally, seeing the Web as a city also helps make sense of other aspects of online life. Craigslist is like the bulletin board at the entrance of the corner store; eBay, a garage sale; Amazon, a bookstore replete with patrons anxious to give you their book tips. You've even got the proverbial wrong-side-of-the-tracks spots via the Web's adult-entertainment underbelly.

Should you believe everything you read on blogs? Hell, no! That's akin to believing everything you hear on the street or in a bar. Thinking of the Web as a city, rather than a newspaper, and bloggers as individual citizen voices provides implications for all net-citizens. Consider the source (don't trust strangers), and find out if the information comes from the government, a newspaper, a big corporation, someone with an agenda, or some Nigerian oil minister's ex-wife who is just dying to give you $20 million.

Blogs and bloggers are now important and valuable alternative sources of information, not unlike your next-door neighbor. Take them with a grain of salt . . . but ignore them at your peril. Just remember that nobody ever said your neighbor was the same as a newspaper. The challenge for marketers

---

[2] www.freerepublic.com/focus/f-news/1210662/posts?page=47#47

[3] http://littlegreenfootballs.com/weblog/?entry=12526

[4] www.powerlineblog.com/

and PR people is to make sense of the voices out there (and to incorporate their ideas into our own). Organizations have the power to become tremendously rich and successful by harnessing the millions of conversations found in Web City.

The Four Uses of Blogs for Marketing and PR

As you get started with blogs and blogging, you should think about four different ways to use them:

1. To easily monitor what millions of people are saying about you, the market you sell into, your organization, and its products.
2. To participate in those conversations by commenting on other people's blogs.
3. To work with bloggers who write about your industry, company, or products.
4. To begin to shape those conversations by creating and writing your own blog.

There are good reasons for jumping into the blog world using these four steps. First, by monitoring what people are saying about the marketplace you sell into as well as your company and products, you get a sense of the important bloggers, their online voices, and blog etiquette. It is quite important to understand the unwritten rules of blogging, and the best way to do that is to read blogs. Next, you can begin to leave comments on the blogs that are important for your industry or marketplace. That starts you on the way to being known to other bloggers and allows you to present your point of view before you create your own blog. Many organizations cultivate powerful relationships with the bloggers who write about their industry. You should work with bloggers so they know as much as possible about what you do. Finally, when you feel comfortable with blogs and bloggers, you can take the plunge by creating your own blog.

In my experience, corporate PR departments' concerns about blogs always focus on issues of actually writing them. But if you've monitored blogs and know that there are, say, a dozen influential bloggers writing about your space, and that those blogs have thousands of loyal readers, you can show a PR person the importance of simply monitoring blogs. Some of the more popular blogs have readerships that are larger than that of the daily newspaper of a major city. PR people care about the readership of the *Boston Globe*, right? Then they should care about a blog that has a similar number of readers. If you become known within your organization as an expert in monitoring blogs, it is a much smaller leap to gaining permission to create your own.

Monitor Blogs—Your Organization's Reputation Depends on It

"Organizations use blogs to measure what's going on with their stakeholders and to understand corporate reputation," says Glenn Fannick,[5] a text mining and media measurement expert at Dow Jones. "Reputation management is important, and media measurement is a key part of what PR people do. Companies are already measuring what's going on in the media; now they need to also measure what's going on with blogs."

Text mining technologies extract content from millions of blogs so you can read what people are saying; in a more sophisticated use, they also allow for measurement of trends. "You can count massive numbers of blogs and look for words and phrases and see what's being said as a whole," Fannick says. "You really need to rely on technology because of the massive volumes of blogs and blog posts out there. There is an unprecedented amount of unsolicited comments and market intelligence available on blogs. It is a unique way to tap into the mind of the marketplace. It is an interesting and fertile ground."

As a starting point, all marketing and PR people need to go to blog search engines and run a query on their organization's name, the names of their products and services, and other important words and phrases such as executives' names. Technorati[6] is an excellent blog search engine. It allows you to instantly see if any of the *112 million* blogs that it tracks have any information you need to know. Google Blog Search is another popular blog search engine. I can't imagine an organization that wouldn't find value in knowing what's being said about them or their products or the industry or market they sell into on blogs.

---

[5] http://fannick.blogspot.com/
[6] www.technorati.com/

More sophisticated marketers then start to analyze trends. Is your product getting greater or fewer blog mentions compared to your nearest competitor's product? Are the blog posts about your company positive or negative in tone? How does that compare with the ratios from six months ago? "It's naive to think that what your stakeholders think is not important," Fannick says. "Opinions are offered on blogs, and understanding the sum of those opinions is very important. You can't just make decisions on what you think your products do; you need to make decisions on the perceptions of what people are actually doing with your products. Seeing the blogosphere as a source of market intelligence is now vital for companies."

So become an expert in what's being said about your organization on blogs. There's never been a better time for marketers to get a true feel for what's going on in the real world. Bloggers provide instantaneous and unsolicited comments on your products, and this free information is just waiting for you to tap into it.

Comment on Blogs to Get Your Viewpoint Out There

Once you've got a sense of who is out there blogging about your company, its products, and the industry and marketplace you work in, it's time to think about posting comments. Most blogs have a feature that allows anyone to comment on individual posts. Leaving comments on someone's blog is one of the best ways to participate in a conversation. You have the opportunity to offer your viewpoint, adding to the ongoing discussion. However, it takes an understanding of blogs and blogging etiquette to pull it off without sounding like a corporate shill. The key is to focus on what the blog post says, and comment on that. As appropriate, you can point to your blog (if you have one) or your web site as your contact information, but make sure that in addition to contact information you provide some content of relevant value.

One of the currencies of social media is that when you participate, people find out who you are. When you leave a comment on someone else's blog post, you can link to your profile on the Web. All the blogging tools have a place where you can leave a virtual calling card, your own Web URL where people who read your comment (especially the blogger him- or herself) can find out who you are and perhaps contact you.

If you have a blog, then you're all set—just include your blog URL in that comment field. However, most people don't have a blog. What the heck do you do then?

I've seen many solutions, most very limiting:

1. Leave no URL (in which case nobody can find you).
2. Leave a LinkedIn or Facebook profile URL (this has limitations, because people must ask to be your friend in order to see your full profile).
3. Leave a company home page (this shows your affiliation, but nothing about you personally).

I've found an alternative solution that works very well. Create a public Google profile[7] for yourself and then use that as the URL that you point people to when you leave a comment on a blog or join a social networking site like Twitter. You can include a photo, a bio, and contact details. It's really cool—and it's free.

I chose to make my Google profile[8] simple because I want people to visit my site or my blog. You can make yours much more detailed if you wish (see the examples on the sign-up page). Once you've got a public profile, use it as your calling card all over the Web. Here's just one example: Link to your Google profile from your Amazon review page so the authors of the books you review can see who you are.

Work with the Bloggers Who Talk about You

On Election Day 2008, an amazing 25 percent of Barack Obama voters were already directly linked to him through social media, including blogs, Facebook, Twitter, and other social sites according to *The Nation*. Putting aside politics and just considering the election from a marketing standpoint, I am absolutely convinced that Obama won the U.S. presidential election because he was the candidate who most strongly embraced social media. Way back before he even declared himself a candidate, Obama and his staff and volunteers jumped into the online world.

---

[7] www.google.com/support/accounts/bin/answer.py?answer=97703&topic=14962

[8] www.google.com/profiles/davidmeermanscott

Kevin Flynn,[9] who worked on the Obama Campaign's New Media Blogging Team, was part of a Chicago-based core group of online campaigners. "I was part of the blogging team, and in the midst of the new media braintrust," he says. "I ended up working on the social media efforts for fifteen states. Each state had their own blog, which had localized content, and I built contacts with people in each state who sent me stories, photos, and other information for the blogs. People were excited to have someone in the organization who wanted to help, so they all fed me great content. Once they saw their photos on the national campaign pages, they got even more excited."

During the campaign, Flynn was responsible for editing and creating posts for a collection of state blogs that included Alaska, Arizona, Georgia, Hawaii, Kansas, and Texas. "The Obama candidacy was exciting for his supporters and those of us working in the campaign," Flynn says. "The technology is easy. If you provide people with the technology tools and there is excitement, then people will make it successful."

Of course, the Obama campaign marketed itself in many more ways than just through social media. But the use of television, direct mail, door-to-door outreach, and rallies have been used for decades and are subject to limitations. "There is no way to talk back with traditional marketing like radio and TV," Flynn says. "With blogging, it creates a conversation and the campaign gets feedback. If there is interest in a topic, then the campaign can change quickly. People can get involved because it is two-way instead of just one-direction. You can grow when there is a dialogue."

Prior to working on the Obama campaign, Flynn had worked in the Chicago financial markets, so he has an ideal perspective to offer advice to corporations on blogging and social media. "Don't be afraid of change," he says. "Don't be afraid to hear things that are uncomfortable, because only by hearing things will you be able to adjust and grow. In this rapidly changing world, you need to listen; otherwise you won't be able to survive."

Of course, the staff and volunteers from the Obama campaign worked very closely with the bloggers who cover politics and provided them with valuable information that helped them to write better posts. While some enlightened organizations do focus on influencing important bloggers

---

[9] www.kevinflynnonline.com/

by reaching out to them, most have a policy of ignoring bloggers, even as they spend a great deal of effort attempting to cultivate relationships with members of the mainstream media. This is a mistake. Bloggers are important voices. Just ask the Obama campaign—bloggers helped elect a president of the United States.

The Obama campaign example shows that making a concerted effort to integrate other bloggers' content into your own works very well. Although this example is from politics, similar strategies for engaging and influencing other bloggers can work for almost any organization. Another organization that's boldly working with bloggers is the New York Islanders professional ice hockey team. The team created what they call the "Islanders Blog Box," a program that provides bloggers with press credentials for games. The program started at the beginning of the 2007–2008 season and was among the first of its kind for a major professional sports team. Each season, about a dozen bloggers are chosen to receive credentials, and the team links to their blogs from its site.[10]

Other organizations set up "blogger days" where people who write blogs that are influential in their industry get the chance to spend the day with the company. They are treated to information about new product releases, have lunch with employees, and sometimes even meet with the CEO or other executives. These outreach programs are critical to providing bloggers with the information they need to tell your story for you.

How to Reach Bloggers Around the World

In mid-2009, a global boutique PR agency called Text 100 examined the communications preferences of bloggers across the globe. Their Web-based survey was designed to clarify bloggers' relationships with PR people and corporations. Some of the findings in the survey of 449 bloggers from 21 countries are worth noting as you contemplate how you will engage with bloggers. The good news is that more than 90 percent of the bloggers surveyed welcome contact from representatives of companies in the area that they write about. However, the way that you approach those bloggers is important.

---

[10] http://islanders.nhl.com/blogbox/blog_box.htm

"Bloggers are united in their desire for distinctive content, particularly around new product developments and reviews, feedback on content posted on their blog, and interviews with key people," says Jeremy Woolf, global social media lead for Text 100, who is based in the company's Hong Kong office. "Photographs are the most frequently used form of supplied content, followed by charts and graphs, and video."

However, Woolf says the study reveals that the bad habits of the PR profession don't work when trying to pitch bloggers. "PR professionals are failing to read the blogs and truly understand their target bloggers' communities," he says. "They seem to expect bloggers to post corporate material, demonstrating a lack of understanding of the medium and the very reason why bloggers blog."

There's no doubt that the vast majority of bloggers welcome contact from organizations. But to be successful, company representatives need to treat bloggers as individuals and to provide them with valuable information that complements the work they're already doing on their blogs. Don't just blindly send them corporate press releases, which are ineffective at best and may even diminish your organization's reputation with the people you're trying to reach out to.

Do You Allow Employees to Send Email? How about Letting Them Blog?

Chapter 15 presents everything you'll need to know to start your own blog. If you already know that you are ready, feel free to jump ahead to learn about how to decide what to blog about, what software you'll need, how to find your voice, and other important aspects. If you're still considering a blog for yourself or your organization, you might be hesitant because of fears that blogging isn't right for your organization.

As I work with companies to help develop a blog strategy, I see much consternation within organizations about the issue of allowing people to blog (or not) and allowing them to post comments on other people's blogs (or not). It's been fascinating to both observe and participate in the debate about blogs in the enterprise. Just like the hand-wringing over personal computers entering the workplace in the 1980s, and also echoing the Web and email debates of the 1990s, company executives seem to be getting their collective knickers in a twist about blogs these days. Remember when executives believed email might expose a corporation to its secrets being revealed to the outside world? Do you remember when only "important employees" were given email addresses? How about when people worried about employees freely using the public Internet and all of its (*gasp!*) "unverified information"?

It's the same debate all over again today with blogs. On one side of the corporate fence, the legal eagles are worried about secrets being revealed by their employees while creating content or commenting on blogs. And on the other, there's the feeling that much of the information being created today is not to be trusted. Corporate nannies want to make certain that their naïve charges don't get into trouble in the big scary world of information.

Well, we're talking about people here. Employees do silly things. They send inappropriate email (and blog posts), and they believe some of the things on TV news. This debate should be centered on people, not technology. As the examples of previous technology waves should show us, attempting to block the technology isn't the answer.

So my recommendation to organizations is simple. Have guidelines about what employees can and cannot do at work, but don't try to make a specific set of blogging guidelines. I'd suggest implementing corporate policies saying that employees can't sexually harass anyone, that they can't reveal secrets, they can't use inside information to trade stock or influence prices, and they shouldn't talk ill of the competition *in any way or via any media*. The guidelines should include email, writing a blog, commenting on blogs (and online forums and chat rooms), and other forms of communication. Rather than focus on putting guidelines on blogs (the technology), it is better to focus on guiding the way people behave. However, as always, check with your own legal advisors if you have concerns.

Some organizations take a creative approach to blogging by saying that all blogs are personal and the opinions expressed are of the blogger, not the organization. That seems like a good attitude to me. What I disagree with is putting in place draconian command-and-control measures saying either that employees cannot blog (or submit comments) or that they must pass all blog posts through the corporate communications people before posting. Freely published blogs are an important part of business and should be encouraged by forward-thinking organizations.

Breaking Boundaries: Blogging at McDonald's

McDonald's, with its famous golden arches, is one of the most recognized brands in the world. Being large and visible means being a convenient target, and McDonald's has endured rounds of vocal people who criticize the company for contributing to Americans' obesity, the accumulation of trash, and other societal ills. Unlike most large organizations that remain nameless and faceless, McDonald's has jumped into blogging by launching Open for Discussion,[11] a blog that focuses on social responsibility at the company. Written by Bob Langert, McDonald's senior director of corporate responsibility, the blog features commentary on sustainability of the environment with titles such as "Conserving Fish Supplies for Today and the Future" and "Designing Packaging with the Environment in Mind."

The blog is well written and updated frequently. Sure, it has a corporate-speak tone to it, but it also feels authentic. Langert says in the About page, "I want to use this blog to introduce you to some of the people, programs, and projects that make corporate social responsibility a reality at McDonald's—to take you along with me as I engage with some of our internal and external stakeholders in various parts of the world and to highlight our accomplishments, as well as the challenges we continue to face."

The company also launched *The McDonald's You Don't Know*, a series of video podcasts available from the McDonald's site via RSS and also via Apple's iTunes music store, YouTube.com, and Google video. The series highlights themes of opportunity, food quality, and community.

Steve Wilson, senior director of global Web communications for McDonald's Corporation, manages a team that delivers the corporate portion of McDonalds.com. In an interview that originally appeared in *EContent*, Wilson told me: "The Internet has so changed the role of information for large global brands like McDonald's. If McDonald's is going to get credibility and trust, we have to participate in the [blogging] community. We can't just jump into a blog storm without having built a dialog first." This is sound advice about blogging from a large consumer brand.

---

[11] www.crmcdonalds.com/publish/csr/home/_blog.html

The Power of Blogs

It is remarkable what a smart individual with passion can do with a blog. People have blogged their way to dream jobs (and book deals) through the ideas they express. Rock bands have built loyal followings and gained record contracts. Political candidates have broken out of the pack. And companies have competed effectively, even against much larger, better-funded players.

"You are what you publish," says Steve Goldstein, CEO of Alacra, whom we met in Chapter 4, discussing AlacraWiki. "It is better to have a reputation than no reputation. Certainly AlacraBlog[12] is valuable for us as a way to get our name out there."

Goldstein was an early CEO blogger, launching AlacraBlog in March 2004. "We didn't know what would happen, but we wanted to try it," he says. "The competitors are really big. By blogging I am able to put a face on [our] company."

Goldstein uses his blog platform as a way to communicate with his clients, prospects, and partners. He uses the blog to tell his constituents things quickly and informally. "I can highlight interesting aspects of the company, like employees and partners, that wouldn't go into a more formal press release," he says. "Internally the blog is important, too. We have a London office, so I use the blog to communicate to employees there."

It's fascinating that there are so few bloggers in the publishing industry, perhaps because publishers are cautious about giving content away for free, or maybe because large publishers feel threatened by blogs. But by starting a blog early and keeping the information flowing, Goldstein has positioned Alacra ahead of many information companies hundreds of times the size of Alacra. "Many publishers don't know what to do about blogging, and very few are doing it," Goldstein says. "For example, there is nobody big at Thomson or Reed Elsevier who blogs."

Get Started Today

There's no doubt that every organization should be monitoring blogs to find out what people are saying about them. I find it fascinating that most of the time when I mention a company or product on my blog I do not get any sort

---

[12] www.alacrablog.com/

of response from that organization. However, about 20 percent of the time, I'll get a comment on my blog from someone at that company or a personal email. These are the 20 percent of companies that monitor the blogosphere and react to what's being said. You should be doing this, too, if you're not already.

It's also clear to me that in most industries and product categories, early bloggers develop a reputation as being innovative. There are still opportunities for "first-mover advantage" in many blog categories. Once you're comfortable with reading and commenting on blogs, get out there and start your own! Chapter 15 contains all the information you'll need to get going.

6 Audio and Video Drive Action

Audio and video on the Web are not new. Clips have been available on web sites since the early days. But until recently, neither audio nor video was used much online because the content was difficult to locate and impossible to browse, and there was no easy way to get regular updates. And since much audio and video content was lengthy—as much as an hour or more—and people had no idea what was in these files without actually watching or listening to them, not many did.

The migration of audio and video from online backwaters to the forefront with valuable content happened because of sites like YouTube and iTunes, with easy ways for people to view and listen. In addition, high-speed Internet connections became the norm, and the technology to create and upload audio and video became simple enough that anybody can do it (including you).

Digging Digg Video

Digg,[1] a technology news web site, uses a video channel to deliver news, commentary, and information to its constituents. But Digg also has a blog and a content-rich web site, and the different marketing tools work together. The Diggnation[2] show is a weekly "tech/web culture show" hosted by Alex Albrecht and Digg founder Kevin Rose. Diggnation is classic thought-leadership content because it is not just about Digg and its products.

---

[1] http://digg.com/

[2] http://revision3.com/diggnation/

Many organizations are creating video to showcase their expertise and provide valuable information to buyers in an easy-to-understand medium. The interview format used in the Diggnation show is very popular, because it is fairly easy to interview guests and post the resulting video. Other common forms of online video include comedies (frequently used to try to garner many views and "go viral"), product overviews, executive speeches, and much more. An added benefit of producing video for your organization is that the media, bloggers, and others in a position to talk you up tend to like to watch video to get story ideas. See Chapter 16 for more information on video and details on how to create your own.

What University Should I Attend?

Many marketers are reluctant to focus on video because they don't see how a video on YouTube or on their company web site will lead to a sale. As I was writing this section of the book, I received an email from a student who attends the University of Pennsylvania. She explained that she chose to apply to the University of Pennsylvania because she saw a Penn video on YouTube[3] as she was researching universities and she fell in love with the school without even having a chance to visit. In the video, singer and five-time Grammy Award winner John Legend explains why he has a deep affection for the University of Pennsylvania, his alma mater.

This story is certainly not unique. People are looking for the products and services that you offer right now. They go to Google and the other search engines, and they ask their friends for advice. Frequently, what they find is a video. Will you be in it?

Many organizations encourage their customers or fan bases to produce videos for them. These customer-generated video efforts often take the form of contests and can be highly successful, especially for a product or service that has a visual impact. For example, Nalgene bottles are virtually indestructible. If you go to YouTube, you'll find hundreds of videos where people try to break them in creative ways, such as running them over with a lawnmower, throwing them out of buildings, and freezing water in them and then hitting them with a hammer. For the makers of the Nalgene bottle, this is a valuable phenomenon, since the company does not have any part in the videos.

---

[3] www.youtube.com/watch?v=gNUiBIlMk1s

The Best Job in the World

I'm often asked: "How do I market a commodity product?" People seem to think that if their product is similar to others, then the new rules of marketing do not apply to them and the only way to sell is a function of lowest price or best distribution. If you've read this far in the book, you ought to be able to predict my answer: Create interesting information and people will find it, share your ideas, and tell your stories. Yes, even if you market a commodity.

Sandy beaches in warm and sunny locations are a commodity product. This may come as a complete shock to people in tourism marketing, but it's true. The traditional approach of showing white beach sand with footprints near lovely blue water and a bikini or two just doesn't cut it because that's what everybody does. How can you stand out?

In 2009, Tourism Queensland[4] created a fantastic video contest called The Best Job in the World.[5] The winner was chosen as Caretaker of the Islands of the Great Barrier Reef. The position had a few minor tasks, but the main thing was to use social media to talk up the islands. The job of blogging and posting videos paid 150,000 Australian dollars for a six-month gig. The contest required each applicant to post a one-minute video explaining why he or she should be chosen as caretaker of Hamilton Island on the Great Barrier Reef. Over 30,000 people applied, and the videos were seen by millions. In addition, thousands of bloggers and media outlets (magazines, radio, television, and newspapers) wrote and broadcast about The Best Job in the World, producing even more buzz about not only the contest but also the location as a tourist destination.

Tourism Queensland created a huge phenomenon. In 2009, when the contest was in full swing, I took a poll of the groups I visit as speaker. By a show of hands, I asked if they had heard of The Best Job in the World. In Washington DC, 20 percent of the room had (the lowest percentage). In Tartu, Estonia, a whopping 60 percent had (the highest). The average, over several thousand people in six countries, was more than 30 percent. Amazing! Imagine if 30 percent of the world had heard of your product through videos people had created for you?

---

[4] www.queenslandholidays.com.au/
[5] www.youtube.com/user/islandreefjob

How did Queensland, Australia get so much attention? I've been to Queensland and the Great Barrier Reef twice. Yes, it is beautiful. But so are many other sandy, beachy, sparkly, bikini-friendly places I've been: Koh Samui, Santorini, Barbados, Puerto Vallarta, and on and on. The answer is simple: Tourism Queensland found a way to get people to share their ideas and tell their stories.

The Best Job in the World was conceived and created by the Brisbane, Australia-based advertising agency, CumminsNitro.[6] Tourism Queensland also worked with Quinn & Co.,[7] a New York public relations firm who handled media relations. I spoke to John Frazier and Melissa Braverman, part of the Quinn & Co. team who worked on the Best Job in the World, to help understand this amazing success.

John Frazier says that the "job announcement" broke in Australia on January 12, 2009 and, by breakfast time in London, the Associated Press was interviewing Tourism Queensland's UK director for a broadcast package which turned up later that day on the morning shows in the United States. Within two days, there were thousands of media pickups. Tourism Queensland set a goal to get 400,000 new visitors to their web site over the course of the one-year campaign. They blew past that in about 30 hours and had a million hits on the second day.

"We learned that if you hit the sweet-spot of the right story at the right time, it will travel like a tsunami all the way around the globe," says Melissa Braverman. "Traditional media (a Reuters exclusive) broke the story, which immediately went viral because it was a chance to have the coolest job in the world at a time when everyone else was getting laid off."

Because so many people saw the announcement about the job opening on both mainstream media and blogs, video applications for the job started to come in at a rapid clip. And because people were hearing about it all over the world, applicants represented many countries. Of course, all that attention also sparked interest and awareness of Queensland, Australia as a tourist destination.

"You can't reheat a soufflé," says Frazier. "There were quickly a number of copycat campaigns that didn't quite take off in as big a way. My best advice is to try to develop an idea that resonates authentically in the lives of real people

---

[6] www.cumminsnitro.com/

[7] www.quinnandco.com/

and then find a way to mount it across as many platforms (such as traditional media, YouTube, Twitter, Facebook) as possible."

Ben Southall from the UK was selected as the ideal candidate and won the job. But the real winner was Tourism Queensland. Frazier estimates there were 1,100 television placements of the story. The video contest for The Best Job in the World was a huge success in drawing attention to the islands of Australia's Great Barrier Reef. At one point, the official Island Reef Job web site was getting 4,000 hits per *second*. According to Peter Lawlor, Queensland, Australia's state tourism minister, preliminary results from a tourism campaign promoting Tropical North Queensland to U.S. tourists drew a 34 percent increase in flight bookings to Cairns, gateway to the area. "The campaign's aim was to increase international visitation to Cairns and the Great Barrier Reef and to raise awareness of the region's unique experiences and attractions. The results so far are outstanding, especially considering current economic difficulties."

Audio Content Delivery through Podcasting

Moving now to the audio-only side of the spectrum, note that the transformation from static audio downloads to radio station–like podcasts, which are much more valuable to listeners (and also more valuable as marketing vehicles for organizations), occurred because of two developments. The first was the ability to add audio feeds and notifications to RSS. This enables listeners who subscribe to an audio feed to download new updates soon after they are released. When audio content was liberated from the need for one large download and went instead to being offered as a series of continuous audio clips, the concept of shows took off. Hosts modeled their shows on radio, producing content on specific subjects catering to distinct audiences. But the podcasting business model is very different from broadcast radio. Radio spectrums can support only a finite number of stations, and radio signals have limited geographic range. To support the technical infrastructure of radio, broadcasters need large audiences and lots of advertising to pay the bills (or donors, in the case of public radio). Contrast that with Internet audio podcasting, which is essentially free (except for minimal hosting fees and some cheap equipment). A podcast show reaches a potentially worldwide audience, allowing anyone to create shows and listen to them.

The second major development was the availability of those podcast feeds through iTunes. Now all iPod users can simply subscribe to a feed (usually at no cost), and then every time they plug their iPod into their computer, the new shows from the feeds they subscribe to automatically download and are copied to the iPod. People who commute and listen to their iPod in the car or on the train, or those who work out with an iPod, suddenly have access to regularly updated shows from the myriad niches that they specifically choose. With podcasting, people instantly liberate themselves from the tyranny of mainstream, hit-driven broadcast radio and can listen to shows based on their specific interests.

Perhaps we should back up for just a moment. The term podcasting confuses some people. A podcast is simply audio content connected to an RSS feed. The medium does not specially require iPods, although that's how the word was derived. You can listen to a podcast on an iPod (or on any other MP3 player) or directly from your computer—no iPod required.

Now marketers have a tool to efficiently create and deliver audio content to people who want to listen. Marketers can easily develop a show that targets their buyers' personas and can thus regularly deliver updated content that is welcome and useful to the audience. By appealing to a niche market and delivering audio that people have chosen to hear, an organization is seen as a thought leader and is first choice for listeners looking to make a purchase.

Putting Marketing Back in Musicians' Control

Music is a classic example of a long-tail business. Before the Web came along, bands that didn't have a major label behind them couldn't hope to get national or global attention. The best they could do was establish a local audience in a city or region, or perhaps with a definable market such as northeastern U.S. college students. Enter podcasting. Now any band or DJ with some simple and easy-to-use equipment can set up as a radio station and get instant global distribution via iTunes and other distribution services.

George L. Smyth hosts the Eclectic Mix podcast,[8] where he challenges listeners to open their minds to new and diverse music and at the same time

---

[8] www.eclecticmix.com/

promotes bands he likes. The banner of his site even has a definition of eclectic, to make sure people understand his approach: choosing what appears to be the best from diverse sources, systems, or styles.

"On each show, I select an artist and spotlight their music," Smyth says. "I play literally anything from classical to punk. My interest in music goes back to my college days, when I would copy records to tape and trade with my friends. I had lost track of music for a while, but recently I've found that there's really great music out there, and I can share it with many more people than with the tapes."

Smyth is evangelical in his description of how podcasting has changed the face of music. "Podcasting of music has been a real success with the under-25 crowd," he says. "Podcasting has allowed people to hear the music of groups that are good but perhaps don't have a big label behind them. In the past there was no choice, but now there is a choice. Many artists will tell you that they just want people to hear the music. If you do listen, maybe you'll like it and want to spend money on tickets and perhaps a download of music from iTunes. Many bands don't make much money from CDs, so they really want people to go to the shows, which is where the big money is for the smaller bands."

Smyth is careful of copyrights and permissions in his podcasts and uses only "podsafe" music (music that the artist has cleared and has said it is permissible to podcast). The more famous bands typically don't allow podcasting (or to be more precise, their record labels don't). But many indie acts embrace podcasting and people like Smyth who promote their music via podcasts. "Uncle Seth is an example of a group that has made it easy for podcasters like me to work with them," Smyth says. "Uncle Seth is an indie band, but they cross genres, and I like to play them."

"Podcasters are a different breed; they're like you and me," says Jay Moonah, musician and songwriter of the Toronto band Uncle Seth. "TV and commercial radio and MTV-type people work and talk from on high. Podcasting is different. It's neat that we've made fans out of some of these podcasters, such as George Smyth of Eclectic Mix. It's fun when they play our music, and then if I e-mail them it is great to start a conversation." Moonah says that indie bands like Uncle Seth that take the lead with podcasting have benefited greatly through wider distribution, which generates new fans.

Editorial note to music fans: Uncle Seth's 2006 single, an upbeat cover of Joni Mitchell's classic song, "Both Sides, Now" (available at iTunes), is killer.

Besides working with other podcasters, Moonah and Uncle Seth also host their own podcast.[9] In each episode, the band debates and discusses wacky topics, and plays exclusive tracks of their music not available anywhere else. "The interesting thing about the show is that we made a conscious effort not to make it just the music," Moonah says. "We wanted to get some of our personality into it. So we went the direction of doing things like talking for an entire show about the first records we ever bought.

"Podcasting has become a real part of the social networking thing," Moonah says. "From a technical aspect, you could do podcasting a long time ago. But for us, the social aspect is really neat; bands and other organizations combine the music and the community and mix them together. For example, there is a community of Canadian Jam bands[10] where we've met a lot of friends. Like other online communities, it has a real-world community associated with it."

As Moonah has honed his expertise with podcasting and musician web sites, he's developed a side business working with bands, labels, and other musicians on podcasting strategy. "Especially in Canada, it's difficult making a living as a musician," he says. "My thing of combining the businesses into a big circle of music and consulting and podcasting really works well for me.

"I like people to understand that podcasting has so many uses," Moonah continues. "It is a legitimate thing, not a toy for kids. So the advice I have for managers and label people is to not jump into your own podcast until you listen to other podcasts. Find podcasts that you like and you think might play you, and submit your music to them to get going. Then think about what you want to do if you want to make your own podcast. The people who make it work are those who understand it. As a band, you can compete with radio via podcasts because you can get onto several podcasts, and then people will hear you several times, just like a radio rotation."

Podcasting: More than Just Music

Smyth's and Moonah's advice about podcasting is important for organizations, not just musicians, that want to reach buyers directly. For content that is best delivered via audio or for buyers who prefer to listen to content, podcasting is

---

[9] http://musicface.com/uncleseth/

[10] www.jambands.ca/

obviously essential. For example, many politicians and churches podcast so that supporters can keep up with speeches and sermons when they can't hear them live. You'll learn more about podcasting, including tips for setting up your own podcast, in Chapter 16.

While the podcasting of music is perhaps an obvious choice given the medium's similarity to radio, all marketers can learn from what the music business has been doing with podcasts. "Podcasting is almost exactly mirroring the Internet of a decade ago," Smyth says. "Ten years ago, I was telling people about the Web and building example sites. But then some larger companies jumped into the Web. I see the same thing with the evolution of podcasting, with some big organizations jumping in, like NPR."

As a component of a larger content-marketing strategy, podcasting is also an increasingly important part of the marketing mix. For example, customer service departments increasingly deliver how-to podcast series to keep users of their products informed. Companies that market to people who are on the road often (such as traveling salespeople) and have downtime in cars or on airplanes have had success reaching people with entertaining podcasts. For many organizations, podcasting for marketing purposes is not an either/ or decision. Instead, podcasting coexists with blogging, a great web site, e-books, and other online marketing tools and programs in a cohesive marketing strategy.

Grammar Girl Podcast

Mignon Fogarty, creator of the Grammar Girl podcast and founder of the Quick and Dirty Tips podcast network, has been podcasting since 2006. Grammar Girl[11] provides short, friendly tips to improve writing. Covering the grammar rules and word choice guidelines that can confound even the best writers, Grammar Girl makes complex grammar questions simple. I should know. I never know when I should use "whom," so I avoid it altogether. However, this is exactly the sort of grammar problem the podcast solves.

"I get an overwhelming amount of feedback from my audience," Fogarty says. "A little over a year ago, I had to hire a part-time assistant to help field my messages because they were taking all my time. I get a lot of grammar questions, which I try to answer; a lot of 'I love you' messages; and a lot of

---

[11] http://grammar.quickanddirtytips.com/

people disagreeing with my recommendations. Grammar can get pretty contentious, and people absolutely love it (in a gotcha kind of way) when I make a mistake or typo."

Creating a podcast show is a great way to get your information into the market. Instead of hyping your products and services, an informational show brands you as someone worthy of doing business with. In Fogarty's case, her sound ideas lead people to want to purchase her book, *Grammar Girl's Quick and Dirty Tips for Better Writing*. The free podcast drives her book sales.

"The fan interaction is definitely different from offline marketing," Fogarty says. "I feel weird even calling the people fans because they feel more like friends with the constant messages that go back and forth. (Someone on Facebook recently said I am 'the most helpful person he doesn't know.') The immediacy of the feedback is also different from offline marketing. I hear within 24 hours (usually faster) if something I'm doing is working or not. If I post a link or a contest on Twitter, I can usually tell within five minutes whether it's getting traction or not."

When Fogarty was ready to release her book, the podcast and her participation in other social networking sites like Twitter and Facebook allowed her to launch the book to her existing fan base. "When I went out on my book tour, the crowds were much bigger than expected, and I believe it is at least in part because of all the groundwork I laid on social networks for over a year before the book came out," she says. "During the first three or four stops on my book tour, bookstores ran out of books. In Atlanta, they ran out of books before I even arrived. A lot of the people who came out were people I had connected with on Twitter or Facebook, and I had posted messages about where I was going to be to both of those services multiple times."

The Grammar Girl podcasts have now been downloaded more than *twenty million* times, and Fogarty has dispensed grammar tips on *Oprah* and appeared on the pages of the *New York Times*, the *Wall Street Journal*, and *USA Today*. *Grammar Girl's Quick and Dirty Tips for Better Writing* is a *New York Times* bestseller. "Having an established network of people is really valuable when you're launching something new," Fogarty says.

Podcasting and online video are great ways to connect with an audience and develop a following who will be eager to buy your products. Chapter 16 provides details on how to start a video or podcast series of your own.

7

The New Rules of News Releases

Guess what? Press releases have never been exclusively for the press.

My first job in the mid-1980s was on a Wall Street trading desk. Every day, I would come to work and watch the Dow Jones Telerate and Reuters screens as they displayed specialized financial data, economic information, and stock prices. The screens also displayed newsfeeds, and within these newsfeeds were press releases. For decades, financial market professionals have had access to company press releases distributed through BusinessWire, PRNewswire, and other electronic press release distribution services. And they weren't just for publicly traded corporations; any company's release would appear in trading rooms within seconds.

I distinctly remember traders intently watching the newswires for any signs of market-moving events. Often the headline of a press release would cause frenzy: "Did you see? IBM is acquiring a software company!" "It's on the wire; Boeing just got a 20-plane order from Singapore Airlines!" For years, markets often moved and stock prices rose and fell based on the raw press release content issued directly by companies, *not* on the news stories written minutes or hours later by reporters from newswire outlets like Reuters and Dow Jones (and later Bloomberg).

Press releases have also been available to professionals working within corporations, government agencies, and law firms, all of which have had access to raw press releases through services like NewsEdge, Dow Jones Factiva, and LexisNexis. These services have been delivering press releases to all kinds of professionals for competitive intelligence, research, discovery, and other purposes for decades.

Of course, since about 1995, the wide availability of the Web has meant that press releases have been available for free to anyone with an Internet connection and Web browser.

> Millions of people read press releases directly, unfiltered by the media. You need to be speaking directly to them!

As I tell this story to PR pros, I hear cries of "Hang on! We disagree! The role of public relations and the purpose of the press release as a tool are about communicating with the *media*." For an example of this thinking, look to Steve Rubel, one of the most influential PR bloggers in the world. He responded to my ideas about press releases by writing a post on his blog, titled "Direct to Consumer Press Releases Suck."[1]

Let's take a look at the objections of traditional PR folks. According to the Public Relations Society of America (PRSA),[2] "Public relations is the professional discipline that ethically fosters mutually beneficial relationships among social entities." In 1988, the governing body of the PRSA—its Assembly—formally adopted a definition of public relations that has become the most accepted and widely used. "Public relations helps an organization and its publics adapt mutually to each other." Nowhere does this description mention the media. PR is about reaching your audience.

I think many PR professionals have a fear of the unknown. They don't understand how to communicate directly with consumers and want to live in the past, when there was no choice but to use the media as a mouthpiece. I also think there's a widely held view about the purity of the press release as a tool for the press. PR professionals don't want to know that hundreds of millions of people have the power to read their releases directly. It's easier to imagine a closed audience of a dozen reporters. But this argument is based on fear, not the facts; there is no good reason why organizations shouldn't communicate directly with their audiences, without a media filter, via releases.

---

[1] www.micropersuasion.com/2006/01/directtoconsume.html

[2] www.prsa.org/

Obviously, the first word of the term *press release* throws off some people, particularly PR professionals. On my blog and on other sites, a semantic debate played out. The consensus of the dozens of professional communicators who weighed in was to call releases aimed at consumers "news releases." This sounds good to me, so from this point on I'll refer to direct-to-consumer releases as *news releases*.

News Releases in a Web World

The media have been disintermediated. The Web has changed the rules. Buyers read your news releases directly, and you need to be speaking their language. Today, savvy marketing and PR professionals use news releases to reach buyers directly. As I mentioned in Chapter 1, this is not to suggest that media relations are no longer important; mainstream media and the trade press must be part of an overall communications strategy. In some markets, mainstream media and the trade press remain *critically* important, and of course, the media still derive some content from news releases. But your primary audience is no longer just a handful of journalists. Your audience is millions of people with Internet connections and access to search engines and RSS readers. Here, then, are the rules of this new direct-to-consumer medium.

The New Rules of News Releases

- Don't just send news releases when big news is happening; find good reasons to send them all the time.
- Instead of just targeting a handful of journalists, create news releases that appeal directly to your buyers.
- Write releases that are replete with the keyword-rich language used by your buyers.
- Include offers that compel consumers to respond to your release in some way.
- Place links in releases to deliver potential customers to landing pages on your web site.
- Optimize news release delivery for searching and browsing.
- Add social media tags for Technorati, DIGG, and del.icio.us so that your release can be found.
- Drive people into the sales process with news releases.

You need to fundamentally change the way you use news releases. If you follow these specific strategies for leveraging this once-lowly medium by turning it into one of the most important direct marketing tools at your disposal, you will drive buyers straight to your company's products and services at precisely the time that they are ready to buy.

If They Find You, They Will Come

Several years ago, I was preparing a keynote speech called "Shorten Your Sales Cycle: Marketing Programs that Deliver More Revenue Faster" for the Software Marketing Perspectives Conference & Expo. To be honest, I was kind of procrastinating. Facing a blank PowerPoint file, I decided to hit Google in search of inspiration.

I entered the phrase "accelerate sales cycle" to see if there was anything interesting I could use in my presentation. The highest-ranked listings for this phrase were from WebEx, a company that provides online collaboration services. What was most interesting to me was that the links pointed to *news releases* on the WebEx site. That's right; at the top of the Google search results was a news release about a new WebEx product, and right there in the first sentence of the news release was the phrase I was looking for: "accelerate sales cycle."

> WebEx Launches WebEx Sales Center: Leader Expands Suite of Real-Time Collaborative Applications
>
> *Enhance Team Selling Process, Engage Prospects Throughout Sales Cycle, and Enable Managers to Monitor and Measure Web Sales Operations*
>
> *SAN JOSE, Calif.*—WebEx Communications, Inc. (NASDAQ: WEBX), the leading provider of on-demand collaborative applications, today launched WebEx Sales Center, a new service that helps companies accelerate sales cycles, increase win rates, and close more deals by leveraging online sales calls . . .

Then I went over to Google News[3] and checked out the same phrase. Sure enough, WebEx also had the number-one listing on Google's news search with a very recent news release: *Application Integration Industry Leader*

[3] http://news.google.com/

Optimizes Marketing and Sales Processes with WebEx Application Suite. The news release, about a WebEx customer, had been sent through PRNewswire[4] and had a direct Web link to the WebEx site to provide additional information. WebEx also provided links in some news releases directly to free trial offers of their services. How cool is that?

"That is exactly our strategy," says Colin Smith, director of public relations for WebEx. "Google and news keywords have really transformed the news release as a distribution vehicle. Our thinking is that, especially for companies that have an end-user appeal, news releases are a great channel."

It's certainly no accident that I found WebEx; I was searching on a phrase that Smith had optimized for search. His research had shown that buyers of the communications services that WebEx provides search on the phrase "accelerate sales cycle" (and also many others). So when I searched on that phrase, WebEx was at the top of the listings.

As a result, WebEx provided me with an excellent (and real) example of a company that had optimized the content of news releases to include relevant terms such as the one I was looking for. And WebEx has greatly benefited from their efforts. In addition to the consumers they already reach online, they've added to their audience by getting the information to someone who tells other people about it (me!); I've used this example in speeches before well over 10,000 marketing and Web content professionals and executive audiences, and it was also downloaded more than 250,000 times as part of my *New Rules of PR* e-book. And now you're reading it here, too.

"People are saying that press releases are dead," Smith says. "But that's not true for direct-to-consumer news releases." As Smith has developed his news release strategy to reach buyers directly, he has had to refine his writing and PR skills for this evolving, but very much alive, medium. "I learned the very structured *AP Style Guide* way to write releases," he says. "But that's changed as keywords and phrases have suddenly become important and the scale and reach of the Internet have opened up end users as a channel."

Smith doesn't let keywords dominate how he writes, but he tries to be very aware of keywords and phrases and to insert key phrases, especially, into releases whenever he can. "We don't think that a single keyword works, but phrases are great," he says. "If people are doing a specific search, or one with

---

[4] www.prnewswire.com/

company names that are in our release, then the goal is that they will find our news release."

Driving Buyers into the Sales Process

Smith is careful to include product information in the end-user-focused news releases he crafts for WebEx. "We try to think about what's important to people," he says. "We put free trial offers in the releases that are about the product." About 80 percent of the releases that WebEx puts out are product or customer related. Since WebEx is a public company, the other 20 percent are earnings and other regulatory releases. "WebEx is a great mix of real end-user stories," he says. "People get why you need Web meetings, so it is easy to tell the story using news releases."

Because the Web meeting story is a compelling one even for those who don't know the product category, Smith also looks for ways to create a viral marketing buzz. For example, he pays attention to major events in the news where WebEx online collaboration would be useful.[5] "We donated free service for limited use during the time that Boston traffic was snarled as a result of the Big Dig tunnel closures. We did the same thing for the New York City transit strike." Smith knows that people are likely to consider WebEx services during this kind of unusual situation. Offering the service for free often creates loyal future users.

Direct-to-consumer news releases are an important component of the marketing mix at WebEx. "We do track metrics, and we can see how many people are going from the release to the free trial," Smith says. The numbers are significant. But with such success, there's also a danger. "We don't want to abuse the news release channel," Smith says, explaining that the company also has a media relations strategy, of which news releases are a part. "We want the news releases to be interesting for journalists, but also to provide consumers with things to do, such as get the free trial."

WebEx is successful in using news releases to appeal to all constituents—the financial markets players who monitor the company's stock, the journalists who write (and speak) about WebEx products and services, and also the consumers who are searching for what WebEx has to offer. WebEx, and thousands of other innovative organizations like it, prove that a direct-

---

[5] www.webexone.com/go/bigdig

to-consumer news release strategy can coexist within an organization that cares about media relations.

Since the first edition of this book was released, WebEx was acquired by Cisco Systems, Inc., a major networking and communications technology company. Colin Smith now works in Cisco's Corporate Communications department at the company's California headquarters.

Reach Your Buyers Directly

Under the old rules, the only way to get published was to have your news release picked up by the media.

We've come a long way. The Web has turned all kinds of companies, nonprofits, political campaigns, individuals, and even churches and rock bands into just-in-time and just-right publishers. As publishers, these organizations create news releases that deliver useful information directly onto the screens of their buyers—no "press" involved!

8

Going Viral: The Web Helps Audiences Catch the Fever

Amazingly, if you toss a Mentos candy into a bottle of Diet Coke, you get a marketing explosion. More tangibly, the mint/cola reaction triggers a geyser that sprays 10 feet or more. This phenomenon was popularized in video experiments produced by Fritz Grobe and Stephen Voltz[1] on their eepybird site. After their initial success, Grobe and Voltz made a video of an extreme experiment to answer the following question: "What happens when you combine 200 liters of Diet Coke and over 500 Mentos mints?" Web audiences were mesmerized by the result—it's insane—and caused a classic viral phenomenon. In only three weeks, four million people viewed the video. Hundreds of bloggers had written about it. Then mainstream media jumped in, with Grobe and Voltz appearing on *Late Night with David Letterman* and *The Today Show*.

Imagine the excitement in Mentos marketing offices when the videos took off online—millions of Mentos exposures at no cost (more on this later). The price tag to get results like that from traditional marketing might have totaled tens, if not hundreds, of millions of dollars.

Minty-Fresh Explosive Marketing

For marketers, one of the coolest things about the Web is that when an idea takes off, it can propel a brand or company to fame and fortune *for free*. Whatever you call it—viral, buzz, or "word-of-mouse" marketing—having

---

[1] http://eepybird.com

other people tell your story drives action. Many viral phenomena start inno-cently. Somebody creates something—a funny video clip, a cartoon, or a story—to amuse friends, and one person sends it to another and that person sends it to yet another, on and on. Perhaps the creator might have expected to reach at most a few dozen friends. One of the first examples I remember was the "dancing baby" from the mid-1990s. It was grainy and low-tech, but it was cool and it spread like crazy. Instead of reaching a few hundred friends and colleagues, dancing baby struck a nerve and reached millions.

The challenge for marketers is to harness the amazing power of viral. There are people who will tell you that it is possible to create a viral cam-paign, and there are even agencies that specialize in the area. But when orga-nizations set out to go viral, the vast majority of campaigns fail. Worse, some companies set up fake viral campaigns where people who are employed by the company or in some way compensated write about a product. The Web is hyperefficient at collective investigative reporting and smoking out trickery, so these campaigns rarely succeed and may even cause great harm to reputa-tions. Often a corporate approach is some gimmicky game or contest that just feels forced and advertisement-like. I think it is virtually impossible to create a Web marketing program that is *guaranteed* to go viral. A huge amount of luck and timing are necessary. A sort of homemade feel seems to work, while slick and polished doesn't. For example, the Numa Numa Dance that was so popular several years ago was about as homemade as you can get—just a guy with a Web camera on his computer—and it helped to popularize the song and sell a bunch of downloads.

Of course, it's not just crazy dancing that goes viral. The formula is a com-bination of some great (and free) Web content (a video, a blog entry, or an e-book) that is groundbreaking or amazing or hilarious or involves a celeb-rity, plus a network of people to light the fire, and all with links that make it very easy to share. While many organizations plan viral marketing campaigns to spread the word about their products or services, don't forget that some-thing may go viral *that you didn't start* (like Mentos and Diet Coke), and it may show you or your products in either a positive or negative light. You need to be monitoring the Web for your organization and brand names so you are alerted quickly about what people are talking about. And if a positive viral explosion that you didn't initiate begins, don't just hang on for the ride—push it along!

Monitoring the Blogosphere for Viral Eruptions

Every day, on blogs, podcasts, video, and Twitter, people promote and pan products. Consumers tell good and bad tales in which products and services play a starring role. Sadly, most companies are clueless about what's going on in the blogosphere. At a minimum, marketing professionals need to know immediately when their brand names or executives are mentioned in a blog (refer back to the discussion about monitoring blogs in Chapter 5). Beyond mention-counting, analysis is important. What are the significant trends in words and phrases currently popular in the blogosphere, as they relate to your organization, product, and industry? On the day that the Diet Coke and Mentos experiments went viral, there was a tenfold spike in the number of blog posts mentioning Mentos. If you follow the word "Mentos," you'd want to know what was going on, so you could either respond to the crisis or leverage the positive development. At the least, you should learn the reason for the spike and alert company managers; when the *Wall Street Journal* calls for comment, "Huh?" is not the savviest response.

Over at Alexa,[2] a service that measures the reach and popularity of web sites, the comparisons between the viral eepybird site created by Grobe and Voltz to showcase their videos and the official Mentos site[3] are remarkable. Marketers use Alexa to figure out what sites are hot and use that information to make their own sites better. The three-month average web site ranking among all sites on the Web after the release of the video was 282,677 for the official Mentos site, while eepybird was 8,877.

"The whole Mentos geyser phenomenon seems to bubble up every few years," says Pete Healy, vice president of marketing for Perfetti Van Melle USA, makers of Mentos. "But this was the first time it came around that there was an infrastructure where people could post videos online. We contacted the two guys at eepybird and said that we really liked the way the Mentos brand was represented. We had recently conducted a meeting about our brand personality, and we decided that if our brand was a person, it would be like Adam Sandler—quirky, tongue-in-cheek, and fun. Because the eepybird video had those qualities, we were delighted."

---

[2] www.alexa.com/

[3] http://us.mentos.com

Healy recognized that he had an opportunity and worked to push the viral excitement forward. First, he linked to the video from the official Mentos site. Then he offered Grobe and Voltz the company's support. "When they appeared on *Late Night with David Letterman* and *The Today Show*, we were there with our 'Mentos ride,' a classic convertible with Mentos branding, giving away samples on the street to add support." Soon after, Healy decided that there might be others who would want to create their own video, so the company launched a Mentos geyser video contest. The top prize was 1,000 iTunes downloads and a year's supply of Mentos, 320 rolls, and according to Healy, over 100 videos were submitted and posted to the site, which was viewed nearly a million times. (Incidentally, note the wisdom of choosing iTunes downloads as a prize; the folks at Mentos reasonably suspected that the kinds of media-savvy people who would submit entry videos are likely to be the kinds of people who would be more interested in free music downloads than in traditional prizes like shopping sprees or free trips. This contributes to the authentic feel of Mentos's attempts to further spread this viral phenomenon.)

"The power to influence what a brand means to others is something that poses a dilemma, but also an opportunity, for the owners of a brand," says Healy. "It has always been true that what a brand means is determined by a consumer, the end user. Now there is a feedback loop that didn't exist before. The Internet is like the town plaza or the town square. For any company that is marketing a brand, the first thing is to be genuine in communicating what the brand is about, the personality of the brand. If we had pretended that the Mentos brand is more than it is, then we would have gotten shot down."

Interestingly, while Healy supported and helped drive the viral aspects of the videos, marketers at Coca-Cola tried to distance the Diet Coke brand from the phenomenon. "When the Mentos and Diet Coke video became big, Coca-Cola took a few shots from the market, because they felt that the eepybird site didn't fit the Diet Coke brand. They took hits from bloggers." Healy says. "As long as we keep in mind that we are just a candy manufacturer, creators of a small pleasure, we can work with interesting things that might happen to our brands on the Web."

Healy did an excellent job pushing the Mentos and Diet Coke buzz without getting in the way by being too much of a corporate nanny. Too often, corporate communications people at large companies distance themselves from what's going on in the real world of blogs, YouTube, Twitter, and chat rooms. But it's even worse when they try to control the messages in ways that the marketplace sees as inauthentic.

Creating a World Wide Rave

When I finished writing the first edition of this book, I became obsessed with the phenomenon of people spreading ideas and sharing stories. How amazing is it that something you create has the potential to keep spreading from one person to the next and, in the process, expose your ideas to people you don't even know? I was so fascinated with this idea that I wrote a book about it, *World Wide Rave: Creating triggers that get millions of people to spread your ideas and share your stories.* That book was released in March 2009, between the first and second editions of this book. I'm adding a short section here to provide you with the basic ideas of *World Wide Rave*, in the hope that you might create your own.

A World Wide Rave is when people around the world are talking about you, your company, and your products—whether you're located in San Francisco, Dubai, or Reykjavík, it's when global communities eagerly link to your stuff on the Web. It's when online buzz drives buyers to your virtual doorstep. And it's when tons of fans visit your web site and your blog because they genuinely want to be there.

> You can trigger a World Wide Rave, too—just create something valuable that people want to share, and make it easy for them to do so.

The World Wide Rave is one of the most exciting and powerful ways to reach your audience. Anyone with thoughtful ideas to share—and clever ways to create interest in them—can become famous and find success on the Web. The challenge for marketers is to harness the amazing power of the World Wide Rave. The process is actually quite simple; anyone can do it, including you. However, if you're already an experienced marketer, you need to know that achieving success requires a far different approach than what you're likely doing now. Many of the easy techniques for triggering a World Wide Rave are the exact opposite of what you've learned on the job or have been taught in school. Similarly, if you're a CEO, business owner, or entrepreneur, you should know that these ideas are likely precisely what your agency partners and marketing staff tell you *not* to do.

Let's look at the important components for generating a World Wide Rave of your own. As you read the next few paragraphs, consider how completely different these ideas are from what you're likely doing today.

Rules of the Rave

Of course, it's obvious as hell that in order for thousands or even millions of people to share your ideas and stories on the Web, you must make something worth sharing. But how do you do that? Here are the essential components. This list is so important, and each item such a strong predictor of success, that I call them your *Rules of the Rave.*

- **Nobody cares about your products (except you).** Yes, you read that right. What people do care about are themselves and ways to solve their problems. People also like to be entertained and to share in something remarkable. In order to have people talk about you and your ideas, you must resist the urge to hype your products and services. Create something interesting that will be talked about online. But don't worry—because when you're famous on the Web, people will line up to learn more and to buy what you offer!

- **No coercion required.** For decades, organizations of all kinds have spent buckets of money on advertising designed to coerce people into buying products. *Free shipping! This week only, 20 percent off! New and improved! Faster than the other guys!* This product-centric advertising is *not* how you get people talking about you. When you've got something *worth sharing*, people will share it—no coercion required.

- **Lose control.** Here's a component that scares most people silly. You've got to lose control of your "messages"; you need to make your valuable online content totally free (and freely sharable); and you must understand that a World Wide Rave is not about generating "sales leads." Yes, you can measure success, but not through business-school Return On Investment (ROI) calculators.

- **Put down roots.** When I was a kid, my grandmother said, "If you want to receive a letter, you need to send a letter to someone first." Then when I was in college, my buddies said, "If you want to meet girls, you have to go where the girls are." The same thing is true in the virtual world of the Web. If you want your ideas to spread, you need to be involved in the online communities of people who actively share.

- **Create triggers that encourage people to share.** When a product or service solves someone's problem or is very valuable, interesting, funny, or just plain outrageous, it's ready to be shared. To elevate your online content to the status of a World Wide Rave, you need a trigger to get people talking.

- **Point the world to your (virtual) doorstep.** If you follow the Rules of the Rave as I've described them, people *will* talk about you. And when they do, they'll generate all sorts of online buzz that will be indexed by the search engines, all relating to what your organization is up to. Forget about data-driven search engine technologies. The better approach to drive people to your stuff via the search engines is to create a World Wide Rave. As a result, your organization's web sites will quickly rise to prominence in the rankings on Google, Yahoo!, and the other search engines.

That's it. Simple, right?

Sure, generating a World Wide Rave is as simple as can be. You should be thinking of how you can create an initiative that will get people to spread your ideas and share your stories. When people are talking about *you*, then you're reaching many more people than you would otherwise. Let's take a look at an example.

Film Producer Creates a World Wide Rave by Making Soundtrack Free for Download

As I say many times in these pages, a great way to generate interest in products and services is to make select content available for free online. There's no doubt that free content sells. So it was with great interest that I had an opportunity to connect with Ryan Gielen, executive producer of *The Graduates*,[4] to learn about his strategy of making the soundtrack of his film available for free download. *The Graduates*, released in 2009, is an award-winning comedy about four friends who head to the beach without a care in the world. Prior to release, the film had been developing a loyal following among the 18- to 34-year-old demographic following a dozen sold-out festival and sneak preview screenings. It had been advertised solely by word-of-mouth and a free soundtrack download.

The film features the music of some incredible indie bands (The New Rags, Plushgun, Sonia Montez, The Mad Tea Party, Our Daughter's Wedding, and

---

[4] www.thegraduatesmovie.com/

The Smittens) that are popular with the buyer personas who might see the movie. So the idea of making the entire soundtrack available for free[5] is a brilliant strategy.

Of course, the bands also benefit because new listeners are exposed to their music and, if they like it, may decide to buy an album or see them live. "We're a very indie film, with very indie bands on our soundtrack," Gielen says. "Both the bands and the film need as much promotional help as possible, because we're competing with studio films, major marketing budgets, stars. We don't compete exclusively with low-budget films. We compete with everyone. So what do we have to offer our potential audience to set us apart? A great film and a great soundtrack isn't enough—we need people to know about it."

Gielen created special access codes that consumers can enter on the movie site to get instant downloads of the entire soundtrack. He also sells the music for those without the code, making the free download seem more valuable. These codes are given away at film festivals, at places where the members of the film's buyer personas congregate, at the various bands' live shows, and more. "We felt it made sense to give away the soundtrack to build loyalty, show off the product, and compensate for a zero-dollar marketing budget, all in one fell swoop," he says.

I wondered about the musicians whose music was given away. Did any of them resist? "My producers and I all loved this idea, and, when we carefully explained it to the musicians, they came along. I think it helped that everyone was aware of how hard the producers and I are working to promote the film and the individual bands on the soundtrack."

Interestingly, Gielen does not see this model catching on with major films. "Movie studios will probably be very slow to adopt this model, possibly because they load soundtracks with famous music that is too expensive to give away," he says. "Music licensing is an enormous headache for indie filmmakers. We all agreed early on that we would go out and find great bands that hadn't been discovered because that would help us license the music, and they would be excited by the exposure. I expect that if we had pitched this to established, signed bands, we would've been laughed out of the room. The media landscape is so broad that we literally had 9,000 bands submit music, something like 100,000 songs to choose from. If our little film takes off, people all over the country will discover the new music. The worst-case

---

[5] http://thegraduatesmovie.com/music/   (use code: worldwiderave)

scenario for even an established band is that we just crafted a $100,000 music video for them. The Rolling Stones should laugh us out of the room, but this is a good opportunity for many, many bands." The strategy has worked well for Gielen. "The free soundtrack has been a real success," he says. "The totally free music promo opened us up to many more people."

So what can you give away to create a World Wide Rave of your own?

Viral Buzz for Fun and Profit

It can be difficult to purposely create viral marketing buzz. But I do believe it's possible—otherwise I wouldn't have written an entire book about World Wide Raves! I think the way to create viral programs is a lot like the way that venture capitalists invest in startup companies and that studios create films. A typical venture capitalist has a formula that states that most ventures will fail, a few might do okay, and 1 out of 20 or so will take off and become a large enterprise that will pay back investors many times the initial investment. Record companies and movie studios follow the same principles, expecting that most of the projects that they green-light will have meager sales but that the one hit will more than pay back the cost of a bunch of flops. The problem is that nobody knows with certainty which movie or venture-backed company in the portfolio will succeed, so it requires a numbers game of investing in many prospects. The same goes for viral efforts. Create a number of campaigns and see what hits, then nurture the winners along.

The Virgin Mary Grilled Cheese Sandwich and Jerry Garcia's Toilet

Consider GoldenPalace.com, the Internet casino that has cornered the market on eccentric eBay purchases for viral promotional purposes.[6] The online casino is the proud owner of dozens of offbeat knickknacks such as Pete Rose's corked baseball bat, William Shatner's kidney stone, Jerry Garcia's toilet, and the famous Virgin Mary grilled cheese sandwich. The marketers at GoldenPalace.com also grab unusual advertising space sold on eBay, such oddities as a woman's cleavage, the opportunity to tattoo a logo on someone's forehead, and billboard space on the back of a person's wheelchair. Some of

[6] www.goldenpalaceevents.com/auctions

this stuff, all purchased on eBay, generates significant viral marketing buzz for GoldenPalace.com. For example, when Shatner's kidney stone was nabbed, it seemed like every TV station, newspaper, and online outlet reported on the sale: "Shatner Passes Kidney Stone to GoldenPalace.com," the headline ran. "Ha-ha-ha," the reporters and bloggers went, dismissing the money spent as foolish. But each story referenced GoldenPalace.com! At a mere $25,000, this foray into a place where no man has gone before was the viral marketing and advertising bargain of the century. And kudos, too, to Shatner, who got his name plastered all over the place (and donated the cash to Habitat for Humanity).

The professional eBay bidders at GoldenPalace.com know that not every one of the hundreds of quirky purchases they make will be a hit with bloggers and the media. But they can count on some of them, maybe 1 out of 20, hitting the mark in just the right way.

Clip This Coupon for $1 Million Off Ft. Myers, FL Home

When there is a glut of luxury homes on the market, what can a homeowner do to make his property stand out? Get people talking about it, of course! Homeowner Rich Ricciani decided to offer potential buyers a coupon good for $1 million off the price of his $7 million Ft. Myers, FL, home. He created a site for the coupon[7] and placed it in newspapers in lieu of a typical real estate advertisement. This creative approach sure beat simply reducing the price of the home on the real estate Multiple Listing Service database.

Ricciani worked with Lani Belisle of VIP Realtors to list the home and book the advertising space for the coupon, which initially ran in the Sunday edition of the *Ft. Myers News-Press*. Then it was time for Tina Haisman Public Relations[8] to get the word out. Haisman used PRWeb to send a well written, search engine optimized press release complete with photos, an embedded YouTube video, and links to the coupon and the home's web site. "I also used PR MatchPoint to compile a list of real estate writers in the south and northeastern U.S., and I personally targeted the big news outlets such as CNN, FOX, NBC, and more," Haisman says.

---

[7] www.themilliondollarcoupon.com/
[8] www.haisman.com/default.htm

In Southwest Florida, the story appeared on the front pages of both the *Fort Myers News-Press* and in the *Naples Daily News,* and it aired on WINK-TV and local radio stations. "*Florida Weekly* named The Million Dollar Coupon the Best Marketing Stunt of 2009!" Haisman says. "Within four days of its release, the Million Dollar Coupon story went viral on real estate blogs nationwide, creating a world wide buzz."

As a result, it aired on television stations in major cities around the country, and the homeowner even did a live interview on Neal Cavuto's *Your World* show on FOX News. Major papers, including the *Los Angeles Times,* covered it, and the idea also appeared in the *Huffington Post.* The team then ran the coupon in the Sunday *New York Times,* the *Wall Street Journal,* and the *Boston Globe.* I love the selection of the *Globe,* chosen because Ft. Myers, FL, is the home of the Boston Red Sox spring training facility—an excellent example of buyer persona profiling. Bloggers talked about it and many people were buzzing about it on Twitter.

Some may call this strategy a gimmick. Nonsense. When people are talking about you, your product stands out in a crowded market. And guess what? This kind of marketing is fun! If you're a realtor, it sure beats pounding wooden signs into front yards. The Million Dollar Coupon web site registered more than 2,500 unique visitors in just a few weeks. While as of this writing the home has not yet sold, it certainly stands out from the crowd.

When You Have Explosive News, Make It Go Viral

Although I've said that I think it is difficult to dream up campaigns that will definitely go viral and become a World Wide Rave, there are times that an organization possesses news that is so important to the target market they serve that they just know the news has significant viral potential. The hiring of a famous CEO away from another company, a merger or acquisition announcement, or a huge celebrity endorsement deal might be just the thing that lights up the blogs in your marketplace. If that's the case, it is important to get that news out in order to create the maximum effect. (Of course there is the opposite example—bad news—which also goes viral, and which you would prefer to contain or minimize. But in this chapter, let's just focus on the kind of good news that you want to get out to as wide an audience as possible.) If you want to push news along to maximum effect, it's critical to have a plan and a detailed timeline of whom you will tell the news to and when.

When Outsell, Inc.,[9] a research and advisory firm for the information industry, had just completed but not yet released a report, titled "Click Fraud Reaches $1.3 Billion, Dictates End of 'Don't Ask, Don't Tell' Era," that was the first to quantify, in real dollars and advertiser sentiment, the click-fraud problems that plague advertisers on search engines, they knew they were sitting on big news. The Outsell report, based on a study of 407 advertisers responsible for about $1 billion in ad spending, told the explosive story of a problem threatening the core business model of search engines like Google. The analysts at Outsell revealed the scope of the problem of fraudulent clicks on Web advertisements that appear as part of search results, clicks that companies doing the advertising were paying for. Outsell analysts knew that they had a story with viral potential.

"At first we hinted at the report in our client newsletter," says Chuck Richard, vice president and lead analyst at Outsell and the author of the report. "We always make certain that the paying clients get access to reports before they hit the media. But internally and with our PR firm, Warner Communications,[10] we thought it was going to be big." Outsell had a logistical problem in that the report was to be released to clients over the U.S. Independence Day holiday weekend. The PR firm sent a media advisory, headlined "Outsell, Inc. Pegs Click Fraud as $1.3 Billion Problem that Threatens Business Models of Google, Others; Study Shows 27% of Advertisers Slowing or Stopping Pay-Per-Click Ads Due to Fraudulent Billings," to selected media. The advisory offered an early look at the report to approved media under an embargo period—stories could not appear until Wednesday, July 5 at the earliest. Verne Kopytoff of the *San Francisco Chronicle* spent the holiday weekend researching the problem identified by Outsell, interviewing Richard, and reaching out for comment from spokespeople at the search engines. His story, "Click Fraud a Huge Problem: Study Finds Practice Widespread; Many Cut Back Online Ads," was the first to break.

"The viral aspect came from bloggers and built over the course of a week or so," Richard says. Within just five days, over 100 bloggers had picked up the

[9] www.outsellinc.com/

[10] www.warnerpr.com/

story, including heavy hitters such as *John Batelle's Searchblog*, Jeff Jarvis's *BuzzMachine, ClickZ News Blog*, Danny Sullivan at *Search Engine Watch*, and *paidContent.org*. After the story broke, Richard was busy doing interview after interview for mainstream media, resulting in a wave of nearly 100 stories in just the first week. Outlets including NPR, MSNBC, *Barron's*, the *Financial Times*, *AdAge*, *eWeek*, the *Boston Globe*, the *Los Angeles Times*, ABC News, *ZDNet*, *BusinessWeek Online*, and *TheStreet.com* all ran stories online, in print, and via broadcast media.

In the following weeks, Richard, now seen in the market as an expert in click fraud, received many press requests based on an existing Arkansas click-fraud class-action settlement that Google was proposing. Within a week, Google announced it would start providing statistics on the fraudulent clicks it intercepted, one of the key changes called for in the Outsell study; many media referenced this development in follow-up stories. Richard believes that the online buzz has prompted the paid search business to finally accept that it can't escape having its own click-fraud tracking, auditing, and certification processes. "This is great news for users, publishers, and advertisers," Richard says.

"For a small company to have access to this kind of reach of journalists and bloggers is remarkable," Richard says. "It couldn't have happened this way even a few years ago. The exposure has made a fundamental difference in [people's] awareness of the firm. Many of our clients have contacted us to say 'congratulations,' that they were happy to see us be more visible. And I've gotten on the prime source lists of many reporters who cover the space, and they proactively call me for comment on stories now." Indeed, *BusinessWeek* wrote a cover story, "Click Fraud: The Dark Side of Online Advertising," and quoted the Outsell report.

But Richard is also aware of how a significant news item or report can influence a company, or even an entire industry. "It's given us a reminder of our responsibility," he says. "If something like this can affect a company's share price or performance or investor inquiries on earnings calls, we need to be confident on our opinions."

The Outsell example clearly illustrates that a piece of news, properly delivered to the market, can go viral. But with careful nurturing over the news cycle and an awareness of traditional news media's and bloggers' roles in promoting ideas, the story can reach much larger audiences and help a smart organization to reach its goals.

Viral marketing—creating a World Wide Rave by having others tell your story for you—is one of the most exciting and powerful ways to reach your audiences. It's not easy to harness the power, but with careful preparation when you are sitting on news and with clever ideas for what has the potential to create interest, any organization has the power to become famous on the Web.

9 The Content-Rich Web Site

If you've read from the beginning of the book, at this point you might be tempted to think that each of the media that innovative marketers use to reach buyers—including blogs, podcasts, news releases, and all the rest—is a standalone communications vehicle. And while each certainly could be a self-contained unit (your blog does not need to link to your corporate site), most organizations integrate their online marketing efforts to help tell a unified story to buyers. Each medium is interrelated with all the others. Podcasts work with blogs. A news release program works with an effective web site and online media room. Multiple web sites for different divisions or countries come together on a corporate site. No matter how you choose to deploy web content to reach your buyers, the place that brings everything together in a unified place is a content-rich web site.

As anyone who has built a web site knows, there is much more to think about than just the content. Design, color, navigation, and appropriate technology are all important aspects of a good web site. Unfortunately, in many organizations these other concerns dominate. Why is that? I think it's *easier* to focus on a site's design or technology than on its content. Also, there are fewer resources to help web site creators with the content aspects of their sites—hey, that's one of the reasons why I wrote this book!

Often the only person allowed to work on the web site is your organization's *webmaster*. At many companies, webmasters—the kings of technology—focus all their attention on cool software plug-ins; on HTML, XML, and all sorts of other 'MLs; and on nitty-gritty stuff like server technology and

Internet Service Providers. But with a webmaster in charge, what happens to the content? In other organizations, webmasters are pushed aside by graphic designers and advertising people who focus exclusively on creating web sites that look pretty. At these organizations, well-meaning advertising agencies obsess over hip designs or hot technology such as Flash. I've seen many examples where site owners become so concerned about technology and design that they totally forget that great *content* is the most important aspect of any web site.

Thus, the best web sites focus primarily on content to pull together their various buyers, markets, media, and products in one comprehensive place where content is not only king, but president and Pope as well. A great web site is an intersection of every other online initiative, including podcasts, blogs, news releases, and other online media. In a cohesive and interesting way, the content-rich web site organizes the online personality of your organization to delight, entertain, and—most important—inform each of your buyers.

Political Advocacy on the Web

The Natural Resources Defense Council (NRDC) is the nation's most effective environmental action organization. According to its web site,[1] the organization uses law, science, and the support of 1.2 million members and online activists to protect the planet's wildlife and wild places and to ensure a safe and healthy environment for all living things. What makes the organization interesting is the vast amount of web content available on its site; the various media that its marketers deploy; and the tools it provides to online activists and political bloggers in order to spread the group's message. The professionals at NRDC, which was named by *Worth* magazine as one of America's 100 best charities, know that more than one million members are the best storytelling asset available. By developing a terrific web site to enlist people to donate their online voices, NRDC expands the team and its message-delivery capabilities considerably.

The site includes environmental news, resources, and information on topics such as Clean Air & Energy; Clean Drinking Water & Oceans; Wildlife & Fish; and Parks, Forests, & Wetlands. In addition, it offers online

---

[1] www.nrdc.org/

publications, links to laws and treaties, and a glossary of environmental terms. The NRDC delivers the organization's message via audio, video, and text and also encourages others to support the cause through giving their time and money and through reusing online content.

Throughout the site, widgets (small applications found on web sites and blogs) and links are available for bloggers to use in helping spread the message. Prominent widgets include social bookmarking tools to add tags to del. icio.us and Digg (to make it easier for people who use those sites to find information from NRDC). The site also offers independent bloggers and web site owners "badges" (graphical images that look like banner ads) that they add to their blog or site and then link back to NRDC to show support. For example, people who wish to help find solutions to both global warming and dependency on oil might put a biofuels badge[2] on their blog or web site; the badge links to NRDC content about biofuels. The badges available include small ones that look like the RSS links found on many blogs and larger ones similar to banner ads. The NRDC has also created Squidoo lenses such as "Understanding Global Warming (from the experts at NRDC),"[3] and it encourages its constituents to do the same. (A Squidoo lens is a web page built by someone with expertise on a topic—for more about Squidoo, see Chapter 14.)

"I came to NRDC from NPR initially, doing media relations," says Daniel Hinerfeld, associate director of communications for NRDC. "But because I'm in the L.A. office and we have entertainment industry contacts, I've started creating multimedia content for the site. We have a video called *Lethal Sound*[4] narrated by Pierce Brosnan that was my first big taste of multimedia." The video, which has been a hit on the festival circuit, details evidence linking sonar to a series of whale strandings in recent years. To encourage people to take action, the landing page for the video has multiple widgets and tools. From this page viewers can easily send messages to elected officials, donate money, and send online postcards to friends. Links to additional content, such as an NRDC press release titled "Navy Sued Over Harm to Whales from Mid-Frequency Sonar" and a detailed report titled "Sounding the Depths II," are just a click away. All this well-organized content, complete with easy ways to link to related information and to share content on blogs and with friends,

---

[2] www.nrdc.org/badges/biofuels.asp
[3] www.squidoo.com/globalwarmingprimer/
[4] www.nrdc.org/wildlife/marine/sonar.asp

is pulled together on the site and contributes greatly to the NRDC leadership position. And online content experts at NRDC are constantly looking for new ways to deliver their important messages.

"We created a podcast channel[5] with broadcast-quality, journalistic-style packages," Hinerfeld says. "Our communications strategy is not just to reach the media, but to also reach the constituents directly." Hinerfeld draws extensively from his experience at NPR when he produces shows for the NRDC podcasts. "I always try hard to include points of view that are at odds with our own," he says. "I think it makes it more interesting, and it reinforces our own position. For example, when we conduct interviews with our own staff, we challenge people with difficult questions, not just softballs, much like a journalist would. Going this route makes it authentic. People don't want PR, they want something that's real."

Hinerfeld says that multimedia is very exciting because it gives NRDC an opportunity to reach younger constituencies. "I've come across people who are huge consumers of podcasts, and many listen to them during long commutes," he says. "We use this sort of content to bond with people in a different, less wonky way. We also profile our younger staff members, which is a way to personalize the institution." Some staff members have MySpace profiles and use them to spread the word as well (more on MySpace is in Chapter 14).

NRDC is very well known within the news media that cover environmental issues on Capitol Hill. But the site content, the audio and video, and the site components that are offered to bloggers to spread the message (and cause it to go viral) make the organization much more approachable, especially to online activists and the younger MySpace generation. The NRDC staffers are active participants in the market and on the sites and blogs their constituents read. All these efforts make their content authentic, because it is contextually appropriate for the audiences the group needs to reach.

Content: The Focus of Successful Web Sites

The NRDC site is an excellent example of a web site that is designed to reach buyers. For the NRDC, the "buyers" are the more than one million members, advocates, and activists who use the site to work to protect the planet's wildlife and wild places and to promote a healthy environment.

---

[5] www.onearth.org/multimedia/podcast

Unfortunately, the vast majority of sites are built with the wrong focus. Yes, appearance and navigation are important: Appropriate colors, logos, fonts, and design make a site appealing. The right technologies such as content-management systems make sites easier to update. But what really matters is the *content*, how that content is organized, and how it drives action from buyers.

To move content to its rightful place in driving a successful marketing and PR strategy, content must be the single most important component. That focus can be tough for many people, both when their agencies push for hip and stylish design and when their IT departments obsess about the architecture. It is your role to think like a publisher and begin any new site or site redesign by starting with the content strategy.

Reaching a Global Marketplace

In 2009, I delivered presentations in countries including New Zealand, Turkey, and the Dominican Republic. As I traveled to my keynote speeches in each of the Baltic countries (Latvia, Lithuania, and Estonia), I was struck by how plugged into the web their residents are. For example, among Estonia's population of just 1.3 million people are 806,000 Internet users. My high-speed connections in this part of the world were much faster than in most parts of the United States.

The incredibly successful marketers I met in each of these small countries impressed me greatly with their outward thinking. When you live in a country like Latvia, your home market is tiny, requiring you to sell your products and services internationally. It also requires that you think deeply about your buyers in the global marketplace.

Consider LessLoss Audio Devices,[6] a company based in Kaunas, Lithuania. LessLoss creates amazing (and fabulously expensive) high-end audio products and has become famous among rabid audiophiles worldwide for power cords, filters, cables, and other equipment. LessLoss sells all over the world, and its site has a deliberately global focus. The e-commerce and SEO platform is managed by Globaltus,[7] also a Lithuanian company.

---

[6] www.lessloss.com/

[7] www.globaltus.com/

The LessLoss site includes amazingly detailed information about the audio devices, together with terrific photos. For example, there's an essay on "The Concept of Noise," which details why a sound-preserving technique known as power filtering is important. After all, when you sell power cables that can cost a thousand U.S. dollars, they had better be good. (And it's probably a good idea to explain *why* they're so good.)

"It is amazing how people from such a small country can reach customers worldwide and prove to be well respected," says Tomas Paplauskas, CEO of Globaltus. "The power of the Internet gives the opportunity to reach huge markets. Just imagine how few of these amazing power cords you could sell in Lithuania. There are no more local businesses—all businesses are global."

I think there is an important lesson here. We can all learn from the successful companies in these small countries, companies that have learned to create content-rich web sites to reach a global audience. And we can all reproduce their success. The marketplace is the outside world, not just your home city or state.

Putting It All Together with Content

As you're reading through this discussion of unifying your online marketing and PR efforts on your web site, you might be thinking, "That's easy for a smaller organization or one that has only one product line, but I work for a large company with many brands." Yes, it is more difficult to coordinate wide varieties of content when you have to juggle multiple brands, geographic variation, languages, and other considerations common to large companies. But with a large, widely dispersed organization, putting it all together on a corporate site might be even more important because showing a unified personality reaps benefits.

"The key is the collaboration between the different business units, the corporate offices, and the departments," says Sarah F. Garnsey, head of marketing and web communications at Textron Inc.[8] "At Textron, each business has its own independently operated web site, which makes coordination difficult because each is a well-defined brand that may be more familiar to people than our corporate brand."

---

[8] www.textron.com/

Textron Inc, a global company with yearly revenues of $14 billion and more than 37,000 employees in 33 countries, is recognized for strong brands such as Bell Helicopter, Cessna Aircraft, E-Z-GO (golf cars), and many others. The company has several dozen web sites, typically for the individual brands, such as Bell Helicopter.[9] "Through search logs we learned that many people were searching for product and business information on the corporate [Textron] site," Garnsey says. "That was a wakeup call for us, because we had thought that people were going to the business sites for this information. So we've built out the corporate site with more content about each of the businesses." On a visit to the new site, I was able to watch a video featuring Cessna Aircraft[10] CEO Jack Pelton, check out a lot of great photos of the products, and read feature stories about employees such as John Delamarter, who's the program manager of Lycoming's Thunderbolt Engine and who discussed his pride and pleasure in his work. Textron has a well-organized online media room and, because the company's stock is traded on the New York Stock Exchange, there is also an Investor Relations section on the site.

"We work with the businesses to showcase interesting things, and we try to have fresh content on the site and update it with new weekly stories," Garnsey says. "But the content is only as good as the management of the content and the processes. With a large site, rigor of process is required that many companies might underestimate. It takes coordination and management. For example, I can't make the content in the recruiting section of the site compelling unless I get the complete cooperation of the human resources department. People had grown to believe that you just throw the content at a webmaster and it all just works. But it doesn't—the days of the guy with the server under the desk are over."

Garnsey has a set of processes and procedures to make certain that the Textron site meets the needs of buyers and that everything on it works well, and she has a small team that works with her to coordinate with the people who manage division and product-company web sites. "We have a content management process to make sure everything is fresh, has been reviewed, and is passed by legal," she says. "But a primary component is that we make sure that the voice of the customer is captured and built into all of our

---

[9] www.bellhelicopter.textron.com/
[10] www.cessna.com/

electronic communications. We work on how to draw users into the content and use the site to form a relationship with them. Even if they don't purchase something from us right away, maybe they will become interested in the company stock or in something from one of the brands like Cessna." To make sure the site follows best practice, Garnsey brings people into a lab for annual usability tests and research. "We also do an audit of all of our dot-com sites every year to make sure that all sites comply with the standards," she says. "And each year we hold a web Summit of all the Textron people working on web initiatives from all over the company. We try to foster a community of people who otherwise would have no reason to speak with each other   because the individual businesses don't have a lot in common."

Great Web Sites: More Art than Science

The more I research web sites—and I've checked out thousands over the past several years—the more I realize that the best ones unite many important factors in a way that is difficult to describe. They just feel right—as if the creator of the site cares a great deal and wants her passion to shine through. Like a sprinkling of fairy dust, the effect is important but indescribable. However, I'm convinced that the key is to understand buyers (or those who may donate, subscribe, join, or vote) and build content especially for them.

Consider Sasha Vujacic:[11] The Official web site of "The Machine," a professional athlete fan page for the point guard/shooting guard of the Los Angeles Lakers' triangle offense. Sasha was a member of the Slovenian junior national team and was drafted by the Los Angeles Lakers in the 2004 NBA Draft. The Sasha site is beautifully designed and contains a huge amount of information about the player, including videos, photos, and much more. And get this: There's content in multiple languages (English, Italian, Slovenian, and even Chinese and Japanese) because Sasha has fans from all over the world. His multilanguage content appeals to different buyer personas.

The Sasha Vujacic Twitter feed[12] updates on the site, and there is an RSS feed of "regularly updated insider information and stories that you may publish on your web site automatically as Sasha publishes them." The best part of the site is that it gives off the vibe that Sasha is approachable. There are many

---

[11] www.sashavujacic18.com/

[12] http://twitter.com/SashaVujacic

casual photos of him, and there's a tool where fans can ask him questions and can even create their own T-shirt design and send it to him. If Sasha likes the design, he posts it on his official online store.

Vladimir Cuk and his firm Attention Interactive built the site for Sasha. But more importantly, Cuk and his firm developed a terrific strategy for Sasha to interact with his fans and the media. "The site is a hit with fans and NBA officials alike," Cuk says. Sasha and his management team are amazed at how the site looks and at the level of interaction and response from the fan community, according to Cuk. Other players have noticed as well and are intrigued about the possibilities of engaging more intimately with the public via the web and social media, Cuk also notes.

When Cuk was pitching Sasha's people for the business, he was up against the traditional public relations firms that frequently work with other NBA players. Sasha and his manager asked very intelligent questions during the meetings and came away ready to try what (to date) is a nontraditional promotion strategy for a pro basketball player. Most players use the media exclusively to deliver messages and are removed from interacting directly with fans. Not Sasha.

Effective sites like Sasha's draw on the passion of the people who build them and reflect the personality of someone dedicated to helping others. As you develop content to further your organizational goals, remember that a successful approach is often more art than science. The content you offer must have distinctive qualities, and your personality needs to show. A well-executed web site, like a quality television program or film, is a combination of content and delivery. But on the web, many organizations spend much more time and money on the design and delivery aspects than on the content itself. Don't fall into that trap. Perfecting that critical mix of content, design, and technology is where the art comes in. Adding personality and authenticity and reaching particular buyer personas makes the challenge even more daunting. Just remember, there is no absolute right or wrong way to create a web site; each organization has an individual and important story to tell.

Now let's spend some time on the specifics of how you can implement these ideas for your own organization. Part III of this book starts with a discussion of how you build a comprehensive marketing and PR plan to reach your buyers directly with web content. Once armed with your plan, continue to the chapters that follow, which will give you advice for developing thought leadership content and writing for your buyers. Finally, I provide detailed information on how to implement a news release program, build an online media room, create your own blog and podcast, and work with social-networking sites. Because I'm convinced of the value of hearing from innovative marketers who have had success with these ideas, I continue to sprinkle case studies throughout the remaining chapters to give you some examples of how others have implemented these ideas and to help you get your own creative juices flowing.

Action Plan for Harnessing the Power of the New Rules

10 You Are What You Publish: Building Your Marketing and PR Plan

Does your company sell great products? Or, if you don't work in a traditional company, does your organization (church, nonprofit, consulting company, school) offer great services? Well, get over it! Marketing is not *only* about your products! The most important thing to remember as you develop a marketing and PR plan is to put your products and services to the side for just a little while and focus your complete attention on the *buyers* of your products (or those who will donate, subscribe, join, or apply). Devoting attention to buyers and away from products is difficult for many people, but it always pays off in the form of bringing you closer to achieving your goals.

Think Starbucks for a moment. Is the product great? Yeah, I guess the three-dollar cup of coffee I get from Starbucks tastes pretty good. And most marketers, if given the opportunity to market Starbucks, would focus on the coffee itself—the product. But is that really what people are buying at Starbucks, or does Starbucks help solve other buyer problems? Maybe Starbucks is really selling a place to hang out for a while. Or, for that matter, isn't Starbucks a convenient place for people to meet? (I use Starbucks several times a month as a place to connect with people or conduct interviews.) Or do people use Starbucks for the free wireless Internet connections? Maybe Starbucks saves 10 minutes in your day because you don't have to grind beans, pour water into a coffee maker, wait, and clean up later. For some of us, Starbucks just represents a little splurge because, well, we're worth it. I'd argue that Starbucks does all those things. Starbucks appeals to many different buyer personas, and it sells lots of things besides just coffee. If you were marketing

Starbucks, it would be your job to segment buyers and appeal to them based on their needs, not just to talk about your product.

The approach of thinking about buyers and the problems our organizations solve for them can be difficult for many marketers, since we've constantly been told how important a great product or service is to the marketing mix. In fact, standard marketing education still talks about the four *P*s of marketing—product, place, price, and promotion—as being the most important things. That's nonsense. In order to succeed on the Web under the new rules of marketing and PR, you need to consider your organizational goals and then focus on your buyers *first*. Only when you understand buyers should you begin to create compelling Web content to reach them. Yes, marketers often argue with me on this. But I strongly believe that the product or service you sell is secondary when you market your organization on the Web.

So, I will ask you to put aside your products and services as you begin the task for this chapter: building a marketing and PR plan that follows the new rules. While the most important thing to focus on during this process is buyers, we will do that in the context of your organizational goals. Trust me—this will be like no marketing and PR plan you've created before.

What Are Your Organization's Goals?

Marketing and PR people have a collective difficulty getting our departmental goals in sync with the rest of the company. And our management teams go along with this dysfunction. Think about the goals that most marketers have. They usually take the form of an epic to-do list: "Let's see; we should do a few trade shows, buy Yellow-Pages ads, maybe create a new logo, get press clips, produce some T-shirts, increase web site traffic, and, oh yeah, generate some leads for the salespeople." Well, guess what? Those aren't the goals of your company! I've never seen "leads" or "clips" or "T-shirts" on a balance sheet. With typical marketing department goals, we constantly focus on the flare-up du jour and thus always focus on the wrong thing. This also gives the marketing profession a bad rap in many companies as a bunch of flaky slackers. No wonder marketing is called the "branding police" in some organizations and is often the place where failed salespeople end up.

Many marketers and PR people also focus on the wrong measures of success. With web sites, people will often tell me things like, "We want to have ten thousand unique visitors per month to our site." And PR measurement is often similarly irrelevant: "We want ten mentions in the trade press and three national magazine hits each month." Unless your site makes money through advertising so that raw traffic adds revenue, traffic is the wrong measure. And simple press clips just don't matter. What matters is leading your site's visitors and your constituent audiences to where they help you reach your real goals, such as building revenue, soliciting donations, gaining new members, and the like.

This lack of clear goals and real measurement reminds me of seven-year-olds playing soccer. If you've ever seen little children on the soccer field, you know that they operate as one huge organism packed together, chasing the ball around the field. On the sidelines are helpful coaches yelling, "Pass!" or "Go to the goal!" Yet as the coaches and parents know, this effort is futile: No matter what the coach says or how many times the kids practice, they still focus on the wrong thing—the ball—instead of the goal.

That's exactly what we marketers and PR people do. We fill our lists with balls and lose sight of the goal. But do you know what's even worse? Our coaches (the management teams at our companies) actually encourage us to focus on balls (like sales leads or press clips or web site traffic statistics) instead of real organizational goals such as revenue. The VPs and CEOs of companies happily provide incentives based on leads for the marketing department and on clips for the PR team. And the agencies we contract with— advertising and PR agencies—also focus on the wrong measures.

What we need to do is align marketing and PR objectives with those of the organization. For most corporations, the most important goal is profitable revenue growth. In newer companies and those built around emerging technologies, this usually means generating new customers, but in mature businesses, the management team may need to be more focused on keeping the customers that they already have. Of course, nonprofits have the goal of raising money; politicians, to get out the vote; rock bands to get people to buy CDs, iTunes downloads, and tickets to live shows; and universities, to get student applications and alumni donations.

So your first step is to get with the leaders of your organization—your management team or your associates in your church or nonprofit or your spouse if you run a small business—and determine your business goals. If you run a nonprofit, school, church, or political campaign, consider your goals for donations, applications, new members, or votes. Write them down in detail. The important things you write down might be "grow revenue in Europe by 20 percent" or "increase new-member signups to one hundred per month in the fourth quarter" or "generate a million dollars in Web donations next quarter" or "generate five paid speaking engagements in the upcoming year."

Now that you have the marketing and PR plan focused on the right goals (i.e., those of your organization), the next step is to learn as much as you can about your buyers and to segment them into groups so you can reach them through your Web publishing efforts.

Buyer Personas and Your Organization

Successful online marketing and PR efforts work because they start by identifying one or more buyer personas to target, so you need to make buyer personas a part of your planning process. A buyer persona (which we touched on back in Chapter 3) is essentially a representative of a type of buyer that you have identified as having a specific interest in your organization or product or having a market problem that your product or service solves. Building buyer personas is the first step and probably the single most important thing that you will do in creating your marketing and PR plan. Consider the U.S. presidential elections of 2004. Marketers for the two major candidates segmented buyers (voters) into dozens of distinct buyer personas. Some of the names of the buyer personas (sometimes called "microtargets" in the political world) became well known as the media began to write about them, while many other persona labels remained internal to the candidates. Some of the better-known buyer personas of the 2004 presidential election were "NASCAR Dads" (rural working-class males, many of whom are NASCAR fans) and "Security Moms" (mothers who were worried about terrorism and concerned about security). By segmenting millions of voters into distinct buyer personas, the candidates built marketing campaigns and PR programs that appealed specifically to each. Contrast this approach with a one-size-fits-all campaign that targets everybody but appeals to nobody.

Another example I quite like for illustrating the point of buyer personas is the market for tricycles. The user of the most common tricycle is a preschool child. Yet a preschooler doesn't buy her own tricycle. The most common buyer personas for children's tricycles are parents and grandparents. So what problem does the tricycle solve? Well, for parents, it might be that the child

BOARDING PASS

1 006 2348989073 3
GKM7IM

DELTA
FUERST/FRANK

SILVER/ELITE
DL2000880076

FLIGHT **DL1442** DATE **07MAY** CLASS **U**

OPERATED BY
DELTA AIR LINES INC

ORIGIN **ATLANTA**

DESTINATION **PROVIDENCE**

COACH

DEPARTURE GATE **A13** "SUBJECT TO CHANGE"

SEAT **26C** EXIT
ZONE 2

DEPARTS **935A**

BRD TIME **855A**

BOARDING PASS

FUERST/FRANK

SILVER/ELITE
DL2000880076

FLIGHT **DL1442** DATE **07MAY**

ORIGIN **ATLANTA**

DESTINATION **PROVIDENCE**

OPERATED BY DELTA AIR LINES INC

SEAT **26C** EXIT
ZONE 2

ATL189426/KI

PROVIDENCE
PUD   DL   1442

5006 **DL915935**
PNR: GKM7IM
FUERST/FRANK

PROVIDENCE
PUD   DL   1442

5006 **DL915936**
PNR: GKM7IM
FUERST/FRANK

0412-71441

has been asking for one and the purchase quiets the child down. Parents also know that the child is growing quickly and will want a two-wheeler with training wheels soon enough, so a basic trike is typically enough in their eyes. However, grandparents buy tricycles to solve the problem of providing an extravagant gift, so they often buy the expensive models to show their love to the child and his or her parents. When you think about tricycles from the perspective of buyer personas, you can see how the marketing might be different for parents and grandparents.

You, too, need to segment buyer personas so you can then develop marketing programs to reach each one. Let's revisit the college example from Chapter 3 and expand on it. Remember that we identified five different buyer personas for a college web site: young alumni (those who graduated within the past 10 or 15 years), older alumni, the high school student who is considering college, the parents of the prospective student, and existing customers (current students). That means a well-executed college site might target five distinct buyer personas.

A college might have the marketing and PR goal of generating 500 additional applications for admission from qualified students for the next academic year. Let's also pretend that the college hopes to raise $5 million in donations from alumni who have never contributed in the past. That's great! These are real goals that marketers can build programs around.

The Buyer Persona Profile

After identifying their goals, the marketing people at the college should build a buyer persona profile, essentially a kind of biography, for each group they'll target to achieve those goals. The college might create one buyer persona for prospective students (targeting high school students looking for schools) and another for parents of high school students (who are part of the decision process and often pay the bills). If the school targets a specific type of applicant, say student athletes, they might build a specific buyer persona profile for the high school student who participates in varsity sports. To effectively target the alumni for donations, the school might decide to build a buyer persona for younger alumni, perhaps those who have graduated in the past 10 years.

For each buyer persona profile, we want to know as much as we can about this group of people. What are their goals and aspirations? What are their problems? What media do they rely on for answers to problems? How can we reach them? We want to know, in detail, the things that are important for each buyer persona. What words and phrases do the buyers use? What sorts of images and multimedia appeal to each? Are short and snappy sentences better than long, verbose ones? I encourage you to write these things down based on your understanding of each buyer persona. You should also read the publications and web sites that your buyers read to gain an understanding of the way they think. For example, college marketing people should read the *US News and World Report* issue that ranks America's Best Colleges as well as the guidebooks that prospective students read, such as *Countdown to College: 21 To-Do Lists for High School: Step-By-Step Strategies for 9th, 10th, 11th, and 12th Graders* and *The Ultimate College Acceptance System: Everything You Need to Know to Get into the Right College for You.* Reading what your buyer personas read will get you thinking like them. By doing some basic research on your buyers, you can learn a great deal, and your marketing will be much more effective.

The best way to learn about buyers and develop buyer persona profiles is to interview people. I have no doubt that representatives of the two presidential candidates interviewed many NASCAR Dads and Security Moms to build profiles for these and many other buyer personas they identified. Similarly, the marketing person at our hypothetical college must interview people who fit the personas the school identified. The college marketing people might learn a great deal if they turned the traditional in-person college admissions interview around by asking prospective students questions such as the following: When did you first start researching schools? Who influenced your research? How did you learn about this school? How many schools are you applying to? What web sites, blogs, or pod-casts do you read or subscribe to? Once you know this first-hand information, you should subscribe to, read, and listen to the media that influence your target buyer. When you read what your buyers read, pay attention to the exact words and phrases that are used. If students frequent Facebook or other social-network sites, so should you, and you should pay attention to the lingo students use. By triangulating the information gathered directly from several dozen prospective students plus information from the media that these students pay attention to, you easily build a buyer persona for a high school student ready to apply to a college like yours.

"A buyer persona profile is a short biography of the typical customer, not just a job description but a person description," says Adele Revella,[1] who has been using buyer personas to market technology products for more than 20 years. "The buyer persona profile gives you a chance to truly empathize with target buyers, to step out of your role as someone who wants to promote a product and see, through your buyers' eyes, the circumstances that drive their decision process. The buyer persona profile includes information on the typical buyer's background, daily activities, and current solutions for their problems. The more experience you have in your market, the more obvious the personas become."

This may sound a bit wacky, but I think you should go so far as to name your persona the way that the campaigns did with NASCAR Dads and Security Moms. You might even cut out a representative photo from a magazine to help you visualize him or her. This should be an *internal name only* that helps you and your colleagues to develop sympathy with and a deep understanding of the real people to whom you market. Rather than a nameless, faceless "prospect," your buyer persona will come to life.

For example, a buyer persona for a male high school student who is a varsity athlete and whom you want to target might be named "Sam the Athlete" and his persona might read something like this: "Sam the Athlete began thinking about colleges and the upcoming application process way back when he was a freshman in high school. His coach and parents recognized his athletic talent and suggested that it will help him get into a good college or even secure a scholarship. Sam knows that he's good, but not good enough to play on a Division 1 school. Sam first started poking around on college web sites as a freshman and enjoyed checking out the athletic pages for the colleges in his home state and some nearby ones. He even attended some of these colleges' games when he could. Sam has good grades, but he is not at the top of his class because his sports commitments mean he can't study as much as his peers. He has close friends and likes to hang out with them on weekends, but he is not heavily into the party scene and avoids alcohol and drugs. Sam frequents Facebook, has his own Facebook page, and has a group of online friends that he frequently Instant Messages with. He is hip to online nuance, language, and etiquette. Sam also reads *Sports Illustrated Magazine*. Now that he is a junior, he knows it is time to get serious about college

---

[1] www.buyerpersona.com/

applications, and he doesn't really know where to start. But to learn, he's paying more attention to the applications pages than the athletic pages on college web sites."

Okay, so you're nodding your head and agreeing with this buyer persona profiling thing. "But," you ask, "how many buyer personas do I need?" You might want to think about your buyer personas based on what factors differentiate them. How can you slice the demographics? For example, some organizations will have a different profile for buyers in the United States versus Europe. Or maybe your company sells to buyers in the automobile industry and in the government sector, and those buyers are different. The important thing is that you will use this buyer persona information to create specific marketing and PR programs to reach each buyer persona, and therefore you need to have the segmentation in fine enough detail that when they encounter your Web content, your buyers will say: "Yes, that's me. This organization understands me and my problems and will therefore have products that fit my needs."

Marketers and PR pros are often amazed at the transformation of their materials and programs as a result of buyer persona profiling. "When you really know how your buyers think and what matters to them, you eliminate the agony of guessing about what to say or where and how to communicate with buyers," says Revella. "Marketers tell me that they don't have time to build buyer personas, but these same people are wasting countless hours in meetings debating about whether the message is right. And of course, they're wasting budgets building programs and tools that don't resonate with anyone. It's just so much easier and more effective to listen before you talk."

Reaching Senior Executives

Many people ask me about reaching senior executives via the Web. That executives do not use the Web as much as other people is a commonly held belief, one that I've never bought. Frequently, business-to-business marketers use this misperception as an excuse for why they don't have to focus on building buyer personas and marketing materials for senior executives. Based on anecdotal information from meeting with many of them, I have always argued that executives are online in a big way. However, I've never had any solid data to support my hunch until now.

Forbes Insights, in association with Google, recently released a new study called *The Rise of the Digital C-Suite: How Executives Locate and Filter Business Information.*[2] The findings clearly show that the Web is considered by executives to be their most valuable resource for gathering business information, outstripping at-work contacts, personal networks, trade publications, and so on. In fact, 74 percent of respondents rated the Internet as very valuable (5 on a 5-point scale).

"The common perception is that top executives at the largest companies do not use the Internet, but the reality is just the opposite," says Stuart Feil, editorial director of Forbes Insights. "These findings show that C-level executives are more involved online than their counterparts, and younger generations of executives—those whose work careers have coincided with the growth of the PC and the Internet—are bringing profound organizational change to these companies."

The Importance of Buyer Personas in Web Marketing

One of the simplest ways to build an effective web site or to create great marketing programs using online content is to target the specific buyer personas that you have created. Yet most web sites are big brochures that do not offer specific information for different buyers. Think about it—the typical web site is one-size-fits-all, with the content organized by the company's products or services, not by categories corresponding to buyer personas and their associated problems.

The same thing is true about other online marketing programs. Without a focus on the buyer, the typical press release and media relations program is built on what the organization wants to say rather than what the buyer wants to hear. There is a huge difference. Companies that are successful with direct-to-consumer news release strategies write for their buyers. The blogs that are best at reaching an organizational goal are not about companies or products but rather customers and their problems.

Now that you've set quantifiable organizational goals and identified the buyer personas that you want to reach, your job as you develop your marketing and PR plan is to identify the best ways to reach buyers and develop

---

[2] www.forbes.com/forbesinsights/

compelling information that you will use in your Web marketing programs. If you've conducted interviews with buyers and developed a buyer persona profile, then you know the buyer problems that your product or service solves, and you know the media that buyers turn to for answers. Do they go first to a search engine? If so, what words and phrases do they enter? Which blogs, chat rooms, forums, and online news sites do they read? Are they open to audio or video? You need to answer these questions before you continue.

In Your Buyers' Own Words

Throughout the book, I often refer to the importance of understanding the words and phrases that buyers use. An effective Web marketing plan requires an understanding of the ways your buyers speak and the real words and phrases they use. This is important not only for building a positive online relationship with your buyers, but also for planning effective search engine marketing strategies. After all, if you are not using the phrases your buyers search on, how can you possibly reach them?

Let's take a look at the importance of the actual words buyers use, by way of an example. Several years ago, I worked with Shareholder.com to create a Web content strategy to reach buyers of the company's new Whistleblower Hotline product and move those buyers into and through the sales cycle. The Shareholder.com product was developed as an outsourced solution for public companies to comply with rule 301 (the so-called "Whistleblower Hotline" provision) of the U.S. Sarbanes-Oxley legislation that passed in 2002 in the wake of corporate scandals such as Enron. Most importantly, we interviewed buyers (such as chief financial officers within publicly traded companies) who were required to comply with the legislation. We also read the publications that our buyers read (such as *CFO*, *Directors Monthly*, and the *AACA Docket* of the American Corporate Counsel Association); we actually downloaded and read the massive Sarbanes-Oxley legislation document itself; and we studied the agendas of the many conferences and events that our buyers attended that discussed the importance of Sarbanes-Oxley compliance.

As a result of the buyer persona research, we learned the phrases that buyers used when discussing the Sarbanes-Oxley whistleblower hotline rule, and so the content that we created for the Shareholder.com web site[3] included

---

[3] www360.shareholder.com/home/Solutions/Whistleblower.cfm

such important phrases as: "SEC mandates," "complete audit trail," "Sarbanes-Oxley rule 301," "confidential and anonymous submission," and "safe and secure employee reporting." An important component of the web site we created (based on our buyer persona research) was thought-leadership–based content, including a Webinar called "Whistleblower Hotlines: More than a Mandate" that featured guest speakers Harvey Pitt (former chairman of the U.S. Securities and Exchange Commission) and Lynn Brewer (author of the book *House of Cards: Confessions of an Enron Executive*). Because this Webinar discusses issues of importance to *buyers* (not only Shareholder.com products), and the guest speakers are thought leaders that buyers are interested in learning from, 600 people eagerly watched the presentation live.

"The Webinar was very important because when we launched the product we were starting from a position with no market share within this product niche," says Bradley H. Smith, director of marketing/communications at Shareholder.com. "Other companies had already entered the market before us. The Webinar gave us search engine terms like 'Harvey Pitt' and 'Enron' and offered a celebrity draw. Search engine placement was important because it created our brand as a leader in Whistleblower Hotline technologies even though we were new to this market. Besides prospective clients, the media found us, which resulted in important press including prominent placement in a *Wall Street Journal* article called 'Making it Easier to Complain.'"

Shareholder.com then took the service to the Canadian market where the legislation was called "Ontario Securities Commission and The Audit Committees Rule of the Canadian Securities Administrators Guidelines Multilateral Instrument 52-110" (quite a mouthful). Smith and his colleagues interviewed buyers in Canada and did some buyer persona research to determine if there were any differences in the words and phrases used in Canada. There were! Unlike the other U.S. companies attempting to enter the Canadian market for hotline solutions by just using their U.S. marketing materials, Shareholder.com created a separate set of Web content for Canadian buyers. Used in the pages for these buyers were specific phrases that were used by Canadian buyers (but not buyers in the U.S.), such as "governance hotline," "conducting a forensic accounting investigation," and the exact name of the Canadian legislation.

Because the marketers at Shareholder.com had done extensive buyer persona research and had created Web content with the words and phrases used by buyers, the Shareholder.com pages were visited frequently and linked to often, and they became highly ranked by the search engines. In fact, at the time of this writing, Shareholder.com is number one out of 258,000 hits on Google for the phrase "whistleblower hotline." As a result of traffic driven from the search engines and great Web content for both U.S. and Canadian buyers (such as Webinars), the product launch was a success. "In the four months immediately after the Webcast, we signed 75 clients," Smith says. "Furthermore, the Webcast archive of the event continued to work for us throughout the year, advancing our brand presence, generating sales leads, and contributing to the strongest Shareholder.com standalone product launch ever."

Figuring out the phrases for your market requires that you buckle down and do some research. Although interviewing buyers about their market problems and listening to the words and phrases they use is best, you can also learn a great deal by reading the publications that they read. Check out any blogs in your buyers' space (if you haven't already), and study the agendas and topic descriptions for the conferences and seminars that your buyers frequent. When you have a list of the phrases that are important to your buyers, use those phrases not only to appeal to them specifically, but also to make your pages appear in the search engine results when your buyers search for what you have to offer.

What Do You Want Your Buyers to Believe?

Now that you have identified organizational goals, built a set of one or more buyer personas, and researched the words and phrases your buyers use to talk about and search for your product, you should think about what you want each of your buyer personas to *believe* about your organization. What are the messages that you will use for each buyer persona? Think back again to the 2004 U.S. presidential election. Once they had identified buyer personas such as NASCAR Dads and Security Moms, the campaigns had to create a set of messages, web sites, TV ads, direct mail campaigns, and talking points that the candidates would use in speeches to these groups. For example, George W. Bush appealed to Security Moms with speeches and advertising that claimed that families would be safer from the threats of terrorism with his "stay the course" approach if he were reelected rather than if John Kerry were elected.

In the 2008 election, Barack Obama focused on his buyer personas and identified as crucially important the concept of "change." Everywhere you saw the Obama campaign, you saw nods to this theme: on the podium where the candidate was speaking, on T-shirts and buttons, on posters, and of course on the Web. The Obama campaign shrewdly understood that, when primary voters pulled the lever to vote for Obama, they were buying into the idea of the need for change. They were choosing an idea, not just a man. The Obama campaign clearly understood, and articulated, what they wanted their buyer personas to believe that the candidate would bring.

You must do the same thing with your buyer personas. What do you want each group to believe about your organization? What messages will you use to reach them on the Web? Remember, the best messages are not just about your product. What is each buyer persona really buying from you? Is it great customer service? The "safe choice"? Luxury? For example, Volvo doesn't just sell a car; it sells *safety*.

And don't forget that different buyer personas buy different things from your organization. Think about Gatorade for a moment. For competitive athletes, Gatorade has been the drink of choice for decades. I found some interesting messages on the Gatorade web site,[4] including "If you want to *win*, you've got to replace what you *lose*," and "For some athletes, significant dehydration can occur within the initial 30 minutes of exercise." These are interesting messages, because they target the buyer persona of the competitive athlete and focus on how Gatorade can help those athletes win.

Now I'm not an expert on Gatorade's buyer personas, but it seems to me that they could further refine their buyer personas based on the sports athletes play or on whether they are professionals or amateurs. If tennis players see themselves as very different from football players, then Gatorade may need to create buyer persona profiles and messages to target both sports separately. Or maybe women athletes make up a different buyer persona for Gatorade than men.

But there's another buyer persona that I have never seen Gatorade address. I remember back to my early twenties, when I lived in an apartment in New York City and was single and making the rounds in the party circuit and late-night club scene. To be honest, I was partying a little too hard some weeknights, skulking home in the wee hours. Of course, I then had to make it down to my Wall Street job by 8:00 A.M. I discovered that drinking a large bottle of Gatorade on the walk to the subway stop helped make me feel a lot

---

[4] www.gatorade.com/

better. Now I don't *actually* expect Gatorade to develop messages for young professionals in New York who drink too much, but that buyer persona certainly has different problems from those that Gatorade solves for athletes. Imagine advertising for this buyer persona: "Last night's third martini still in your system? Rehydration is not just for athletes. Gatorade."

Of course, the point is that different buyer personas have different problems for your organization to solve. And there's no doubt that your online marketing and PR programs will do better if you develop messages for each buyer persona, instead of simply relying on a generic site that uses one set of broad messages for everyone.

Developing Content to Reach Buyers

You must now think like a publisher. You should develop an editorial plan to reach your buyers with focused content in the media that they prefer. Your first action might be to create a content-rich web site with pages organized by buyer persona. This does not mean you need to redesign the entire existing web site, nor does it necessitate a change in the site architecture. You can start by just creating some new individual pages, each with specialized content customized for a particular buyer persona, creating appropriate links to these pages, and leaving the rest of the site alone. For example, our hypothetical college might create content for each of the buyer personas they identified. Sam the Athlete (the high school student who is a varsity athlete and a candidate for admission) should have specific content written for him that describes what it is like to be a student athlete at the college and also gives tips for the admission process. The college could include profiles of current student athletes or even a blog by one of the coaches. In addition, appropriate links on the homepage and the admissions pages should be created for Sam. An appropriate homepage link such as "high school athletes start here" or "special information for student athletes" would attract Sam's attention.

At the same time, the college should develop pages for parents of high school students who are considering applying for admission. The parents have very different problems from those of the students, and the site content designed for parents would deal with things like financial aid and safety on campus.

As you keep your publisher's hat on, consider what other media your organization can publish on the Web to reach the buyers that you have identified. A technology company might want to consider a white paper detailing solutions to a known buyer problem. Perhaps you have enough information to create an e-book on a subject that would be of interest to one or more of your buyer personas. You may want to develop a series of a dozen direct-to-consumer news releases focusing on a series of issues that you know your buyer is interested in. Or it might be time to start a blog, a podcast, or online video channel to reach your buyers.

Consider creating an editorial plan for each buyer persona. You might do this in the form of a calendar for the upcoming year that includes web site content, an e-book or white paper, a blog, and some news releases. Notice as you build an editorial plan and an editorial calendar for the next year that you're now focused on creating the compelling content that your buyers are interested in. Unlike the way you might have done it in the past (and the way your competitors are marketing today), you are not just creating a big brochure about your organization. You're writing for your buyers, not your own ego.

Bozeman, MT-based RightNow Technologies,[5] a provider of customer relationship management software, rebuilt its company web site around buyer personas. "The RightNow persona development exercise was broader than just for creating web site content but was designed for all marketing content," says Steve Bell, product marketing manager for RightNow. "The goal of the web site project was to turn RightNow.com into a web site that sells. We created the new web site with conversion paths (entry points into the buying process) for each persona, and more overall conversion points than the original site."

To help the Web development team at RightNow build appropriate information for the site, detailed buyer personas were created for four different personas:

- **Atul**—Director of Information Technology (a technical evaluator for a company that's considering RightNow Technologies' products)
- **Chuck**—Customer Services Director (an operational prospect for RightNow Technologies—someone who manages a team that would use the product to do their jobs)
- **Olivia**—Senior Vice President (a RightNow Technologies strategic prospect—the top executive in the department that will use the product to do their jobs)

---

[5] www.rightnow.com/

- **Trinh**—Financial Analyst (a RightNow Technologies information seeker who wants to know more about the company itself)

Bell and his team developed details about these buyer personas. The best way to do this is to interview representatives of each group. As an example, some details about Chuck's goals include:

- Chuck wants to improve his team's efficiency, due to his inability to fund new hires to keep up with demand.
- Chuck wants to decrease his staff's call and email volume, so they can spend more time with customers who really need help instead of routinely answering the same questions.
- Chuck needs to find a solution that doesn't involve complicated IT and can be implemented quickly.
- Chuck wants to improve customer satisfaction, but he assumes that will happen if he can reduce his team's call and email volume.

It's worth clarifying that the detailed information about your buyer personas is for your internal information and shouldn't be posted onto the site. However, what you learn helps you to create valuable information to be posted on the public site. For example, on the RightNow homepage, there is a list of questions on the left-side navigation. The pages that these links point to are specifically built around buyer personas and address problems that these personas face.

- *I need to transform my call center.*
- *I need to capture customer feedback.*
- *I need to add live chat.*

"Chuck's content is built around his specific needs ('I need to . . . '), which are illustrated on the home page and take him down a specific conversion path," Bell says. "Olivia, who is more senior, is more focused on strategy and is more brand-conscious, so a big part of the banner areas on the home page are dedicated to her, such as 'Weathering the Storm.' The CEO blog and the customer experience strategies are also targeted at Olivia. There was a brand new technology section dedicated to Atul."

According to Bell, the results have exceeded expectations. RightNow has seen significant improvement in important Web measurements of the new site, compared to the previous one: a fourfold increase in overall conversions, a fivefold increase in live demo request conversions, and an increase in Flash demo conversions by a factor of more than three.

As the RightNow Technologies example shows, there are clear benefits to marketing based on detailed understanding of buyer personas. In particular, when you stop talking about you and your products and services and instead use the Web to educate and inform important types of buyers, you will be more successful.

Obama for America

I want you to stop, take a deep breath, and let me close this chapter on building your marketing and PR plan by making a few observations about why Barack Obama was elected to be the 44th president of the United States. Of course, this is a book about the new rules of marketing and PR, not a book about presidential politics. These are not political observations but, rather, thoughts about the amazing success Obama and his campaign team had in embracing voters using the new rules of marketing and PR. If you are an American citizen, it doesn't matter who you (or I) supported or voted for during the 2008 U.S. presidential election. *Everyone* (those who work in companies large and small, nonprofits, independent consultants, job seekers, musicians . . . well, everyone) can learn from Obama's victory. I certainly have. After all, who would have predicted in 2006 that a young, skinny, half-black man with a strange name—Barack Hussein Obama—and funny ears, who had served less than one term in the U.S. Senate, could be elected to the most powerful position in the world, despite facing more than 20 other candidates, many of them better known and better funded? There is no doubt in my mind that Obama was elected because his campaign used the ideas that I describe in this book. Mind you, I'm not saying his aides had copies of it on the campaign bus. But I am saying that the campaign observed and acted on the very same online opportunities that we've been discussing in this book, and they did it better than just about anyone else.

> Barack Obama is the most successful "new marketer" in history. Study his campaign so that you can adapt the ideas for your business.

"Voters in 2008 were not just passive followers of the political process," says Aaron Smith, research specialist at the Pew Internet & American Life Project and author of the project's April 2009 report *The Internet's Role in Campaign 2008*.[6] "They used a wide range of digital tools and technologies to get involved in the race, to harness their creativity in support of their chosen candidate, and to join forces with others who shared their same political goals."

Smith's findings indicate the widespread use of the Web to research candidates and support campaigns. The 2008 election was the first in which more than half the voting-age population used the Internet for political purposes. Some 55 percent of all adults—and 74 percent of all Internet users—said they went online for news and information about the election or to communicate with others about the race. The research found that social media platforms such as blogs, social networking sites, and video-sharing sites played a key role in 2008, as voters went online to share their views with others and try to mobilize them to their cause.

As you read these remarkable statistics from Smith's report, please be aware that the numbers are likely very similar as they relate to your own business. It is clear that the Web and social media are now a mainstream way for people to do research. Are people finding you, your company, and its products and services the way they found Barack Obama?

- 45 percent of wired Americans watched videos online related to politics or the election. Young adults led the way in their online video consumption, as nearly half of all 18- to 29-year-olds watched online political videos this election cycle.
- 33 percent of Internet users shared digital political content with others—whether by forwarding political writing or multimedia content over email, or by sharing information with others through other online mechanisms.
- 52 percent of those with a social networking profile used their social network site for political purposes.

While I was not personally active in the political campaigns of the 2008 U.S. presidential election, I did spend a great deal of time studying the

---

[6] www.pewinternet.org/Press-Releases/2009/The-Internets-Role-in-Campaign-2008.aspx

marketing aspects of the candidates. Here are my thoughts on why Obama won the election, presented as tips so you can apply them to your own business:

Focus on buyer personas. As we learned in Chapter 5 from Kevin Flynn, who worked on the Obama social media team, the campaign targeted buyer personas (voters) on a state-by-state basis. There was specific focus on getting out each and every one of the Obama "base" of supporters to vote as well as a strong focus on undecided voters.

Don't underestimate the importance of social media and the new rules of marketing and PR. The other campaigns seemed to be fighting using the play-books of past campaigns, the old rules of marketing and PR. Hillary Clinton was relying on what worked to elect Bill Clinton. John McCain was relying on what worked to elect George W. Bush. The Obama campaign realized that for him to become president, he had to deliver information online primarily, not as an afterthought. The number of people the campaign reached on the Web is staggering: According to *The Nation*, 13 million people signed up for the Obama campaign email list, more than 5 million "friended" Obama on Facebook, 2 million joined MyBO[7] (an online organizing site where people could sign up to support the campaign as a volunteer), and more than 1 million people subscribed to campaign text messages on mobile phones.

Embrace citizen journalists. My friend Steve Garfield,[8] author of the book *Get Seen: Online Video Secrets to Building Your Business*, is a well-known video blogger. He's got tens of thousands of followers. During the primaries, Garfield attended several rallies held by various candidates. When he asked to go to the media section at a Hillary Clinton rally in Boston, he was turned away (because he was "not a real journalist") and had to cover it from the back of the crowd. However, Obama's campaign immediately brought him up to the media section where he was placed with print reporters from the major dailies and TV crews from the networks. The Obama campaign understood that citizen journalists (bloggers, podcasters, video bloggers) have immense power.

Clearly and simply articulate what you want people to believe. From the beginning, Obama was about "change." The word "change" was everywhere in

[7] http://my.barackobama.com/

[8] http://stevegarfield.com/

his campaign, so much so that the entire world knew what Obama stood for. I asked a group of 300 people in Riyadh, Saudi Arabia what was the one word they thought of when I said "Barack Obama," and all in the room said "CHANGE." Quick: What did the following candidates stand for? John McCain, John Edwards, Hillary Clinton, Mitt Romney, or any others. Hard to say, isn't it?

Remember that people don't care about products and services; instead, they care about themselves and about solving their problems. The Obama campaign understood that his job was to solve the problems facing voters. He also knew that voters were buying into solutions, not just an individual. Did you notice in speeches how often Obama referred to his audience compared to how often he referred to himself? For example, in his inauguration address,[9] new President Obama used what I call inclusive language (such as "our," "we," and "us") a total of 142 times in 20 minutes, while he used what I call internal language ("me," "I," and "my") just 3 times. (Yes, I counted.) The other candidates talked about *themselves* a hell of a lot more than Obama did.

Don't obsess over the competition. Obama rarely talked about his competition. Once in a while he would, but mainly he talked about the problems facing voters. McCain talked a lot about Obama. Interestingly, Clinton and McCain both tried to associate themselves with the "change" word (the competition's word), but both failed because people already associated it with Obama.

Put your fans first. Obama used many techniques to craft an inclusive campaign and alert fans about developments first. For example, I found out on Obama's Twitter feed that Joe Biden was to be Obama's running mate. It was stunning to me that Obama told his fans *before* mainstream media. (Of course, smart reporters were following his Twitter feed and learned at the same time as Obama supporters.)

Don't interrupt your buyers. Do you like getting phone calls from telemarketers at dinnertime? McCain supporters seemed to think so, since they unleashed a barrage of so called robocalls, which seemed to have backfired.

Negativity doesn't sell. Obama's theme of hope and the idea that life can be better with change was uplifting to many people. The campaigns based on fear didn't work.

---

[9] www.youtube.com/watch?v=VjnygQ02aW4

Get your customers to talk about you. Obama tapped over 3 million donors who together provided $640 million to the campaign. The majority contributed small amounts online. Once someone donates money, he or she has a vested interest in the candidate and will tend to talk about them on social networking sites and in person. So to get the word out—lots of small donors are better than a few fat cats.

Take time for your family. (Yes, this really is a marketing observation, because it has to do with positioning and what a candidate stands for.) Obama frequently took time to be with his wife and daughters when he could have done another rally somewhere. He took several days at the end of the race to spend time with his ailing grandmother. While he was pulled away from "work," I think people respected his devotion to family and they saw something they liked in this attitude.

Marketers can learn a great deal from political campaigns (just like, once upon a time the campaigns learned from us). I encourage you to take a look at these lessons from the Obama campaign and apply them to your business. As you are developing your own marketing and PR plan using the new rules, think back to the inspirational marketing and PR unleashed by Obama's team during the U.S. presidential election of 2008.

Stick to Your Plan

If you've read this far, thank you. If you've developed a marketing and PR plan that uses the New Rules of Marketing and PR and you're ready to execute, great! The next 10 chapters will give you more specific advice about implementing your plan.

But now I must warn you: Many people who adhere to the old rules will fight you on this strategy. If you are a marketing professional who wants to reach your buyers directly, you will likely encounter resistance from corporate communications people. PR folks will get resistance from their agencies. They'll say the old rules are still in play. They'll say you have to focus on "the four Ps." They'll say you need to talk only about your products. They'll say that using the media is the only way to tell your story and that you can use press releases only to reach journalists, not your buyers directly. They'll say that bloggers are geeks in pajamas who don't matter.

They are wrong.

As the dozens of successful marketers profiled in this book say, the old rules are old news. Millions of people are online right now looking for answers to their problems. Will they find your organization? And if so, what will they find?

Remember, on the Web, you are what you publish.

11 Online Thought Leadership to Brand Your Organization as a Trusted Resource

If you've read this book starting from the beginning, I hope I've been able to convince you that Web content sells. (If you've skipped ahead to this chapter, welcome!) An effective online content strategy, artfully executed, drives action. Organizations that use online content well have a clearly defined goal—to sell products, generate leads, secure contributions, or get people to join—and deploy a content strategy that directly contributes to reaching that goal. People often ask me: "How do you recommend that I create an effective _____?" (fill in the blank with *blog, podcast, white paper, e-book, email newsletter, Webinar*, and so on). While the technologies for each form of online content are a little different, the one common aspect is that through all of these media, your organization can exercise thought leadership rather than simple advertising and product promotion; a well-crafted white paper, e-book, or Webinar contributes to an organization's positive reputation by setting it apart in the marketplace of ideas. This form of content brands a company, a consultant, or a nonprofit as an expert and as a trusted resource.

Developing Thought Leadership Content

What is thought leadership, and how do you do it?

The first thing you need to do is put away your company hat for a moment and—you guessed it—think like one of your buyer personas. The content that you create will be a solution to those people's problems and *will not mention your company or products at all!* Imagine for a moment that you are a marketer at an automobile tire manufacturer. Rather than just peddling your tires, you might write an e-book or shoot a video about how to drive safely in the snow, and then promote it on your site and offer it for free to other companies (such as automobile clubs and driver's education schools) to put on their sites. Or imagine that you run a local catering company and you have a blog or a web site. You might have a set of Web pages or podcasts available on your site. The topics could include "Plan the Perfect Wedding Reception" and "What You Need to Know for the Ideal Dinner Party for Twelve." A caterer with a podcast series like this educates visitors about their problems (planning a wedding or a dinner party) but does *not* sell the catering services directly. Instead, the idea here is that people who learn through the caterer's information are more likely to hire that caterer when the time comes.

Mark Howell, a consultant for Lifetogether,[1] is a pastor who works with Christian organizations and uses a thought leadership blog to get his message out. "My primary targets are people who are working in churches or Christian organizations that are trying to figure out better ways to do things," he says. "So I keep my content to things that seem secular but have broad application to churches. For example, I recently did a post called 'Required Reading: Five Books Every Leader Needs' where I tie broader business trends and marketing strategies to churches."

What makes Howell's blog work is that he's not just promoting his consulting services but instead is providing powerful information with a clear focus, for readers that just might hire him at some point. "My personal bias, and what I write about, is that for a lot of leaders in churches, the personal passion for what they are doing could be enhanced if they just got a taste for what more secular writers, such as Tom Peters, Guy Kawasaki, and Peter Drucker, are saying," Howell says. "There are so many ideas out there, and if I could just give people a sense of what some of these thinkers are saying, then my hope is that they can see that there is application for church leadership."

Forms of Thought Leadership Content

Here are some of the common forms of thought leadership content (of course, there may be others in your niche market). We've seen many of these media

---

[1] www.strategycentral.org/

in earlier chapters, but let's focus now on how they can help your company establish itself as a thought leader.

White Papers

"White papers typically [argue] a specific position or solution to a problem," according to Michael A. Stelzner,[2] author of *Writing White Papers*. "Although white papers take their roots in governmental policy, they have become a common tool used to introduce technology innovations and products. A typical search engine query on 'white paper' will return millions of results, with many focused on technology-related issues. White papers are powerful marketing tools used to help key decision makers and influencers justify implementing solutions." The best white papers are *not product brochures*. A good white paper is written for a business audience, defines a problem, and offers a solution, but it does not pitch a particular product or company. White papers are usually free and often have a registration requirement (so the authors can collect the names and contact information of people who download it). Many companies syndicate white papers to business web sites through services such as TechTarget[3] and Knowledge Storm.[4]

E-Books

Marketers are using e-books more and more as a fun and thoughtful way to get useful information to buyers. As I have mentioned, the book you are reading right now started as an e-book called *The New Rules of PR*, released in January 2006. For the purposes of marketing using Web content, I define an e-book as a PDF-formatted document that solves a problem for one of your buyer personas. E-books come with a bit of intrigue—they're like a hip younger sibling to the nerdy white paper. I recommend that e-books be presented in a landscape format, rather than the white paper's portrait format. Well executed e-books have lots of white space, interesting graphics and images, and copy that is typically written in a lighter style than the denser white paper. In my view, e-books (as marketing tools) should always be free, and I strongly suggest that there be no registration requirement. Here are a few e-books to

---

[2] www.writingwhitepapers.com/

[3] www.techtarget.com/

[4] www.knowledgestorm.com/

check out: *How to Tell if Someone is Lying: The Lie Detection Ebook* by Martin Soorjoo[5] and *Healthy Mouth, Healthy Sex!: How your oral health affects your sex life* by Dr. Helaine Smith.[6]

Email Newsletters

Email newsletters have been around as long as email but still have tremendous value as a way to deliver thought leadership content in small, regular doses. However, the vast majority of email newsletters that I see serve mostly as another advertising venue for a company's products and services. You know the type I'm talking about—each month you get some lame product pitch and a 10-percent-off coupon. Consider using a different type of email newsletter, one that focuses not on your company's products and services, but simply on solving buyers' problems once per month. Let's consider the hypothetical tire manufacturer or caterer that we discussed above. Imagine the tire manufacturer doing a monthly newsletter about safe driving or the caterer writing one on party planning.

Webinars

Webinars are online seminars that may include audio, video, or graphics (typically in the form of PowerPoint slides) and are often used by companies as a primer about a specific problem that the company's services can solve. However, the best Webinars are true thought leadership—like the traditional seminars from which they get their name. Often, Webinars feature guests who do not work for the company sponsoring the Webinar. For example, I participated as a guest speaker on a Webinar series called Inbound Marketing University,[7] sponsored by HubSpot. Inbound Marketing University featured 10 sessions, each with a different speaker. Nearly 4,000 people attended at least one of the sessions the first time they were offered. "Inbound Marketing University developed a tight-knit community of marketers who view HubSpot as a trusted resource and leader in inbound marketing," says Mike Volpe, vice president of marketing at HubSpot. "Having received so much valuable information and tools for free, many were quite interested in learning more

---

[5] www.communicationdownloads.com/Links.aspx

[6] http://helainesmithdmd.blogspot.com/2008/03/healthy-mouth-healthy-sex-free-e-book.html

[7] www.inboundmarketing.com/university

about HubSpot and our paid software for their own companies or clients." Inbound Marketing University was so successful, that it is now repeated regularly for new students.

Wikis

Wikis as thought leadership content are started by organizations that want to be seen as important players in distinct marketplaces. "You can use wikis to reach the people you want to reach and help them to organize content," says Ramit Sethi, co-founder and vice president of marketing for Pbworks,[8] a company that provides wiki software tools. "So if you're in a company, you can use a wiki to allow your users to add their own Frequently Asked Questions, and other people can supply answers, which helps everyone. People love being a part of the community, and they really like that a wiki gives them a way to discuss their interests." Sethi says that the personality and culture of an organization play an important role in the decision to start a company-sponsored wiki. "Companies that are a little bit fearless about letting people write their opinions make the best candidates for a wiki," he says. "But the most important thing is that you need to build something that is worth talking about, and you need to make it really easy. People don't want to install all kinds of software; they just want to get typing." (If you're interested in wikis, you might want to re-read the section in Chapter 4 where Steve Goldstein shared his experience creating a wiki for Alacra.)

Research and Survey Reports

Research and survey reports are used by many companies. By publishing results for free, organizations offer valuable content and get a chance to show off the kind of work they do. This can be an effective approach as long as your research or survey is legitimate and its statistically significant results are interesting to your buyers. (You will read about a survey report created by Steve Johnson a little later in this chapter.)

Photos, Images, Graphs, and Charts

Don't underestimate the value of an image to tell a story. If your product has visual appeal (sporting goods and real estate come to mind), you can create

---

[8] http://pbworks.com/

interesting content based on images. If your expertise lends itself to "how-to" instruction (example: "Learn how to surf"), photos can be particularly useful. Expertise that can be depicted as a chart (example: "Real-estate values in Fairfield County 1976–2010"), also stands to be especially useful to your buyers.

Blogs

As we've seen already, a blog is a personal web site written by someone who is passionate about a subject and wants the world to know about it. The benefits rub off on the company that he or she works for. Writing a blog is the easiest and simplest way to get your thought leadership ideas out and into the market. See Chapter 15 for information on how to start your blog.

Audio and Video

Podcasts (ongoing series of audio downloads available by subscription) are very popular as thought leadership content in some markets. Some people prefer just audio, and if your buyers do, then a podcast of your own might be the thing for you. Video content, vodcasts, video blogs, and vlogs (lots of names, one medium) are regularly updated videos that offer a powerful opportunity to demonstrate your thought leadership, since most people are familiar with the video medium and are used to the idea of watching a video or television program to learn something. An easy and fun way to create audio and video content is to host an interview show with guests who have something interesting to say. The intelligence of the guests rubs off on you as you interview them. Consider interviewing customers, analysts who cover your marketplace, and authors of books in your field. See Chapter 16 for information on audio and video.

How to Create Thoughtful Content

While each technique for getting your thought leadership content into the marketplace of ideas is different, they share some common considerations:

- Do not write about your company and your products. Thought leadership content is designed to solve buyer problems or answer questions and to show that you and your organization are smart and worth doing business with. This type of marketing and PR technique is *not* a brochure or sales pitch. Thought leadership is *not* advertising.

- Define your organizational goals first (see Chapter 10). Do you want to drive revenue? Get people to donate money to your organization? Encourage people to buy something?
- Based on your goals, decide whether you want to provide the content for free and without any registration (you will get many more people to use the content, but you won't know who they are), or you want to include some kind of registration mechanism (much lower response rates, but you build a contact list).
- Think like a publisher by understanding your audience. Consider what market problems your buyer personas are faced with and develop topics that appeal to them.
- Write for your audience. Use examples and stories. Make it interesting.
- Choose a great title that grabs attention. Use subtitles to describe what the content will deliver.
- Promote the effort like crazy. Offer the content on your site with easy-to-find links. Add a link to employees' email signatures, and get partners to offer links as well.
- To drive the viral marketing effects that we looked at in Chapter 8, alert appropriate reporters, bloggers, and analysts that the content is available and send them a download link.

Write What You Know

Dr. Kevin Harrington, owner of Harrington Family Chiropractic, reaches his buyers by publishing information online. Lots of it. He's got a web site,[9] blog,[10] and Twitter feed;[11] he produces videos; and he's active on Facebook.[12] He first established an online presence for his practice with a web site in 2004. But he started to see real benefit a few years later, when he began emailing his patients links to relevant articles after their visits. "People loved it," he

---

[9] http://harringtonfamilychiro.com/
[10] http://drkevdc.wordpress.com/
[11] http://twitter.com/drkevdc
[12] www.facebook.com/DrKevinHarrington

says. "I started to become a portal of information for people, so I started a blog to create more original information."

So how does a chiropractor with a busy practice find the time to write valuable information *and* keep up with the business? "I try to spend a half an hour each day looking through the health sites for things that might be interesting to my readers," Harrington says. "And I try to blog a few days a week, but I try to write things that are concise so it doesn't take too long."

Harrington's blog includes posts such as "TV Reduces Young Kids' Language Development" (note that this is not directly related to his business but still important to his buyer personas) and "Can Overtraining Your Knees Lead to Hip Pain?" After he finishes a new blog post, he adds links to the post on Facebook and sends it to his followers via Twitter.

I found one of Harrington's techniques to be really clever. On the new patient forms that people fill out during their first visit, among the usual health-related questions he also asks the following: "In an effort to keep our patients educated, we often use social media. Are you active in Facebook, Twitter, or texting?" When a patient says yes, Harrington goes to work immediately. "I friend people on Facebook right there in the office before they leave," he says. "People are amazed. And when I go to their Facebook page later, I try to comment on things that I see." He also uses video both to connect with patients and to aid in treatment, telling them something like this: "When you get home, I want you to do some exercises. I will send you a link to a video on my site so you can see me explaining the exercises." Patients love it.

"Since I have been active in social media, I have seen a 20-percent increase in business," Harrington says. "As an example, I was following a college friend on Facebook and I learned that her back hurt, so I reached out to her. Now she's a patient."

Harrington advises other entrepreneurs to get themselves out there. "This kind of information is not about me," he says. "It's not a sales thing. It is information that is valuable for people. Don't worry about being perfect, just try it."

Leveraging Thought Leaders Outside of Your Organization

Some organizations recruit external thought leaders that buyers trust, which is an effective technique for showing your buyers that you are plugged in and work with recognized experts. You might have a thought leader from your industry guest blog for you, author a white paper, participate on a Webinar, or speak to your clients at a live event. For example, Cincom Systems, Inc., a software industry pioneer, publishes the *Cincom Expert Access*[13] e-zine that is read by over 200,000 people in 61 countries. *Cincom Expert Access* delivers information from several dozen business leaders, authors, and analysts such as Al Reis, author of *The Fall of Advertising and the Rise of PR*; Dan Heath, author of *Made to Stick*; and Guy Kawasaki, author of *Reality Check*. I am also a member of Cincom's Ask the Expert network. *Cincom Expert Access* provides concise, objective information from personalities that Cincom's clients trust, sometimes in an irreverent, humorous manner, to help readers do their jobs better.

How Much Money Does Your Buyer Make?

"People often ask me, 'Steve, how much should we be paying our product managers?' " says Steve Johnson,[14] an instructor at Pragmatic Marketing, the premier product marketing firm for technology companies. "I used to just throw out a number that sounded about right. But I realized that my estimated salary figure was based on old data, back from the days when I hired product managers." Because Pragmatic Marketing conducts training for product managers, the company is seen as the expert on all things related to that job function. This situation created a terrific opportunity for some thought leadership. "We realized that we didn't really know current benchmarks, so we decided to find out." After all, customer compensation is often a key demographic for understanding your buyer persona.

Johnson composed a survey to gather data from the thousands of people in the Pragmatic Marketing database. "We said, 'If you tell us your salary and other information about your job via the anonymous survey, we will tell you everyone's salary in the form of benchmarks,' " he says. The results were an instant hit with the Pragmatic Marketing buyer persona—product managers—and the survey has become an annual undertaking. "Our email newsletter goes out to thousands and thousands of people. In October we say 'Heads up, next month we're doing the annual salary survey.' Then in November we

---

[13] www.internetviz-newsletters.com/cincom/
[14] www.productmarketing.com

announce that the survey is live and invite people to take it. We get hundreds of responses in just a few days, aggregate the data, and publish the results on the Web.[15] In 2009, for example, we learned that the average U.S. product management compensation is $100,341 in salary and that 79 percent of product managers get an annual bonus that averages $12,467. But we also learned other information, such as that product managers send and receive almost 100 emails a day and spend roughly two days a week in internal meetings— 15 meetings per week. But 55 percent are going to 15 meetings or more each week, and 35 percent attend 20 or more meetings."

Johnson sees tremendous benefits in survey-based thought leadership. "First of all, the data is really useful," he says. "Now I command the authority to say something like '95 percent of Product Managers have completed college and 44 percent have completed a master's program.' But more importantly, the buyers we are trying to reach to sell training services to, product managers, recognize us as the thought leaders in product management because we have up-to-date information on what's really going on with technology product managers. And the data that sits on our web site is fantastic for search engine marketing because anyone looking for information about product managers in technology businesses will find us."

This is a new world for marketers and corporate communicators. The Web offers an easy way for your ideas to spread to a potential audience of millions of people, instantly. Web content in the form of true thought leadership holds the potential to influence many thousands of your buyers in ways that traditional marketing and PR simply cannot.

To embrace the power of the Web and the blogosphere requires a different kind of thinking on the part of marketers. We need to learn to give up our command-and-control mentality. It isn't about "the message." It's about being insightful. *The New Rules of Marketing and PR* tell us to stop advertising and instead get our ideas out there by understanding buyers and telling them the stories that connect with their problems. The new rules are to participate in the discussions going on, not just try to shout your message over everyone else. Done well, Web content that delivers authentic thought leadership also brands an organization as one to do business with.

---

[15] www.pragmaticmarketing.com/publications/survey

12 How to Write for Your Buyers

Your buyers (and the media that cover your company) want to know what specific problems your product solves, and they want proof that it works—in plain language. Your marketing and PR is meant to be the beginning of a relationship with buyers and to drive action (such as generating sales leads), which requires a focus on buyer problems. Your buyers want to hear this in *their* own words. Every time you write—yes, even in news releases—you have an opportunity to communicate. At each stage of the sales process, well-written materials will help your buyers understand how you, specifically, will help them.

Whenever you set out to write something, you should be writing specifically for one or more of the buyer personas that you developed as part of your marketing and PR plan (see Chapter 10). You should avoid jargon-laden phrases that are overused in your industry, unless this is the language the persona actually uses. In the technology business, words like *groundbreaking*, *industry-standard*, and *cutting-edge* are what I call gobbledygook. The worst gobbledygook offenders seem to be business-to-business technology companies. For some reason, marketing people at technology companies have a particularly tough time explaining how products solve customer problems. Because these writers don't understand how their products solve customer problems, or are too lazy to write for buyers, they cover by explaining myriad nuances of how the product works and pepper this blather with industry jargon that sounds vaguely impressive. What ends up in marketing materials and news releases is a bunch of talk about "industry-leading" solutions that purport to help companies "streamline business process," "achieve business objectives," or "conserve organizational resources." *Huh?*

An Analysis of Gobbledygook

Many of the thousands of web sites I've analyzed over the years and the hundreds of news releases and PR pitches I receive each month are laden with meaningless gobbledygook words and phrases. As I'm reading a news release, I'll pause and say to myself, "Oh, jeez, not another flexible, scalable, groundbreaking, industry-standard, cutting-edge product from a market-leading, well positioned company! I think I'm gonna puke!" Like teenagers overusing catch phrases, these writers use the same words and phrases again and again—so much so that the gobbledygook grates against all our nerves. Well, duh. Like, companies just totally don't communicate very well, you know?

I wanted to see exactly how many of these words are being used, so I created an analysis for doing so. I first analyzed gobbledygook in 2006 and published the findings on my blog and as an e-book called *The Gobbledygook Manifesto.*[1] In 2006, the most overused words and phrases included *next generation, robust, world class, cutting edge, mission critical, market leading, industry standard, groundbreaking,* and *best of breed.*

I then conducted an extensive, revised analysis in early 2009. For this new round, I first needed to select overused words and phrases, so I turned to the following sources:

- The overused words and phrases from the 2006 analysis, which I got by polling select PR people and journalists.
- Suggestions from readers, who posted comments about the original analysis on my blog.
- Seth Godin's *Encyclopedia of Business Clichés.*
- *This Paperclip Is a Solution,* a survey given to general business and trade publication editors by Dave Schmidt, VP of public relations services at Smith-Winchester, Inc.
- The book *Death Sentences: How Cliches, Weasel Words and Management-Speak Are Strangling Public Language,* by Don Watson.

[1] http://changethis.com/pdf/37.03.Gobbledygook.pdf

Then I turned to the Dow Jones Enterprise Media Group for help. The folks at Dow Jones used text-mining tools found in their Dow Jones Insight product to analyze news releases sent by companies in North America during 2008. The data we gathered came from all 711,123 press releases distributed through Business Wire, Marketwire, GlobeNewswire, and PR Newswire. Dow Jones Insight identified the number of uses of the 325 gobbledygook phrases in each release.

The results were staggering.[2] The winner for the most overused word or phrase in 2008 was *innovate* which was used in 51,390 press releases, followed closely by *unique, leading provider, new and improved, world class* and *cost effective*. Each of these terms was used over 10,000 times in press releases from 2008. The problem is that these words are so overused that they have become meaningless. If anything, using these terms makes the reader feel as if the company is just releasing dozens of copycat "me too" statements.

To help you analyze your own writing, I also worked closely with the people at HubSpot to create Gobbledygook Grader,[3] a software tool that you can use to evaluate your written content (press releases, brochure copy, etc.). Simply cut and paste text into Gobbledygook Grader and it will check for use of the 325 gobbledygook, jargon, clichéd, overused, hype-filled words and phrases that I identified. You'll even receive a grade together with the full report.

Poor Writing: How Did We Get Here?

When I see words like *flexible, scalable, groundbreaking, industry standard*, or *cutting-edge*, my eyes glaze over. What, I ask myself, is this supposed to mean? Just saying your widget is "industry standard" means nothing unless some aspect of that standardization is important to your buyers. In the next sentence, I want to know what you mean by "industry standard," and I also want you to tell me why that standard matters and give me some proof that what you say is indeed true.

People often say to me, "Everyone in my industry writes this way. Why?" Here's how the usual dysfunctional process works and why these phrases are

---

[2] http://solutions.dowjones.com/campaigns/2009/gobbledygook/

[3] http://gobbledygook.grader.com/

so overused: Marketers don't understand buyers, the problems buyers face, or how their product helps solve these problems. That's where the gobbledygook happens. First the marketing person bugs the product managers and others in the organization to provide a set of the product's features. Then the marketing person reverse-engineers the language that they think the buyer wants to hear based *not on buyer input* but on what the product does. A favorite trick these ineffective marketers use is to take the language that the product manager provides, go into Microsoft Word's find-and-replace mode, substitute the word *solution* for *product*, and then slather the whole thing with superlative-laden, jargon-sprinkled hype. By just decreeing, through an electronic word substitution, that "our product" is "your solution," these companies effectively deprive themselves of the opportunity to *convince* people that this is the case.

Another major drawback of the generic gobbledygook approach is that it doesn't make your company stand out from the crowd. Here's a test: Take the language that the marketers at your company dreamed up and substitute the name of a competitor and the competitor's product for your own. Does it still make sense to you? Marketing language that can be substituted for another company's isn't effective in explaining to a buyer why *your* company is the right choice.

I'll admit that these gobbledygook phrases are mainly used by technology companies operating in the business-to-business space. If you are writing for a company that sells different kinds of products (shoes, perhaps), then you would probably not be tempted to use many of the above phrases. The same thing is true for nonprofits, churches, rock bands, and other organizations—you're also unlikely to use these sorts of phrases. But the lessons are the same. Avoid the insular jargon of your company and your industry. Instead, write for your buyers.

"Hold on," you might say. "The technology industry may be dysfunctional, but I don't write that way." The fact is that there is equivalent nonsense going on in all industries. Here's an example from the world of nonprofits:

The sustainability group has convened a task force to study the cause of energy inefficiency and to develop a plan to encourage local businesses to apply renewable-energy and energy-efficient technologies which will go a long way toward encouraging community buy-in to potential behavioral changes.

What the heck is that? Or consider this example from the first paragraph of a well-known company's corporate overview page. Can you guess the company?

Since its founding in 1923, [Company X] and its affiliated companies have remained faithful to their commitment to produce unparalleled entertainment experiences based on the rich legacy of quality creative content and exceptional storytelling. [Company X], together with its subsidiaries and affiliates, is a leading diversified international family entertainment and media enterprise with four business segments: media networks, parks and resorts, studio entertainment, and consumer products.

Effective Writing for Marketing and PR

Your marketing and PR is meant to be the beginning of a relationship with buyers (and journalists). As the marketing and PR planning process in Chapter 10 showed, this begins when you work at understanding your target audience and figure out how they should be sliced into distinct buying segments or buyer personas. Once this exercise is complete, identify the situations each target audience may find themselves in. What are their problems? business issues? needs? Only then are you ready to communicate your expertise to the market. Here's the rule: When you write, start with your buyers, not with your product.

Consider the entertainment company blurb above. The marketing and PR folks at Disney (did you guess it was Disney's corporate overview page[4] I quoted from above?) should be thinking about what customers want from an entertainment company, rather than just thinking up fancy words for what they think they already provide. Why not start by defining the problem? "Many television and cinema fans today are frustrated with the state of the American entertainment industry. They believe today's films and shows are too derivative and that entertainment companies don't respect their viewers' intelligence." Next, successful marketers will use real-world language to convince their customers that they can solve their problem. Be careful to avoid corporate jargon, but you don't want to sound like you're trying too hard, either—that always comes across as phony. Talk to your audience as you might talk to a relative you don't see too often—be friendly and familiar but

---

[4] http://corporate.disney.go.com/corporate/overview.html

also respectful: "Like our audience, we care about and enjoy movies and TV shows—that's why we're in this business in the first place. As such, we pledge to always . . . ." Now I have no connection with Disney and don't know about the Disney business. But I have purchased a lot of Disney products: movies, TV shows, videos, and visits to theme parks. It might seem strange to people at Disney to actually write something like I suggest. It might feel strange for the PR and marketing people at Disney to use a phrase like "movies and TV shows" rather than "quality creative content," but it's absolutely essential to establishing a relationship with customers.

The Power of Writing Feedback (from Your Blog)

I want to pause for a moment to share a story about the power of communications and feedback on the Web. When I published the results of this original study on my blog[5] in a post titled "The Gobbledygook Manifesto" (I also sent a news release the next day), there were zero hits on Google for the exact phrase "gobbledygook manifesto." I purposely invented a phrase that I could establish on the Web. Within just three weeks, as a result of several dozen bloggers writing about The Gobbledygook Manifesto and over 100 comments on my blog and others, the exact phrase "gobbledygook manifesto" yielded over 500 hits on Google: zero to 500 in just three weeks. Better yet, readers of my blog and others suggested other overused gobbledygook words and phrases such as *best practices, proactive, synergy, starting a dialog, thinking outside of the box, revolutionary, situational fluency,* and *paradigm shift.*

Dave Schmidt, VP for Public Relations Services at Smith-Winchester, Inc., contacted me to share the results of a survey he conducted of general business and trade publication editors. Schmidt asked the editors about the use of overused words and phrases he's seen and wanted to find out how many editors agreed that each of the phrases was overused in news releases and company-authored articles. He received responses from 80 editors:

- *Leading* (used as an adjective, as in " . . . a leading producer of . . . ")— 94 percent of editors feel is overused. Since everyone wants to be the leading something, there are no longer any true leaders.

---

[5] www.Webinknow.com/2006/10/the_gobbledygoo.html

- "We're excited about . . ." (as used in a quote from management)— 76 percent of editors feel is overused. Companies also say, "We're pleased . . ." and "We're thrilled . . . ." Can you picture an editor running a CEO quote like one of these? You need to quote your spokespeople with words that you would like to see in print.
- *Solutions*—68 percent of editors feel is overused. The word *solutions* has been ruined by overuse in news releases to the point that it is best avoided, even by solutions providers.
- " . . . a wide range of . . ."—64 percent of editors feel is overused. This has become the lazy person's way of avoiding precise writing.
- *Unparalleled*—62 percent of editors feel is overused.
- *Unsurpassed*—53 percent of editors feel is overused.

Thank you to the many people who contacted me with suggestions of overused gobbledygook. I just think it is so cool that you can create something on the Web, use it to get thoughtful information into the market quickly and efficiently, and then have people offer suggestions to make the original writing even better.

Your online and offline marketing content is meant to drive action, which requires a focus on buyer problems. Your buyers want this in their own words, and then they want proof. Every time you write, you have an opportunity to communicate and to *convince*. At each stage of the sales process, well-written materials combined with effective marketing programs will lead your buyers to understand how your company can help them. Good marketing is rare indeed, but a focus on doing it right will most certainly pay off with increased sales, higher retention rates, and more ink from journalists.

13

How Web Content Influences the Buying Process

Today when people want to buy something, the Web is almost always the first stop on their shopping trip. In any market category, potential customers head online to do initial research. The moment of truth is when they reach your site: Will you draw them into your sales process or let them click away?

When buyers use search engines and directories to reach your site, link to it through another site, or respond to a marketing campaign, you have an opportunity to deliver targeted information at the precise moment when they are looking for what you have to offer. Yet marketers often fail to realize the potential of their web sites, which must hook buyers in from the start and hang on to them until the sale is complete. Individuals don't go to the Web looking for advertising; they are on a quest for content. By providing information when they need it, you can begin a long and profitable relationship with them. Editors and publishers obsess over readership, and so should you.

In this chapter, we're going to build on some of the ideas and concepts that I've already introduced in the book. In Chapter 3 we talked about reaching buyers directly with your organization's online content, and Chapter 10 was when we put together a detailed plan to identify buyer personas and target each one with an individualized approach. Remember, great Web content is about your buyers, not about you. Now I'll provide some ideas for how you can make a web site that takes buyers through their consideration process and moves them toward the point where they are ready to buy (or donate, join, subscribe), which, of course, is the goal of all Web content.

While it is important for your web site to have an attractive design and for all of the technical aspects (HTML and so on) to work properly, these aspects are beyond the scope of this book. There are many excellent texts on how to write HTML, XML, ASP, JavaScript, and other Web languages. And there are also great resources for getting the design aspects right—things like colors, fonts, logo placement, and whatnot. While these elements are critical to an overall site, I want to focus on how *content drives action* on web sites, because the content aspect is often overlooked.

To best leverage the power of content, you first need to help your site's visitors find what they need on your site. When someone visits a site for the first time, the site communicates messages to the buyer: Does this organization care about me? Does it focus on the problems I face? Or does the site only include information describing what the company has to offer from its own narrow perspective? You need to start with a site navigation that is designed and organized with your buyers in mind. Don't simply mimic the way your company or group is organized (e.g., by product, geography, or governmental structure), because the way your audience uses web sites rarely coincides with your company's internal priorities. Organizing based on your needs leaves site visitors confused about how to find what *they* really need.

You should learn as much as possible about the buying process, focusing on issues such as how people find your site or the length of a typical purchase cycle. Consider what happens offline in parallel with online interactions so that the processes complement each other. For example, if you have an e-commerce site and a printed catalog, coordinate the content and messages so that both efforts support and reinforce the buying process (i.e., include URLs for your online buying guide in the catalog and use the same product descriptions so people don't get confused). In the B2B world, trade shows should work with Internet initiatives (by collecting email addresses at the booth, for example, then sending a follow-up email with a show-specific landing page at your site). Understanding the buying process in detail, both online and offline, allows you to create Web content that influences the buying decision.

Segmenting Your Buyers

The online relationship begins the second a potential customer hits your homepage. The first thing he needs to see is a reflection of himself. That's why you must organize your site with content for each of your distinct buyer personas. How do your potential customers self-select? Is it based on their job function, or on geography, or on the industry they work in? It's important to create a set of appropriate links based on a clear understanding of your buyers so that you can quickly move them from your homepage to pages built specifically for them.

For example, the New York Public Library (NYPL),[1] an institution that has 50.6 million items in its collections housed at 89 locations and overseen by 3,200 staff members, has a web site that must serve many varied visitors. The NYPL site appeals to a very diverse set of buyer personas (people who use the libraries' services both online and offline), who download materials directly from the site. Here are just a few of the buyer personas that the NYPL site serves:

- Academic researchers from around the globe who need access to the NYPL digital information collections.
- People who live in the Bronx and speak Spanish as a first language. (The library offers introductory classes, conducted in Spanish at the NYPL's Bronx location, on how to use a computer.)
- Tourists to New York City who want to take a tour of the beautiful main library building on Fifth Avenue.
- Film studios, TV producers, and photographers who use the famous NYPL setting. (*Breakfast at Tiffany's*, *Ghostbusters*, and *Spider-Man* are just a few of the movies that have been partially filmed there.)
- Individuals, foundations, and corporations that help support the library with donations.

The NYPL site includes detailed content throughout to reach each of these buyer personas (as well as others). The front page of the NYPL web site is broken into several main sections, including "Find Books & Do Research" (information on what is in the library's catalogs for people who need a particular book), "Libraries" (branch information for those who live in New York City), "Digital Library" (information that anybody in the world can download), "News," "NYPL Live!" (events), and "Support the Library" (membership and giving information for people who want to donate money or time to

---

[1] www.nypl.org/

the NYPL). Each landing page has additional information to make browsing this huge web site easy.

One way many organizations approach navigation is to link to landing pages based on the problems your product or service solves. Start by identifying the situations in which each target audience may find itself. If you are in the supply chain management business, you might have a drop-down menu on the homepage with links that say, "I need to get product to customers faster" or "I want to move products internationally." Each path leads to landing pages built for buyer segments, with content targeted to their problems. Once the prospects reach those pages, you have the opportunity to communicate your expertise in solving these problems—building some empathy in the process—and to move customers further along the buying cycle.

Elements of a Buyer-Centric Web Site

As you build a site that focuses on your buyers and their purchasing process, here are a few other things to consider:

Think about Your Buyers' Preferred Media and Learning Styles

I had a great conversation with Ted Demopoulos,[2] author of *What No One Ever Tells You About Blogging and Podcasting*. We spoke about blogging versus podcasting, people's learning styles, and the choices of what content to put on a site. Ted brought up an interesting point: It's not an either/or decision. "It's worth having your message in different formats," he says. "I love to read. And I often listen to informative audio while driving, biking, or mowing the lawn. But I do not like video. It's not like reading; it progresses at its own rate. I can't watch faster or skim easily, like with text, and it demands total attention, unlike with audio." Of course, other people are the opposite of Ted. They don't like to read but love video content. We all have different learning styles and media preferences. So, on your site, you should have appropriate content designed for your buyers. This does not mean that you need to have every single format, but you should think about augmenting text with photos and maybe some audio or video content. "Not only do people like different formats, but psychologists have shown that people learn better with different

---

[2] www.demop.com/

media," Demopoulos adds. "Marketers should have messages in as many formats as practical. Even though the messages are the same, they will appeal to different groups of people. For example, some will want an e-book, but you can take the same content and turn it into a tele-seminar."

Develop a Site Personality

It is important to create a distinct, consistent, and memorable site, and an important component of that goal is the tone or voice of the content. As visitors interact with the content on your site, they should develop a clear picture of your organization. Is the personality fun and playful? Or is it solid and conservative? For example, on the Google homepage, when people search they can click "I'm Feeling Lucky," which is a fun and playful way to get you directly to the top listing in the search results. That one little phrase, "I'm Feeling Lucky," says a lot about Google. And there's much more. For example, in the collection of more than 100 languages that Google supports, from Afrikaans to Zulu, there is also Google in the language of Elmer Fudd,[3] with everything translated into what Elmer Fudd would say, such as "I'm Feewing Wucky." This is cool, but it wouldn't work for a more conservative company—it would just seem strange and out of place. Contrast that with Accenture's homepage.[4] At the time of this writing, just under the Accenture logo was the phrase "High Performance. Delivered." There is a photo of Tiger Woods and a message ("We know what it takes to be a Tiger.") with an offer ("See findings from our research and experience with over 500 high performers."). Both of these home pages work because the site personality works with the company personality. Whatever your personality, the way to achieve consistency is to make certain that all the written material and other content on the site conform to a defined tone that you've established from the start. A strong focus on site personality and character pays off. As visitors come to rely on the content they find on your site, they will develop an emotional and personal relationship with your organization. A web site can evoke a familiar and trusted voice, just like that of a friend on the other end of an email exchange.

---

[3] www.google.com/intl/xx-elmer/
[4] www.accenture.com/

For an example of a site with very distinct personality that appeals to buyer personas, check out Malware City[5] from BitDefender. Vitor Souza is global communications manager at BitDefender, creator of internationally certified security software used by tens of millions of people and sold in more than 100 countries. As part of a true global company, Souza works from offices in Mountain View, CA, and Bucharest, Romania. BitDefender is a particularly interesting example because the market that BitDefender serves is very competitive, so product differentiation is not easy to accomplish. A cornerstone of the company's marketing approach, Malware City was launched as a standalone site focused on key influencers within the IT security community. The new site was not a redesign of the existing company site but, rather, an informational supplement to the main BitDefender product site.[6]

"We launched Malware City for people who are interested in the latest information on Internet threats," Souza says. "It has a blog from our lab analysts, educational materials for IT guys, and many other interactive tools."

Souza and his team clearly understood that the best online initiatives are those that deliver specific information tailored to a particular buyer persona. The Malware City site was developed to appeal to three different buyer personas:

1. Information technology security press (both mainstream press and social media).
2. BitDefender users.
3. A group Souza describes as "Internet security geeks"—the most important buyer persona for Malware City.

The Malware City site appeals directly to the Internet security geek buyer persona with language like this: "Our citizens are wise warriors fighting malware, willing to share their knowledge in order to breed an army ready to battle security threats. Want to join us? Demonstrate your skills and we will be glad to welcome you into our family." The design is very hip and stylish, with an urban, punk sort of theme—in stark contrast to the slew of boring sites in the technology industry.

---

[5] www.malwarecity.com/
[6] www.bitdefender.com/

"Malware City is the property of BitDefender," Souza says. "We didn't brag about it but didn't hide it either. We want it to be a site dedicated to all interested in their online security, and not only to BitDefender users. Instead of pumping them with irrelevant messages and interrupting their activities, we offer helpful and relevant information that our visitors are interested in," he says. "And we ask nothing in return. We can see from the subscriber's comments or the emails that we received that they consider Malware City a helpful source of information. Other clear evidence is an increasing number of visitors and the fact that they are talking about the site on their blogs, or they are bookmarking it."

Photos and Images Tell Your Story

Content is not limited to words; smart marketers make use of nontext content—including photos, audio feeds, video clips, cartoons, charts, and graphs—to inform and entertain site visitors. Photographs in particular play an important role for many sites. Photos are powerful content when page visitors see that the images are an integrated component of the web site. However, generic "stock" photographs (happy and good-looking multicultural models in a fake company meeting room) may actually have a negative effect. People will know instantly that the photo is not of real people in your organization. Neither you nor your users are generic. On a technical note, while photos, charts, graphs, and other nontext content make great additions to any site, be wary of very large image sizes and of using distracting multimedia content like Flash Video. Visitors want to access content quickly, they want sites that load fast, and they don't want to be distracted.

Include Interactive Content Tools

Anything that gets people involved with the content of a site provides a great way to engage visitors, build their interest, and move them through your sales cycle. Examples of interactive tools include such things as the stock quoting and charting applications found on financial sites and "email your congressman" tools on political advocacy sites. Interactive content provides visitors with a chance to immerse themselves in site content, which makes them more likely to progress through the sales consideration cycle to the point where they are ready to spend money.

Make Feedback Loops Available

Providing a way for users to interact with your organization is a hallmark of a great site. Easy to find "contact us" information is a must, and direct feedback mechanisms like "rate this" buttons, online forums, viewer reviews, and opportunities to post comments provide valuable information by and for site visitors.

Provide Ways for Your Customers to Interact with Each Other

A forum or wiki where customers can share with one another and help each other works well for many organizations as a way to show potential customers that there is a vibrant community of people using their products or services. In other words, an existing set of customers interacting with each other on your site is great marketing!

Create Content with Pass-Along Value that Could Go Viral

Web content provides terrific fodder for viral marketing—the phenomenon where people pass on information about your site to their friends and colleagues or link to your content in their blogs (more on viral marketing is in Chapter 8). When content proves interesting or useful, visitors tend to tell friends, usually by sending them a link. Creating buzz around a site to encourage people to talk it up isn't easy. Creating content that has a pass-along value is never a certain process, because it happens more organically. There are a few things you can do to help the process, though. When creating site content, think carefully about what content users might want to pass along and then make that content easy to find and link to. Make the actual URLs permanent so that no one finds dead links when visiting months (or years) later. To be successful with viral marketing is to say something interesting and valuable and to make it easy to find and share.

Using RSS to Deliver Your Web Content to Targeted Niches

It is so easy for those of us in the media and analyst community to get information via RSS (Really Simple Syndication) that I can't stress its importance enough as a component of a Web marketing strategy; it's my preferred method in my work tracking markets, companies, and ideas. Once information is in RSS format, an RSS-aware browser such as Firefox checks the feed for changes and displays them on a Web page. Having the information come to me is just so much easier than in the days when I had to go looking for it myself. RSS and news aggregation software is easy to use, usually free, and provides a way to get information from any device. I particularly like that RSS provides a powerful information-management tool that bypasses the increasingly crowded and annoying email channel. Having my favorite web sites, media outlets, and blogs feeding RSS is my own custom compilation of exactly what I want to see.

Surprisingly, only a small percentage of organizations deploy RSS for syndicating news and content to the outside world. Even fewer understand how RSS feeds are a preferred way to market to niche customers who have very specific needs. Learn from the way that most major news sites such as the BBC, the *New York Times*, the *Washington Post*, and thousands more deploy RSS. Almost any content that can be broken down into discrete items (such as news releases, blog postings, product updates, or SEC filings) can be syndicated via RSS.

Netflix offers RSS feeds[7] for which video fans sign up to receive updates based on their interests. Available feeds include Netflix Top 100, New Releases, Documentary Top 25, Comedy Top 25, Classics Top 25, and many more, and they all target specific customers who select only the content that interests them. So if I'm a fan of independent films, I subscribe to the RSS feed, and any time independent film–related content changes on the Netflix site, I'm alerted to it via my RSS reader.

What sets this apart from the standard one-size-fits-all marketing model is that it is highly targeted and delivered directly to micro-audiences of interested consumers. Contrast this with the typical way that companies market to their customers on the Web. Often when you become a customer, the organization signs you up for its "special offers" email. After you get two or three of these emails, it becomes painfully obvious that they are just untargeted messages to the entire customer list and have little value for you. No wonder that house email lists suffer from significant opt-out numbers. Note how different the Netflix approach of offering information that has been selected and

---

[7] www.netflix.com/RSSFeeds

is welcome when compared with the old world of blasting generic email ads to the masses.

Link Content Directly into the Sales Cycle

Marketers with the most successful sites specifically design content to draw buyers into the sales cycle. People considering a purchase always go through a certain thought process. In the case of something simple and low-cost, say deciding to download a song from iTunes, the process is likely very straightforward and may only take seconds. But for a major decision such as buying a new car, sending your child to college, or accepting a job offer, the process may take weeks or months. For many business-to-business sales, the cycle may involve many steps and multiple buyer personas (a business buyer and an IT buyer, perhaps) and may take months or even years to complete.

Effective Web marketers take web site visitors' buying cycle into account when writing content and organizing it on the site. People in the early stages of the sales cycle need basic information about their problems and the ways that your organization solves them. Those further along in the process want to compare products and services, so they need detailed information about the benefits of your offerings. And when buyers are ready to whip out their credit cards, they need easy-to-use mechanisms linked directly from the content so they can quickly finish the purchase (or donation, subscription, and so on).

For an example of a very long sales cycle, consider our college example from earlier chapters. High school students apply to colleges in the fall of their senior year and typically make a decision about which school to attend in the spring. But the sales cycle starts much earlier. When students visit colleges in person, they tend to be juniors in high school, but when students first visit college web sites, they are likely freshmen or sophomores. The college web site is often the first place that a student comes into contact with the college, and the site must cater to an audience of young teenagers who won't be ready to apply for admission for two or three years. Creating appropriate content to develop a lasting relationship over a long sales cycle is possible only when an organization knows the buyer personas well and understands the sales process in detail. The college must provide high school students with appropriate content so they get a sense of what college life would be like if they were to attend and what the admission process entails.

A focus on understanding buyers and the sales cycle and developing appropriate content that links visitors through the cycle to the point of purchase is essential for a great site. Based on my years of research, the vast majority of sites are little more than online brochures or vast one-way advertising vehicles. These sites are almost wholly ineffective. The Web offers significant opportunities to those marketers who understand that content is at the forefront of the best sites.

A Friendly Nudge

After you've demonstrated expertise in the market category and knowledge about solving potential customers' problems, you can introduce your product or service. When creating content about your offerings, remain focused on the buyer and her problems, rather than elaborating distinctions between products. As people interact with your content at this middle stage in the buying process, it is appropriate to suggest subscriptions to related content— perhaps an email newsletter, Webinar (Web-based seminar), or podcast. But remember, if you're asking for someone's email address (or other contact details), you must provide something equally valuable in return.

Prospects want to poke, prod, and test your company to learn what sort of organization you are. They also have questions. That's why well-designed sites include a mechanism for people to inquire about products or services. Be flexible but also consistent; offer them a variety of ways to interact with your company, and make contact information readily available from any page on the site (one click away is best). Also keep in mind that, particularly with expensive products, buyers will test you to see how responsive you are, so you must make responding to these inquiries a priority. At this stage, you want people to think: "This is an organization I can do business with. They have happy customers, and they are responsive to me and my needs."

Close the Sale and Continue the Conversation

As the customer approaches the end of the buying process, you must provide tools that facilitate the sale. Buyers may be unsure which of your products is appropriate for them—so you may need to provide online demonstrations or a tool that allows them to enter specific details about their requirements and then suggests the appropriate product.

Once the deal is closed, there's one more step. You must continue the online dialog with your new customer. Add her to your customer email newsletter or customer-only community site where she can interact with experts in your organization and other like-minded customers. You should also provide ample opportunities for customers to give you feedback on how to make the products (and sales process) better.

An Open-Source Marketing Model

Franz Maruna, CEO of concrete5,[8] started an interactive media firm in 2002. His business was building custom web sites and communities for businesses, including some major sites like Indie911.com, Lemonade.com, and School-pulse.com. To create and deploy the sites, concrete5 built their own content management system (CMS). CMS software is used to build and manage Web pages and other online content, and Maruna's firm created a new system because he couldn't find the right tools in a commercially available package. As the concrete5 team built more complex sites, they constantly updated their own CMS system to fit their requirements and their clients' needs.

Maruna eventually became disenchanted with the process of constantly selling new Web-development work, so he decided to focus on what he really liked: the content management system. "In 2007, we spent eight months building a release version of the concrete5 CMS," he says. "My partners and I knew that we had a better mousetrap, but we had a chance to decide what to do with it. So in the summer of 2008 we made the CMS software available to anyone for free and as open-source [i.e., the programming code is available to anyone, without registration; computer-savvy users may make changes to it and build new versions of the software as they see fit]. We decided that bigger and better things would happen for our firm if we let others get onto the bus with us."

Providing a free, open-source software application is a remarkably bold move, but Maruna believes it is a smart one. "We make money on the marketplace (modules and tools that we sell) and on Web hosting," he says. "It's like I give you free beer (the software), but if you want pretzels and peanuts (tools

---

[8] www.concrete5.org/

and hosting), you have to pay. To have a party, you don't need to have a huge bar. All you need is a keg and people will show up. It doesn't take a lot."

Maruna then built a community[9] to spread the word about what the company was doing. "Bloggers started talking about it and people started to tweet. We built our own forums where people can come together. The community is great with real-world bug testing, a super-powerful way to test ideas and concepts. The community has translated the product into a dozen languages."

The concrete5 community includes very active forums. While people from the company participate, they comprise a primarily community-contributed knowledge base. What makes this form of Web content interesting as a marketing and PR tool is that it is totally open for customers and noncustomers alike. Many companies have interactive communities but lock them away in password-protected nooks. At concrete5, it is all out in the open—showing other interested potential users what's really going on.

Through Web content, concrete5 first introduces people to the concepts of an open-source CMS system, then offers free working products. Next, the company encourages users to participate in the online forum and concrete5 blog[10] and then finally makes money by selling enhancements and tools for the software and interactive Web hosting services. All of the resulting Web content serves as the company's marketing engine. As I write this, a bit more than a year has passed since the launch of concrete5, and the CMS application has been downloaded over 50,000 times. The company has an active forum of 5,000 developers and designers who are eagerly helping each other out.

"It is an exciting opportunity when people say both good things and bad things about you," Maruna says. "The focus group is all around you every day, and it's free. As a company, when you start engaging in an open-source way, you then have a community that becomes a passionate support base for you. Do this, and your customers will become your fans and they will go to the end of the world to evangelize your product for you. Beyond the amazing work our open-source community puts in around translating our product, bug-testing it, and creating extensions, they've also sent us copious amounts of beer (thanks!) and flown halfway around the world to meet us. A digital community is awesome if you use it correctly. You don't own it; you

---

[9] www.concrete5.org/community/

[10] http://concretethestudio.com/

participate in it. You can't buy it; you have to work at it. Be a good person, treat the world like you'd treat your family, and they'll do the same."

For every organization, the key to a great web site is to understand buyers and build valuable content especially for them.

But there is one final step. Effective marketers constantly measure and improve. Because it is so easy to modify Web content at any time, you should be measuring what people are doing on the site. Benchmarking elements such as the self-select links and testing different landing page content can help. If you have two offers on a landing page (a free whitepaper and a free demonstration, say) you might measure which one works to get more clicks but also measure how many people who respond to the offer actually buy something. This way you will know not just numbers of clicks, but revenue by offer type, and you can use that in future landing pages. Armed with real data, you make valuable modifications. You might want to just see what happens if you change the order of the links on the home page. Sometimes people just click the thing on top of a list. What happens if something else is on top?

Of course, product superiority, advertising, the media, and branding remain important to the marketing mix. But on the Web, smart marketers understand that an effective content strategy, tightly integrated to the buying process, is critical to success.

14

Social Networking Sites and Marketing

The popularity of social networking sites such as Facebook, Twitter, Link-edIn, and Bebo is phenomenal. Social networking sites make it easy for people to create a profile about themselves and use it to form a virtual network combining their offline friends and new online friends. According to data released by comScore,[1] the social networking category of web sites had nearly 140 million visitors in the U.S. in early 2009. That's nearly three-quarters of U.S. Internet users! MySpace Sites led the category with 71 million visitors, followed by Facebook.com with 67.5 million visitors, and Twitter.com, now the third-ranked social networking site, with 17 million visitors. And it's not just the United States; social networking is extremely popular all over the world. For instance, in Europe, Facebook has seen a 314 percent increase in one year to nearly 100 million visitors. Of course, not all visitors to these sites create their own profiles, but there are millions and millions of people who do—to share their photos, journals, videos, music, and interests with a network of friends.

While these huge numbers are impressive, we can easily lose track of what this means to us as marketers. When we consider the reach of influential people on social networking sites, we should rethink our notions about who can best spread our ideas and tell our stories. Many people tell me that they want to get quoted in important publications like the *Wall Street Journal* or have their products mentioned on television networks like the BBC or on shows like *Oprah*. These "media hits" are seen as the holy grail of marketers. But

---

[1] www.comscore.com/

while mainstream media is certainly important (and who wouldn't want to be on the BBC), is that really the best thing for your business?

At the 2009 South-by-Southwest Interactive Festival,[2] I hung out for a while in the blogger lounge, a place where people who are active in social networking could get Internet connectivity, AC power, and a cold drink while they met their virtual friends in the flesh. As I looked around the room and saw the hundred or so influential people, I realized something important: *The collective voices of the bloggers who were in the South-by-Southwest blogger lounge that day are likely more powerful and have more influence than* the Wall Street Journal. As you think about reaching your audience using social networking, consider who really has the power. Is it mainstream media? Or someone else? And how can you reach them?

Television's Eugene Mirman Is Very Nice and Likes Seafood

"There is no middleman between me and an audience," says comedian Eugene Mirman,[3] known for his work in *Flight of the Choncords*, his book of satire *The Will to Whatevs: A Guide to Modern Life*, and appearances on Comedy Central and late-night television shows. He writes a blog, has a Facebook page,[4] and is on Twitter.[5] "I want to be entertaining on the Web," he says. "That's what's fun for me. While there is a store on my web site, the push is to provide things to entertain people, not to sell." And entertain he does. Mirman's Twitter bio reads: "I am television's Eugene Mirman. I am very nice and like seafood." Sample tweet: "I started a tortilla fire in my toaster oven. Last time I leave to watch a preview of the new Green Lantern movie." He even included a link to a photo of the blackened and burned Mexican food as evidence.

Mirman uses Facebook and Twitter as ways to get his information out to multiple audiences very quickly. For example, immediately after he delivered the 2009 commencement address at Lexington High School in Massachusetts, he posted the video on YouTube[6] and then pointed to it from his blog, as well

---

[2] http://sxsw.com/

[3] http://eugenemirman.com/

[4] www.facebook.com/pages/Eugene-Mirman/17472821218

[5] http://twitter.com/eugeneMirman

[6] www.youtube.com/watch?v=KZlQd2Eg-9w

as from his Twitter and Facebook profiles. The video got 100,000 views in just one week.

Mirman says that he writes what's interesting to him at the time and doesn't worry about productivity. "I want to do things that are funny and I want a lot of people to see it, but I do what I think is good and funny and then hope that others pass it on," he says. "It's easier for me to do what I like, and if it attracts fans, then that's great. And I'm lucky that it has been effective over the years to do it this way. With social media, you can tell a story. If you have a special interest, like cooking, then you can get an audience."

Think back to my metaphor of the Web as a city and social media as a cocktail party, which I discussed in Chapter 4. Cocktail parties are fun. You go because you want to be there. And while the chance of meeting someone who could become a customer is a distinct possibility, that's a by-product of good conversation. Take a tip from Mirman and make sure you bring the right attitude to social media. With that in mind, let's look in detail at several of the most important social networking sites.

Facebook: Not Just for Students

In the time since I wrote the first edition of this book, Facebook has taken off as an online tool for businesspeople to connect to communities and to customers directly. The spark for this remarkable explosion was the September 2006 opening of Facebook to nonstudents. Prior to that time, you needed an email address ending in ".edu" to qualify for an account. According to comScore, in the months prior to allowing open registration, Facebook.com traffic hovered at approximately 14 million unique visitors per month. The number of visitors nearly doubled in the next nine months, reaching 26.6 million in May 2007. As of this writing, Facebook has reached 275 million visitors worldwide. The site reports[7] that 100 million people log onto Facebook at least once each day.

The site connects members via a "friend request" process. Until you approve someone as your Facebook friend, your extended profile remains private. I've found Facebook to be a great way to maintain casual contact with people I meet in person and online. Many have sent me friend requests after reading this book or my blog, and when I speak at a conference, I'm bound to

---

[7] www.facebook.com/press/info.php?statistics

get a handful of friend requests from attendees. It is incredibly rewarding to learn a bit more about the individuals who use the ideas found in this book. And, of course, those people can learn more about me, too.

The most important thing to remember about marketing on Facebook (and other social networking sites) is that it is not about generating hype. The best approaches to Facebook marketing involve three useful ways to deliver information and ideas to a network of people who are interested in you and your products and services: friend-to-friend communication, groups, and applications. The first is generally the easiest and really just requires that you describe yourself via your personal profile. For example, when I publish a new e-book or my next print book, I'll post a message on my Facebook profile so my friends will know what I'm up to. I also post links to new blog posts and speaking engagements. Similarly, back when I set up my profile, I included a short video to give my Facebook friends an idea of what one of my speeches was like. My Facebook friends see my updates via their Facebook feed, basically an ongoing delivery of information from their circle of friends.

A great way for organizations of all kinds to keep interested people informed is to gather them into a Facebook group. All users can create groups, and their membership can be closed (invitation only) or open (anyone may join). There's also a similar place where people can meet called a Facebook fan page, which is a page of information that anybody can see (compared to groups where you must register first). Facebook Groups are typically for more in-depth communications around a subject (such as a product launch), while Facebook fan pages are typically for a loose but longer-term presence. I know this sounds complicated, but it should be further incentive to join some groups and become a fan of a few companies to see what people are doing.

For example, Philip Robertson, director of marketing communications for ooVoo,[8] an application for conducting face-to-face video conversation with friends, family, and colleagues, wanted to establish social media connections soon after ooVoo was launched in mid-2007. "Facebook was quickly becoming a place for people to connect and catch up online," he says. "At the same time, we began to look at different ways to market." Robertson started a Facebook group as a way to communicate with existing ooVoo users and to help

[8] www.oovoo.com/

build a larger population of users as people discussed the service and shared it with their Facebook friends. "We've used the group to promote campaigns such as 'my ooVoo day' where top-tier bloggers used ooVoo to interact with people. We also use it as a way to post new software. People who are fans of the brand can use new software first."

Starting a Facebook group is very straightforward. It takes just a few minutes to set one up, and the process includes a built-in tool for sending invitations to your Facebook friends (and, as appropriate, the friends of your colleagues). You should also mention the group on your organization's regular web site or blog. "We got 250 members to the Facebook group really quickly," Robertson says. "We invited the initial members through our own fan base, and we also invited influential people who can give us feedback on the brand." The ooVoo group has more than 1,500 members as of this writing. There is also an ooVoo Facebook fan page with nearly 10,000 fans.

People join Facebook groups because they want to stay informed, and they want to do it on their own time. Just as with blogs, the best way to maintain a Facebook group is simply to make valuable information available. Unlike intrusive email updates, which arrive only when the sender chooses, Facebook groups can be visited at the member's convenience. "You are not spamming people with information that they are forced to read," Robertson says.

The informal, two-way nature of Facebook's group dynamics is an important aspect for marketers. "Pass-along value is very important," says Robertson. "You can recommend Facebook groups and applications to friends in a much easier and more casual way than you can with e-mail. And people can post information to the group themselves, to actively take part in the brand."

I've had some remarkable experiences with Facebook groups, experiences that never would have happened in the absence of social networking tools. One of the most interesting was with Stephen Quigley's New Media and PR class at Boston University.[9] The class uses this book as one of its texts, and for the last several terms the students have invited me to join their invitation-only Facebook groups. One term's group was called "New Media Rocks My PR World" (love the name), and another set of students went with "Media Socialites" (love this one even more). Here is the Media Socialites' description

---

[9] www.bu.edu/com/about/faculty/stephen_quigley.html

of their group: "Professor Quigley's new batch of student social media sponges, eager to soak up as much information about New Media and PR in a semester as is humanly possible . . . and, in proper social networking fashion, making important connections along the way."

Social networking has given birth to new models for learning. I graduated from Kenyon College in 1983, and in four years I don't recall ever giving textbook authors any thought whatsoever. I certainly never met any of them. But with social media tools like Facebook, smart professors (and students) are now involving textbook authors and other guests, effectively creating virtual classrooms to supplement the physical ones. The students and professors tell me it's transforming their learning process. How about your business? How is social media changing what you do? Take a lesson from these forward-thinking educators and become a part of the discussion.

The final feature I mentioned is the ability to make applications, which are a great way to build your brand on Facebook. As an open platform, Facebook allows anybody to create applications that allow friends to share information on the service in different ways. There are many thousands of applications available on Facebook, and the more popular ones are used regularly by hundreds of thousands of people each day—not bad for a marketing tool that costs nothing to launch and is easy to create. One of my personal favorites is the "Cities I've Visited" application from TripAdvisor.[10] It displays a map on my Facebook page where I can stick a virtual thumbtack in the cities I've visited. Since I am on the road a lot, this is a great way for me to keep track of my world travel.

TripAdvisor's business is providing unbiased hotel reviews, photos, and travel advice, so the "Cities I've Visited" Facebook application is a perfect marketing tool for the company. Facebook applications are a terrific way for marketers to be creative and try something new, and there is always the possibility for an application to catch fire and go viral like "Cities I've Visited." Which, by the way, now has an amazing three million active users.

In short, Facebook is emerging as a primary means for folks to keep in touch with the people and the organizations that are important to them, and it follows that it has become an important marketing tool for many companies. As with other social networking media, success on Facebook comes

---

[10] www.tripadvisor.com/

from being a thought leader and developing information that people *want* to absorb.

Check Me Out on MySpace

Marketing on social networking sites can be tricky because their online communities disdain overt commercial messages. Acceptable marketing and promotion on these sites frequently involves offline brands or personalities creating pages to build and expand an online following rather than directly advertise products. For instance, it is common for members of rock bands to have a MySpace page. Connecticut-based The Alternative Routes has a popular MySpace page[11] with a network as of this writing of over 15,000 friends. People are active on the band's page, having left more than 3,000 comments to date.

Volkswagen has taken a different approach. With tongue planted firmly in cheek, marketers at Volkswagen created a MySpace profile page for Helga,[12] the German character who appears in some of the company's TV commercials. Visitors learn Helga's Likes ("I love the smell of gasoline. Gears turning, oil burning, stomach churning. Go fast or go home. Efficiency.") and Dislikes ("'Pimped rides,' bumper balls, people in the left lane going 40 with the blinker on. Traffic. Scorpios, you can't trust them.") Users can download ringtones, images of Helga, and short audio clips in Helga's strong German accent. My favorite Helga clip features her saying "My xenon headlights are on." The Helga MySpace page works because Helga is obviously a made-up character, and she is fun. And it works (she has over 6,000 friends) because Helga is seen as an engaging, slightly offbeat online character.

Yet another tactic that some smart nonprofit organizations use is to encourage employees to establish a personal page, with details of the cause they support, as a way to spread the word. Supporters of political candidates (as well as some candidates themselves) create pages on social networking sites too. As with all good marketing, it is important to create content that is right for the people you want to reach, and that starts with the choice of which social networking site (or sites) to post your profile.

---

[11] www.myspace.com/alternateroutes
[12] www.myspace.com/misshelga

As you consider a strategy to get yourself out there and onto a social networking site for marketing and PR purposes, just remember that authenticity and transparency are critical. Don't try to fool the community into thinking that the page is something that it is not. (You might want to skip to the discussion of ethics in Chapter 15). Frequent eruptions within these communities happen when members uncover a fraud of some kind, such as an advertising agency creating fake profiles of people applauding products. Yes, you can use social networking sites such as MySpace to build a following, but the approaches that bands like The Alternative Routes and companies like Volkswagen take work best; avoid sleazy fake profiles of people who supposedly use your products.

Tweet Your Thoughts to the World

We really should have seen Twitter[13] coming. After all, one of the most popular elements of the instant messaging craze is the "away message," which gives users the opportunity to tell people what they are doing (a bit like a text version of a telephone voicemail greeting). As blogs (a more long-winded means of answering that question—among others) became more popular, it was probably only a matter of time before blog posts started to look more like away messages. Thus was microblogging born, with Twitter being the most popular service. And popularity is important because of the social nature of Twitter, a service for friends, family, and coworkers to communicate through the exchange of quick, short messages (with a maximum of 140 characters).

People use Twitter to keep their "followers" (people who subscribe to their Twitter feed) updated on their life. For instance, you might "tweet" about who you're having lunch with or the project you're engrossed in, or you might ask your network a question. Users can choose to follow the Twitter updates of anyone they want to hear from: family members, colleagues, or perhaps the author of the last book they read. Because of the severe constraint on the length of tweets, people use Twitter to post information that is important to update their network about but is much more concise than a blog post and more casual than an email. You can update your Twitter feed from a Web browser, a mobile phone, or an instant messaging service, so Twitter is always on. I update my feed a few times a day, tweeting about my travels around the

---

[13] http://twitter.com/

world, who I'm meeting, and what's going on at the conferences and events where I speak. I also frequently send out links to examples of great marketing that people send me, things like e-books, YouTube videos, and blog posts. In this way, Twitter is a way of pointing people to things that I find interesting. As with other forms of social networking, it takes time to build a following. In particular, the best way to get people to pay attention to you is to participate by following others and responding to them, just like you should do in the blogosphere.

Every marketing and PR person should be aware of Twitter and understand how people use it. As a first step, you should immediately high-tail it over to the Twitter search engine[14] to see what people are saying about you, your organization, your products and services, and perhaps your competitors and the category of product you sell. If you've never done this, please do it right now, because it can be an eye-opening experience to see what (if anything) people are saying.

When you're ready to set up your own Twitter profile and begin to tweet, the most important aspect from the marketing and PR perspective is—as I say time and again—don't use this service as an advertising channel to talk up your products and services. If that's your intention, you need to be very careful.

"If you want to use Twitter as a marketing channel, you have to put yourself out there as an interested member of the community," says Scott Monty,[15] digital and multimedia communications manager at Ford Motor Company.[16] "I'm constantly amazed at what a powerful personal and professional network it is for me. Recently, I went online to find a hotel room in New York City, which is usually not a problem, especially with the last-minute travel sites. Only this time, no rooms in midtown were to be had. So I sent a tweet[17] to my network and immediately heard from a number of people with suggestions, including Tim Peter,[18] who works with a group that does luxury reservations. Within a few minutes, I had a reservation at the Mansfield, a boutique hotel in midtown Manhattan. Perfect! Thanks to a well-connected and attentive community, I was able to keep myself off a Central Park bench

---

[14] http://search.twitter.com/

[15] www.scottmonty.com/

[16] www.ford.com/

[17] http://twitter.com/scottmonty

[18] http://twitter.com/tcpeter

for the night. It just goes to show that if you take the time to invest in relationships and being a valued member of a community, it can work in your favor when you need it."

Some companies use Twitter to alert customers to special deals. Because of the broadcast-like nature of microblogging, thousands of potential buyers can receive this information instantaneously. "Woot has used Twitter as a way to alert people to new merchandise that is available, and JetBlue lets people know when they are running airfare specials," Monty says. But as with all new media, it is important to learn the unwritten etiquette of Twitter before using it. "The *Today* show gives updates of feature stories and highlights of shows," Monty says. "When they started on Twitter, they bulk-followed a bunch of people and basically spammed them. Based on the *Today* show Twitter profile, there were 3,500 people whom they were following and only 500 people following them. It annoyed me and my colleagues, because they were trying to build up numbers rather than being a part of the conversation."

With all this online conversation going on, some people think that Facebook, Twitter, and other social networking tools can replace a face-to-face approach to business. I actually think strong social networking ties lead to *stronger* personal relationships because it is easy to facilitate face-to-face meetings that never would have occurred otherwise. For example, before a conference, I might send a tweet saying "I'll be in San Francisco next Tuesday." I'll frequently get a message right back from someone who is planning to be at the same conference, or someone who lives there, and we end up meeting in person. I'll also create an impromptu meeting of my followers—called a TweetUp—which occurs when people who are connected on Twitter have a face-to-face meeting. I've had between 10 and 30 people show up in cities like Wellington, New Zealand; Atlanta; New York City; and Phoenix, Arizona to connect.

Social Networking and Personal Branding

I've had many conversations with people who are new to social networking sites such as Twitter, and often they are puzzled at first about what to do. Hey, I've been there too. We all make mistakes. I recall when I was first getting going with Facebook and my teenage daughter was looking over my shoulder. She rolled her eyes and called me a "big dork" when I wrote a message on my own Facebook Wall (a place for your visitors to write). I found that with my own learning and the experiences with people I've helped over the past few years, getting a few things right at the start makes the experience more fun (and productive). While I'll be writing about Twitter here, the basic ideas apply to all social networking sites.

An important thing to consider is how your online actions are a reflection of your personal branding (the image that you project to the world). As you already know, *people* use Twitter to keep others updated on what they find interesting at that moment. Frequently when I am asked about Twitter and its use in personal branding and marketing, people immediately dive into stuff like "how often should I tweet," "what should I tweet about," "is it cool to DM [direct message] people," and other tweet-related details. Well, that's all fine, but the vast majority of people miss the most basic (and important) personal branding aspect of all.

> What does your Twitter page look like?

Most Twitter pages don't say enough and most have crappy design. While that's fine if you're just communicating with friends, if you care about your personal brand, you need to do better. Much better. And it is so easy! When you first set up your Twitter account, you have choices. And after you've set up the account, you can make these changes to any aspect of your profile at any time (except your Twitter ID) under the "Settings" tab in Twitter.

Twitter ID: (Mine is dmscott.) Choose an appropriate ID. Something like MrSillyGuy is probably not a good idea for most people. However, a silly ID might fit your personal brand, say, if you're a comedian. (As of this writing MrSillyGuy is not taken as a Twitter ID.)

Name: (Mine is David Meerman Scott.) Use your real name. Don't just default to your user ID which so many people seem to do. And don't just use a nickname like "Pookie." You can put your nickname in quotes inside of your real name if you want to. If you really care about your personal brand, you'll want people to know who you really are.

Location: (Mine is Boston, MA.) Use the town or nearest city that makes sense for you. Saying something cute like "earth" or "somewhere in Canada" turns people off who don't know you. Besides, the location is a good way to make local contacts.

Web: (Mine is www.davidmeermanscott.com.) If you have a blog or site, put the URL here. Or maybe your profile on a company web site makes sense for you. This should be somewhere people can go to learn more about *you*. If you don't have a blog or site, I recommend that you create a Google profile and link to that. Go back to Chapter 5 to learn about Google profiles. You can also leave the "Web" link blank if you want, but that says to people that you don't want to be contacted or to have people learn more about you.

Bio: (As I write this, mine is "Marketing speaker and bestselling author of *The New Rules of Marketing and PR* and the new book *World Wide Rave*.") This is where you say something about yourself. You only get 160 characters. As a component of personal branding, this is a critical section. Don't leave it blank. And don't make a mini-resume from a laundry list of attributes like this: "father, brother, surfer, economics major, world traveler, marketer, and rockstar wannabe." (I confess, that would be my list.) I see this sort of thing all the time and it is not good for personal branding because you don't really focus on your particular expertise. Try to be descriptive. And try to be specific.

Photo: Your photo is very important! Don't default to the placeholder that Twitter provides for those with no photo. And don't use something clever as a stand in (like your cat). If you care about your personal brand, you should use a photo of you and not a pet or image of your car. Photos appear very tiny on Twitter—like a postage stamp—so use a close-up shot. If you use a full view of yourself, then you will appear like a stick figure. Remember that your photo conveys a very important first impression when people see your profile for the first time. Are you wearing a hat? Is it a casual shot of you taken while on holiday with a beer in your hand? Or have you chosen a formal head-and-shoulders shot with business attire taken by a professional photographer? Is your son or daughter in the photo with you? There is no real right or wrong, but do keep in mind that each of these choices says a great deal about you.

Background image: The background image of your Twitter page is a place where you can really show off. The default blue background is like when you first open PowerPoint—it's a default. Twitter has some choices, but many people use them, so you will not be unique. Shoot a custom photo in order to really shine. I use a close-up photo of a nifty old typewriter keyboard. It's my personal brand on Twitter.

These choices are really easy to set up, but they're very important for your personal brand. If you are on Twitter, take the time to make some changes today. Again, the same ideas apply on other social networking sites like Facebook and LinkedIn, so don't forget to carefully consider your personal branding on those sites as well.

Connecting with Fans

"Being a touring musician means meeting fans," says Amanda Palmer, lead singer for The Dresden Dolls and punk rock cabaret solo artist. "I go out and meet fans after every gig. It's important to make contact in real life and not just online in social media like Twitter. If you don't meet fans in real life too, then you're a fraud. If you're not comfortable getting into the sweat with them and talking with people at shows, then how can you do it successfully online? I love connecting with fans. Speaking to people at the merchandise table after the show is great. I can stay there forever."

This committed attitude has helped make Palmer a personal branding force of nature, using her infectious personality to connect with fans in person and on the Web. She has amassed a large online following on her blog,[19] her MySpace page[20] (more than 75,000 friends), her Facebook fan page[21] (more than 20,000 fans), and her Twitter feed[22] (more than 50,000 followers). Note that Palmer's band, the Dresden Dolls also has nearly a quarter of a million friends on MySpace.

When The Dresden Dolls formed in 2000, Palmer created an email list from day one. Soon after, the personal connections she established at the band's concerts, which continued in e-mail messages with fans, started to bleed onto the band's personal forum, The Shadowbox.[23] A collection of all things Amanda Palmer and Dresden Dolls, The Shadowbox has accumulated a remarkable quarter of a million fan posts since its launch. "It's like I've built a house and people are hanging around in it," Palmer says.

Palmer is very active on Twitter and uses it as a tool for instant communication with her fans. She frequently answers fans' tweeted questions and comments. Because she truly enjoys her connection with her followers, Twitter comes naturally to her. "It's important to have the makeup that I do," she says. "I love to answer fans' questions, and I love to make people happy. You can't fake being authentic with your fans. It's so easy to see through when other musicians are faking it, such as when some employee of their record labels tweets on behalf of their artists. Fans can see through fake tweets like

---

[19] http://amandapalmer.net/content/

[20] www.myspace.com/whokilledamandapalmer

[21] www.new.facebook.com/amandapalmer

[22] http://twitter.com/amandapalmer

[23] www.theshadowbox.net/

'I'm about to play at a rad club. Get tix here.' Fake artists' blogs are the same. Who cares?"

Palmer frequently uses Twitter to bring together groups of fans quickly and spontaneously when she is on the road. She tweeted a secret gig in Los Angeles one morning and about 350 people showed up five hours later at a warehouse space where she played the piano. It works great for her because, although she's able to get a large number of people to show up, she is not so popular that she would create a dangerously huge mob. "I'm in the sweet spot of popularity," she says. "I can send out a tweet and get 300 people to show up in a couple of days and do a free gig on the beach. I'll play the ukulele, sing, sign, hug, take pictures, eat cake, and generally hang out and connect. And I'll stay as long as it takes to talk with everyone personally. Trent Reznor of Nine Inch Nails can't do that because he's just too popular."

Palmer does struggle with the amount of time she spends connecting with fans both in person and through the tools of social media like Twitter. "I feel guilty sometimes that I'd often prefer to answer questions from fans and do interviews and meet people than work on new music," she says. Interestingly, she has fans who feel the same way; her prolific online *content* has earned a following of its own. "One person at a record store gig and signing came up to me and said, 'I don't really like your music, but I love your blog.'"

How Amanda Palmer Made $11,000 on Twitter in Two Hours

When you have a loyal following on Twitter, it becomes an incredibly powerful tool for accomplishing your goals. You can use Twitter to spread an idea, ask people's opinions, research a problem, or even make some money. "The great thing about Twitter is that the minute I started using it, I realized the possibilities are endless," Palmer says. She proved it one Friday night.

"I tweeted as a joke that I was all alone, again, on a Friday night at my computer, like a loser," Palmer says. "Other people started chiming in, and we were all losers. One of my friends called it a virtual flash mob, and all of a sudden there were a thousand people hanging out and following what was going on, the dialog between the fans. And we started a faux organization called *The Losers of Friday Night on their Computers*. We started making demands of the government like no tax on vodka, government issued sweatpants, free pizza, anything you could possibly need to be a loser on Friday night at your computer. And it was just really funny. It felt like a little piece of loser anarchy on Twitter."

Palmer set up the hashtag (unique code for finding tweets on a particular subject) #LOFNOTC for the Losers, and the thousands of people communicating made the Loser group the number one trending topic on Twitter at that moment. As members chatted, someone suggested the group should make a T-shirt. So without any planning, Palmer said, "Sure let's do it," and used a Sharpie to make a T-shirt design. Someone suggested the slogan "DON'T STAND UP FOR WHAT'S RIGHT, STAY IN FOR WHAT'S WRONG," which was added to the shirt. Palmer's Web marketing company was able to create a quickie site (which went live in just half an hour), and offered the T-shirts for sale at $25 each. The Losers group bought 200 T-shirts that night. Several hundred more were sold the next day after Palmer blogged about it. The total take made via Twitter over just two hours that night was $11,000.

Not many people can get a thousand others to gather on a Friday night, and fewer still can then sell them something as effectively as Palmer did. But that's not the real point here. The point is that Twitter is an increasingly important way for people to connect and communicate, and organizations are using it cleverly to benefit their businesses, their followers, and themselves. So should you.

Which Social Networking Site Is Right for You?

While some people might be tempted to create a page on lots of different social networking sites, this may not be necessary (or even useful), since each one appeals to different users. "While the top social networking sites are typically viewed as directly competing with one another, our analysis demonstrates that each site occupies a slightly different niche," says Jack Flanagan, executive vice president of comScore. "There is a misconception that social networking is the exclusive domain of teenagers, but [our] analysis confirms that the appeal of social networking sites is far broader." In fact, Facebook says that more than two-thirds of its users are out of college and that the fastest growing demographic is those 35 years old and older.

So think about the right social networking sites for you and your business. Besides Facebook, MySpace, and Twitter, here are a few other popular ones to check out.

LinkedIn: The LinkedIn[24] site says: "Professionals use LinkedIn to exchange information, ideas and opportunities. When you join, you create a profile that summarizes your professional accomplishments. Your profile helps you find and be found by former colleagues, clients, and partners. You can add more connections by inviting trusted contacts to join LinkedIn and connect to you." The LinkedIn About page provides a laundry list of things you can do on the site, such as find potential clients, search for jobs, land deals, and get introductions. LinkedIn is an excellent tool if your buyer personas work in businesses.

Squidoo: Unlike other social networking sites that are based on personal profiles of individuals, Squidoo[25] is based on people's expertise in a niche subject. Squidoo is another way for marketers to build an online presence easily and for free. Headed up by "original squid" Seth Godin,[26] creator of "Permission Marketing" and best-selling business author of *Purple Cow*, Squidoo is built around online lenses, which are a way to filter a person's expertise on a subject onto a single page. Interested people check out a lens on a topic and quickly get pointed to useful web sites. A person who makes a lens is a lensmaster, and he or she uses a lens to provide context. "Everyone is an expert," the Squidoo site says, and Squidoo helps everyone share that expertise with the world. Vince Ciulla, a professional automotive technician with over 30 years' experience, has created a Squidoo lens called Auto Repair—Trouble Shooting[27] that points to content on his main site. "Fixing your car is easy," Ciulla says. "The hard part is figuring out what's wrong. My web site and links from my Squidoo lens are how people can get the information they need for free, such as how to replace a brake master cylinder. I also explain things like how the cruise control works."

SecondLife: An online world entirely built and owned by its residents, Second Life[28] is a place where people interact in three virtual dimensions. But this is not a game (there is no goal and nobody is keeping score); rather,

---

[24] www.linkedin.com/

[25] www.squidoo.com/

[26] http://sethgodin.typepad.com/

[27] www.squidoo.com/autorepair_diagnostics

[28] http://secondlife.com/

it is a world with millions of residents and an economy built on the Linden dollar in which millions of U.S. dollars (at the current exchange rate) change hands each month. The Second Life world is teeming with people who use a self-created, in-world avatar to interact with others by buying, selling, and trading things with other residents (and just milling about and chatting). You can purchase land, build a store or business, and make money. Not surprisingly, there is even a sleazy underworld as well. But you don't have to be into commerce; you can just walk around and hang out. Quite a few of the companies that have jumped into Second Life seem to have done so just to be part of a new phenomenon, and many have since closed down their presence there. As with all social networking sites, it is important to consider if your buyer personas are active before jumping in. I hear that many software developers frequent Second Life, so it's no surprise that smart companies like IBM and HP have set up shop there.

Shopping sites: Okay, I know this is an outlier. Most people don't consider shopping sites to be social networking, and they're nothing like the other sites I've mentioned in this chapter. But don't overlook the incredible communities that thrive on sites like Amazon, where customer reviews, profiles of those customer reviewers, and user conversations take place every day. For example, if a new book comes out in your marketplace, why not be the first to review it on Amazon? If you're a real estate agent and you write a thoughtful review on a new book about real estate investing, it may be seen by tens of thousands of people (as well as the author and members of the media). People who then visit your Amazon profile learn about you and your business and some may contact you. Other review-based sites to check out include Rotten Tomatoes (movie reviews), Zagat (restaurant reviews), and Yelp (reviews of local businesses). There are many more such sites. Don't forget to create a useful profile for yourself with contact information.

You Can't Go to Every Party, So Why Even Try?

Think back to our social-media-as-cocktail-party metaphor for a moment. You can't go to every party thrown in your city. There are literally thousands of social networking sites out there, and it is simply impossible to be active in all of them. And once you choose a few parties to attend, you can't meet and have a conversation with each and every person there. You know there are tons of great conversations going on all around you, and you know that you can't be a part of them all.

What do you do at a party? Some people constantly look over the shoulder of the person they are talking to, always on the lookout for a better conversation. Some flit from one person to another every few minutes all night, having many short, superficial conversations. What I like to do at parties is have a few great conversations and be happy that I'm at a wonderful event. I know I can't be with everyone, so I have fun with the people I'm with. What more could I want?

If you're following my analogy here, you should apply the same thing to your participation in social media. For most people and organizations, it's better to be active in a few social networking sites instead of creating profiles on dozens of them and being too busy to spend much time in any one. In my own case, I have my own blog, I am on Facebook and Twitter, and I'm active on a few forums and chatrooms, but that's about it. I'm not on MySpace or LinkedIn or SecondLife. There are thousands of other social media and social networking sites that I choose not to participate in, such as Nexopia, Bebo, Hi5, Tagged, Xing, Skyrock, Orkut, Friendster, Orkut, Xiaonei, Cyworld, and many, many more. Since you can't go to every party, you need to pick and choose. Where do you want to be? Where you can be most helpful? Where are the members of your buyer personas?

Optimizing Social Networking Pages

If you're creating pages on Facebook, MySpace, Twitter, and the other social networking sites, and if you've been following the planning process outlined in Chapter 10, then you're creating content that reaches your buyers and helps you achieve your goals. Although social networking sites aren't advertising, you can still use the sites to lead people into your buying process. For example, The Alternate Routes have links on their MySpace page to the band's latest album, touring schedule, and online ticket purchasing tools; Volkswagen links to the automaker's other sites; Vince Ciulla points people from his Squidoo lens to his web site; and Amanda Palmer links to her blog from her Twitter profile.

Here are some ideas to get the most out of using social networking sites for marketing:

- *Target a specific audience.* Create a page that reaches an audience important to your organization. It is usually better to target a small niche market (e.g., people who want to do their own car repairs but don't know how to diagnose what's wrong).
- *Be a thought leader.* Provide valuable and interesting information that people want to check out. As you will remember from Chapter 11, it is better to show your expertise in a market or at solving a buyer's problems than to blather on about your product.
- *Be authentic and transparent.* Don't try to impersonate someone else. It's a sleazy practice, and if you get caught you can do irreparable harm to your company's reputation. If your mother would say it's wrong, it probably is.
- *Create lots of links.* Link to your own sites and blog, and those of others in your industry and network. Everybody loves links—they make the Web what it is. You should certainly link to your own stuff from a social networking site, but it's important to expand your horizons a bit.
- *Encourage people to contact you.* Make it easy for others to reach you online, and be sure to follow up personally on your fan mail.
- *Participate.* Create groups and participate in online discussions. Become an online leader and organizer.
- *Make it easy to find you.* Tag your page and add it to subject directories. Encourage others to bookmark your page with del.icio.us and DIGG.
- *Experiment.* These sites are great because you can try new things. If it isn't working, tweak it. Or abandon the effort and try something new. There is no such thing as an expert in social networking—we're all learning as we go!

Start a Movement

Clearly, one of the most interesting aspects of social media is that people talk about you, your company, and its products and services. Most of the time, these discussions happen away from your influence. However, it is certainly possible to guide the discussion if you're a bit creative. For example, Ford Motor Company is helping to lead discussions with its Fiesta Movement,[29] a social networking platform built around the new global vehicle of the same

---

[29] www.fiestamovement.com/

name. Ford provided 100 social media "agents" with personalized Fiestas that they can drive for six months and then relate their experiences through a variety of social media sites.

"This is a Euro-spec vehicle that is not yet available in the United States," says Ford's Scott Monty. "We're using this as a combination of test marketing and buzz generation. The agents are creating content all over the Web, and people are talking about the Ford Fiesta on Facebook, Twitter, their blogs, and posting videos and photos on sites like YouTube and Flickr. Ford came on with an approach to social media that showed that we are different. We came at social media from a different perspective, a more personal one, and I think that has made all the difference for us."

Ford's strategy is betting on the continued rise in social media's popularity, and its online numbers reflect the buzz. Agent postings have garnered significant numbers on social media sites through the first quarter of the Fiesta Movement—more than 1.8 million YouTube views, more than 270,000 Flickr views and more than 1.8 million Twitter impressions, resulting in more than 13.2 million interactions.

Social media take the pervasiveness of the Internet one step farther. And while we don't know where they're heading, what is certain is that marketing and PR on the Web will continue to evolve—quickly. Success comes from experimentation. With a service like Twitter or a site like Facebook (or whatever the next new thing is), nobody knows the rules at first. Smart marketers succeed just by trying. Reuters, for example, generated a ton of stories in the mainstream media and on blogs when it opened the first virtual news bureau in Second Life. They got a huge amount of buzz simply by trying something. Similarly, JetBlue and Dell have created huge followings on Twitter because they were early adopters. The trick to benefiting from any new medium is this: Participate in it; don't just try to take advantage of it. Be a *genuine* part of the action! Whatever your social networking site of choice, don't hesitate to jump in and see what you can do.

15

Blogging to Reach Your Buyers

Blogs are now a mainstream vehicle for organizations to get their ideas into the marketplace. The readers of blogs view the information shared by smart bloggers as one of the few forms of real, authentic communication. Audiences consume advertising with skepticism and consider pronouncements by CEOs to be out of touch with reality. But a good blog written by someone within a large or small company, a nonprofit, a church, or a political campaign commands attention.

At the same time, blogs have seen a lot of hype in recent years. Business magazines regularly include breathless enthusiasm about how blogs and blogging hold the power to transform your business. While I absolutely agree that blogs can change your business and your life (as my blog has changed mine), there is still some mystery to blogging if you haven't done it before. This chapter will set out the basics of how to establish your own blog. But I recommend that, before you begin to write, you first monitor blogs in your market space and that you step into the blogosphere by commenting on a few blogs before you write your own. You might want to reread Chapter 5, where I introduced blogs and provided some case studies of successful bloggers. As you begin to comment on other people's blogs, you'll develop your own blogging voice and get a sense of what you like to discuss online. That's great! You're experimenting on someone else's blog real estate. If you're like many people, soon you'll be itching to write your own blog. But if commenting is a painful chore for you, maybe you're not cut out to be a blogger. That's okay—there are many more blog readers than blog writers. This forum isn't for everybody.

It's impossible to tell you everything you need to know about blogging in this one chapter. While the case studies and basic information will certainly get you started, the best thing is to experiment to find your voice. Read other blogs and be aware of what you like and dislike about other bloggers' styles. You might also check Debbie Weil's excellent *The Corporate Blogging Book*.

What Should You Blog About?

People often struggle to decide what to blog about. This is particularly true for marketing and PR professionals, because we have been taught to be slaves to the notion of flogging our products and services with "on message" advertising and press releases; for most organizations, that's exactly the wrong way to blog. The first thing to ask yourself is "Whom do I want to reach?" For many people, the answer is a combination of buyers, existing customers, and influencers such as analysts and the media. You need to find a topic that you are passionate about. If you aren't excited about the topic or if it feels painful to write, you're unlikely to sustain the effort; and if you do manage to keep going, the writing is likely to be forced.

Most first-time bloggers try to cover too much. It is better to start with a narrow subject and leave room to expand. Be authentic. People read blogs because they want to find an honest voice speaking passionately about a subject. You do not have to be harsh or controversial if that is not your style. If you are interesting and provide valuable information, your readership will grow.

Grant D. Griffiths, a Kansas family and divorce lawyer, started his blog[1] in March 2005. "I've learned that in the legal profession, and probably any other profession, you need to be very targeted," Griffiths says. His blog is written for a very specific buyer persona. "I'm not writing my blog for other attorneys; I write for the public. More specifically, I write for people in Kansas who need a family lawyer. My practice blog is my storefront, shingle, office sign, newspaper ad, and yellow-pages ad."

Griffiths has averaged about a dozen email inquires per week since August 2005 from new contacts who find him as a result of his blog. "And on average I get two to three new cases a week from the blog," he says. "If you type in anything related to Kansas and family law into a search engine, then my blog

---

[1] http://gdgrifflaw.typepad.com/

is usually in the top few hits on the first page. I stopped doing yellow-pages ads last year. In talking to other lawyers, I hear they are scared of not doing a yellow-pages ad because they are afraid that if they don't, then they won't get any more business. They don't feel like real lawyers without a yellow-pages ad because it is traditional marketing."

In its "State of the Blogosphere" 2008 report,[2] blog search engine Technorati claimed that it tracked more than 112 million blogs in 81 languages and that about 100,000 new blogs are created every day, which means that, on average, a new blog is created every second of every day. That's a heck of a lot of competition, and you might ask yourself if it is worth the effort. But remember back to the *long tail* theory we discussed in Chapter 2. If you write a niche blog (e.g., a blog about Kansas family law), then you're not competing with 112 million other blogs. You're writing in a space where there are few (if any) other blogs, and you will no doubt find readers who are interested in what you're saying. If you have a small niche, you may interest only a few hundred readers. But you'll reach the right readers—those people who are interested in what you and your organization have to say.

Blogging Ethics and Employee Blogging Guidelines

Some organizations such as IBM[3] and the United States Air Force[4] have created formal guidelines for employee bloggers and published them online for anyone to access. Your organization should decide for itself whether to create such guidelines, and the decision should be determined based on input from marketing, HR, and other departments. I think it is much better for organizations to establish policies about all communications (including verbal communication, email, participation in chat rooms, and the like) rather than to focus on a new medium (blogs). I feel strongly that a company can and should set policy about sexual harassment, disparaging the competition, and revealing company secrets, but there's no reason to have different policies for different media. Once the policy is set, employees should be permitted to blog

---

[2] http://technorati.com/blogging/state-of-the-blogosphere//
[3] www.ibm.com/blogs/zz/en/guidelines.html
[4] www.af.mil/shared/media/document/AFD-090406-036.pdf

away as long as they follow it. No matter what the decisions you make about who should blog and what the rules are, it is always better for the blogger to avoid passing individual posts through a PR department or legal team. However, if your blog posts *must* be reviewed by others in your organization before going live, then have your colleagues focus only on the content, not your actual words. Do not let others in your organization turn your authentic and passionate writing into another form of marketing gobbledygook.

Let's talk about ethics for a moment. All sorts of unethical practices go on in the blogosphere, and you must be certain to hold yourself and your organization accountable for your actions as a blogger. Some organizations have gotten caught using unethical practices on their blogs and have done great harm to their corporate reputations. I've included some of the issues you need to pay attention to, as well as an example of each unethical practice. This is not intended to be a comprehensive list, but rather a starting point for you to think about ethics.

- *Transparency:* You should never pretend to be someone you are not. For example, don't use another name to submit a comment on any blog (your own or somebody else's), and don't create a blog that talks about your company without disclosing that someone from your company is behind it.
- *Privacy:* Unless you've been given permission, don't blog about something that was disclosed to you. For example, don't post material from an email someone sent you unless you have permission.
- *Disclosure:* It is important to disclose anything that people might consider a conflict of interest in a blog post. For example, if I write in my blog about a product from a company that is one of my consulting clients, I put a sentence at the end disclosing my relationship with the company.
- *Truthfulness:* Don't lie. For example, never make up a customer story just because it makes good blog content.
- *Credit:* You should give credit to bloggers (and other sources) whose material you have used in your blog. For example, don't read a great post on someone else's blog, take the idea, change a few words, and make it your own. Besides being good ethical practice, links to other bloggers whose ideas you have used helps to introduce them to your blog and they may link to you.

Again, this is not a complete list. The Word of Mouth Marketing Association has created an *Ethics Code*.[5] I recommend that you read and follow the guidelines. But you should also follow your gut. If sending a post feels funny to you for some reason or makes you uncomfortable, it may be unethical. What would your mother say about that post? If she would tell you it is wrong, it probably is, so don't send it. Please do the right thing.

Blogging Basics: What You Need to Know to Get Started

Unlike web sites, which require design and HTML skills to produce, blogs are quick and easy to set up using off-the-shelf software with easy-to-use features. With just a little basic know-how, you can quickly and easily establish and promote your blog. Here are some specific tips to keep in mind:

- Before you begin, think carefully about the name of your blog and its tagline, which will be indexed by the search engines. It is very difficult to go back and change this information once you have established it.
- Easy-to-use blogging software is available from TypePad,[6] WordPress,[7] and others. Some of the services are free and others require a small subscription fee. Research the services and choose wisely based on your needs, because it is difficult to switch to a different service without losing all the content you have already created. And once your blog has been indexed by search engines, and people have subscribed to your RSS feed or bookmarked your URL, a change to different software is really tough.
- You will need to choose a URL for your blog. The blogging services all offer customizable URLs (such as yourblog.typepad.com). You can also map your blog to your company's domain (www.yourcompany.com/yourblog) or to a custom domain (www.yourblog.com).
- Blogging software makes it easy to choose color, design, and font, and to create a simple text-based masthead. You might consider using a custom

---

[5] http://womma.org/ethics/code/

[6] www.typepad.com/

[7] http://wordpress.org/

graphical image as your masthead—these are easy to design and will make your blog more attractive to readers.

- As you begin your blog, tweak your design, and tentatively try a few posts. I recommend you use password protection for the first few weeks or so. That way you can share your blog with a few friends and colleagues first and make changes before opening it up to the world.

- The look and feel of the blog could be complementary to your corporate design guidelines, but it should not be identical. For many blogs, it is better to be a bit different from the corporate look to signal to readers that the blog is an independent voice, not corporate-speak.

- Blogging software usually allows you to turn on a comments feature so your visitors can respond to your posts. There are several options for you to consider. Some people prefer their blogs to have no comments from readers at all, and that might be the right choice for you. However, one of the most exciting things about blogging is when your readers comment on what you've written. Depending on your blogging software, you may opt for open comments (where people can write comments that are not subject to your approval) or for a system where you need to approve each comment before it appears on your blog. Many bloggers use the approval feature to watch for inappropriate comments. But I encourage you to allow any comments from people who disagree with you—debate is one of the best indications of a well-read blog. Unfortunately, the blogosphere is plagued by the problem of comment spam, so to prevent automated comment robots from vandalizing your blog, some comment systems require people to answer a simple question called a "captcha"[8] before their comments go live (I use this approach, and it works very well).

- Most blogs also have a feature to allow trackbacks, which are messages that another blogger sends to you when she has posted something on her blog that references a post you wrote first. A trackback says to your blog readers, "Hey, if you're reading this original post, you might also be interested in a related post on another blog, so click here." Thus, a trackback is similar to a comment. However, instead of leaving a comment on *your* blog, the other blogger writes a post on her blog and sends you a trackback so your readers know her post is there. Again, because of

---

[8] www.captcha.net/

spam, I recommend you set up your blog so that you must approve trackbacks before they get posted there.

- Pay close attention to the categories you choose for your blog, and add social media tags for services like Technorati, DIGG, and del.icio.us to each post. (Take a look at Chapter 17 for more on social media tags.)
- RSS (Really Simple Syndication) is a standard delivery format for many of your readers. Make certain that your new blog has RSS capability. Most blogging software services have RSS feeds as a standard feature.
- Include an "About" page that includes your photo, biography, affiliations, and information about your blog. Often when people visit a blog for the first time, they want to know about the blogger, so it is important to provide background.
- Encourage people to contact you, make it easy for them to reach you online, and be sure to follow up personally on your fan mail. You'll get a bunch of inquiries, questions, praise, and an occasional detractor if you make it easy for people to contact you. Because of the huge problem with spam, many people don't want to publish email addresses. But the biggest problem is with automated robots that harvest email addresses, so to thwart them, write your email address so humans can read it but the machines cannot. On my web site, for example, I list my email address as david (at) DavidMeermanScott (dot) com.
- Don't write excessively about your company and its products and services. You must resist this urge to blog about what your company offers. Instead blog about a subject of interest to the people you are trying to reach. What problems do your buyers have that you can write about? How can you create content that informs and educates and entertains?
- Involve other blogs and bloggers by becoming a true participant in the online community. Link to and leave comments on other blogs. Let someone else's post serve as the starting point for a conversation that you continue on your own blog. You'll generate much more interest in what you're doing if you are inclusive and integrative.

Pimp Out Your Blog

Before my daughter started eighth grade, she spent the entire week pimping out her school binder. All the cool girls do it, transforming standard plastic three-ring binders with photos, stickers, song lyrics, and other bits and bobs on the outside. She even had a spot for a quote of the day that she updated each morning. Inside, the binder had page dividers she customized and pocket folders with pens and protractors and whatnot.

I got to thinking that the same is true of good blogs. A pimped-out blog shows the blogger's personality. I've pimped out my own blog with lots of cool stuff. On the top is a masthead that I had a friend who's a designer create. In TypePad (which I use for my Web Ink Now blog), if your blog is 800 pixels wide in total, you just have someone design an image that's 770 pixels wide by 100 or 150 pixels high and drop it in—TypePad automatically adds a border and replaces the rather plain-looking text masthead with the new design. Other blog software tools also support graphical mastheads, although the specific requirements and implementation methods will be different.

On the right and left columns of my blog, I have links to Amazon from the cover images of my books. Because these links are part of my Amazon Associates program account, I'm even paid a small commission for every book sold. (Hey, it's not much money, but every few months I can take my family out for a decent dinner on the proceeds.) I've also got links to pages on my site and to my other Web content, such as my blog about my collection of Apollo space artifacts,[9] my Squidoo lens, and through Technorati I've created a link to the blogs that link to mine. Through the use of small logos with embedded links, I send people to the articles I've written for *EContent* magazine, to information about the Newstex Blogs On Demand network that syndicates my blog, and to the homepages of associations with which I'm affiliated. Finally, I have easy sign-up links for people who want to view my blog as an RSS subscription via FeedBurner,[10] and an email subscription option with FeedBlitz[11] so people can get each of my blog posts sent to their email inbox.

One of the downsides of a blog is that the reverse-chronological aspect (most recent post at the top) means that much of your best stuff, which may have been written last month or last year, is hidden away. Thus, I've also included easy navigation links on my blog so people can quickly find the good stuff. For example, I include "The Best of Web Ink Now" with links to a

---

[9] www.apolloartifacts.com/

[10] www.feedburner.com/

[11] www.feedblitz.com/

handful of my most popular posts, a scrolling list of recent comments on the blog, and navigation by category of post.

Pimping out your blog is easy. If you devote a few hours to it, you can make a very cool-looking blog that even my teenage daughter would approve of. Sure, the standard templates offered by the blog software providers are great to get started, but once you are fully committed to blogging, it is important to make your blog personality shine through with links, images, a masthead, photos, and other add-ons.

Building an Audience for Your New Blog

When you send your first few blog posts, you are likely to hear a deafening silence. You'll be waiting for comments, but none will come. You'll check your site statistics and be disappointed by the tiny number of visitors. Don't get discouraged—that's normal! It takes time to build an audience for your blog. When you're just getting started, make sure people know it is there and can find it! Create links to your blog from your homepage, product pages, or online media room. Mention your blog in your email or offline newsletters, and create links to your blog as part of your email signature and those of other people in your organization.

The good news is that blogs that are regularly updated generate high search engine rankings, because the algorithms that are used by Google, Yahoo!, and the other search engines reward sites (and blogs) that update frequently. It is likely that you will get significant search engine traffic once you've been consistently blogging for a while. I typically post three or four times a week to my blog, and most days my blog generates several hundred visitors via search engines. To ensure that your new blog is found by your buyers as they search for what you have to offer, be certain to post on topics of interest and to use the important phrases that people are searching on (see Chapter 10 if you want to review how to identify the words and phrases that your buyers use). Smart bloggers understand search engines and use their blogs to reach audiences directly.

Commenting on other people's blogs (and including a link to your blog) is a good way to build an audience. If you comment (and track back to) blogs in the same space as yours, you might be surprised at how quickly you will get visitors to your new blog. A curious thing about blogging etiquette is that bloggers who are competitive for business offline are usually very cooperative online, with links back and forth from their blogs. It's a bit like all the auto dealers in town congregating on the same street—proximity is good for everyone, so people work together.

Your customers, potential customers, investors, employees, and the media are all reading blogs, and there is no doubt that blogs are a terrific way for marketers to tell authentic stories to their buyers. But building an audience for a blog takes time. Most blog services provide tools for measuring traffic. Use this data to learn which posts are attracting the most attention. You can also learn what sites people are coming from when they visit your blog and what search terms they used to find you. Use this information to continually improve your blog. Once again, think like a publisher.

Tag, and Your Buyer Is *It*

With the total number of existing blogs now in the tens of millions and with the availability of niche blogs on virtually any topic, it is easy to get lost in the blogosphere. The simple truth is that it isn't always easy for people to find a blog post on subjects of interest. Recently, a colleague of mine needed new tires for his car. Instead of just heading to the local retailer to be at the mercy of a salesperson, or poking around tire manufacturer web sites, he went to one of the blog search engines to see what people were writing about tires. He entered the keyword "tires," and sure enough, within a few clicks he reached several blogs that had useful information about purchasing tires. But he also faced a heck of a lot of useless noise with the word *tires* in the results—things like analysis of tires used in a recent NASCAR race, rants about the garbage on the sides of freeways (which includes discarded tires), and even posts about . . . ahem . . . "spare tires" on middle-aged men.

It is precisely this problem—the false hits in word-and-phrase searches, not middle-aged men's lack of exercise—that led blog search engine Technorati to develop a tagging feature that lets bloggers categorize what their posts are about. To use this feature, a blogger simply creates a set of meta-tags for each blog post. So, if someone is looking for a blog post about tires, she can go to Technorati and search on the tag for tires rather than on the keyword. This gets readers much closer to what they are looking for than a simple word search.

From the blogger's perspective, the benefits of adding tags to create increased precision about the post's content, whereby each post reaches more people, are worth the extra effort. For example, I assign each post that I write to multiple appropriate categories, such as "marketing," "public relations," and "advertising." New visitors reach my blog every day as a result of searching on the tags that I had added to blog posts.

Fun with Sharpies (and Sharpie Fans)

I love Sharpie permanent markers. I carry one in my travel bag at all times, because you never know when you might need one. For instance, there was the time that I accidentally gouged the wooden desk leg in a hotel room. I applied a bit of black Sharpie and it was as good as new! Other people dig Sharpies, too, such as the guy who decorated his basement with a Sharpie, teenagers who personalize their sneakers with multicolor Sharpies, celebrities like the Olsen twins who use them to sign stuff, or people like Mike Peyton, a "snake artist" who uses Sharpies in his work creating wooden snakes decorated with fantastic colors.

Thus, it was fun to come across the Sharpie Blog,[12] "a dedicated space where we can showcase some of the really fun, cool, creative stuff that gets made using Sharpie markers." The blog is written by Susan Wassel, better known as Sharpie Susan. I connected on Twitter with Bert DuMars, vice president of e-business and interactive marketing at Newell Rubbermaid (the makers of Sharpies), to learn more about the blog and others developed by the company.

"Customer surveys showed that Sharpies were fun and creative, but the site, because it is just a product site, was not so much fun," DuMars says. "So that led to the idea of a blog about creativity and art. The blog is about showing additional use for the pens."

I like that the Sharpie blog is not a hard sell. A lot of the blog is focused on art, and Sharpie Susan does a great job showing off the work of the artists. "Sharpie King," for example, creates works that can sell for thousands of dollars. Sharpies already had dedicated fan sites, Facebook groups, and video tributes, so the team needed to work with what was already happening. "We didn't want to invade and ruin much of the social media stuff going on around Sharpie," DuMars says. "We wanted to help push it along a bit."

---

[12] http://blog.sharpie.com/

If your brand is fun and useful, consider the approach taken by Sharpie. Showcase your fans' creativity and let them market for you. And remember that sometimes a minimalist approach is best. As DuMars wisely realized, a heavy-handed campaign might have gotten in the way of the good thing that was already happening. By just joining the party and adding to the fun, the folks at Sharpie showed that they enjoy—and appreciate—their fans' efforts.

Blogging Outside of North America

People often ask me about blogging in other countries. They want to know if the marketing approaches I outline work elsewhere. Specifically, many people ask if blogs are a good way to do marketing and PR in Europe and Asia. While I cannot comment on every single country, I can say that blogging is a global phenomenon in countries with widespread web access and that many bloggers from other countries are active in the global blogging community. I've received links and trackbacks from bloggers in something like 50 different countries. It's so cool when a comment or a link comes into my blog from someone in, say, Russia or Finland or Thailand.

There is other clear evidence that blogging is alive and well outside of North America. TypePad offers services in the United Kingdom, Japan, France, Germany, the Netherlands, Spain, Italy, Finland, and Belgium, in addition to the United States. And Technorati, the blog search engine, maintains sites in English, French, German, Italian, Chinese, and Korean. My wife, Yukari Watanabe Scott,[13] a commentator on the Japanese book business, maintains a blog to reach her readers in Japan. This technique is especially important because her readers there are halfway around the world from where we live, near Boston.

One of my favorite blogs is Adrian Neylan's Cablog,[14] a hilarious collection of stories about his life as a taxi driver in Sydney, Australia. This is what blogging is all about: giving a global voice to a common bloke, transforming him into a totally uncommon international media personality. Neylan shares fascinating stories about the people in his taxi's backseat and, in a funny way, tells us a little about ourselves, even though many of us are a dozen time zones away. When I visited Sydney in mid-2009, I hired Neylan to drive me and posted a video interview with him.

[13] http://watanabeyukari.weblogs.jp/youshonews/
[14] www.cablog.com.au/

For a true international blogging success story, consider the example of Linas Simonis, a marketing consultant from Lithuania who established in April 2005 one of the first business blogs[15] in that country. The reaction from the Lithuanian business community was almost immediate. "People didn't know what RSS was in Lithuania at that time, so I created an email subscription to my blog," Simonis says. "By the end of the first year, I had 400 subscribers, and you must remember that less than three-and-a-half million people live in Lithuania, so the equivalent would be something like 40,000 subscribers in the United States."

The business press also took notice. "Now I am quoted as a positioning and marketing expert because of my blog," he says. "Journalists are calling me, not because I pitched them, but because of my blog posts. I did some pitches a while ago, but they were totally unsuccessful. But news on my blog is picked up and used widely by the media. One article on my blog, called 'How to Position Lithuania,' generated two TV appearances on major TV channels in prime time, a radio interview with the country's biggest radio station, and about a dozen pickups in print media. And this was without any effort from my side, without any pitch, all because of great blog content."

But what's really remarkable about Simonis's story is the new business that he generated via his blog. "Three months after I started the blog, my company stopped needing to make cold calls to solicit new business," he says. "The blog and the company web site generated so many requests that we didn't need to actively seek new clients—they come to us. Soon after I started blogging, I was even hired by conference organizers to deliver speeches and seminars, and I had calls from universities to speak to students." Simonis has also started consulting for several corporate clients in Lithuania that wish to establish blogs, and he publishes an English-language blog[16] as a forum to write about positioning strategy in a Web 2.0 world.

What Are You Waiting For?

Everybody I've spoken with about starting a blog has said the same thing (but in slightly different ways). They were all a bit uncomfortable when they started a blog. They felt a little dorky because they didn't know all the

---

[15] www.pozicionavimas.lt/

[16] www.positioningstrategy.com/

unwritten rules. They were even a little scared to push the button on that first post. We've all been there. To get comfortable before you take the plunge, remember back to Chapter 5: You should follow a bunch of blogs in your industry first. What things do you like about those blogs? What's annoying? What would you do differently? Then before you jump into the water by creating your own blog, you can stick your toe in by leaving comments on other people's blogs. Test out your blog voice. Finally, when it feels right, start your own blog. And when you do get going, please send me your URL so I can check it out.

16 Video and Podcasting Made, Well, as Easy as Possible

Creating audio and video content for marketing and PR purposes requires the same attention to appropriate topics as other techniques outlined in this book. It requires targeting individual buyer personas with thoughtful information that addresses some aspect of their life or a problem they face. By doing so, you brand your organization as smart and worthy of doing business with. However, unlike text-based content such as blogs or news releases, audio and video require a modest investment in additional hardware such as microphones and video cameras, as well as software, and, depending on the level of quality you want to achieve, may also necessitate time-consuming editing of the files. Although the actual procedures for podcasting and video are a bit more convoluted than, say, starting a blog, they are still not all that difficult.

Video and Your Buyers

Organizations that deliver products or services that naturally lend themselves to video have been among the first to actively use the medium to market and deliver information about their offerings. For example, many churches routinely shoot video of weekly services and offer it online for anyone to watch, drawing more people into the congregation. Many amateur and professional sports teams, musicians, and theater groups also use video as a marketing and PR tool.

The idea of *companies* using video for Web marketing is still relatively new. Video follows both blogs and podcasting on the adoption curve at organizations that don't have a service that naturally lends itself to video. Some companies are certainly experimenting, typically by embedding video (hosted at YouTube or another video site) into their existing blogs and online media rooms. I'm starting to see video snippets of CEO speeches and quick product demonstrations on corporate blogs, but this is still uncommon within companies.

A Flip Video Camera in Every Pocket

One development that is helping change the relative scarcity of corporate marketing video is the popularity of the Flip video camera.[1] I love mine and take the small and inexpensive digital video camera with me on every business trip. You never know where a great video interview might present itself, like the one I did with Frederick "Fritz" Henderson, CEO of General Motors. Other times, an idea pops up that is best told in video, like the idea in *Do you sell camels?*,[2] which I filmed at the camel market outside Riyadh, Saudi Arabia.

The Flip video camera is quickly becoming an essential tool for marketers to carry at all times. It allows you to always be ready to interview customers, employees, and industry analysts and to quickly post the video on your site or blog. It can also help you shoot short clips showing how your products are made or used. No professionals required.

The thing couldn't be easier to use. There's a big red button on the camera to start and stop filming, and if you want to get fancy, there is also a zoom. That's about it. Even a technology-challenged person like me can use it. The "flip" name comes from the USB drive built into the camera that flips out, making it simple to upload videos to a connected device and then on to You-Tube, Vimeo, or other video-sharing sites. Really, it's that easy. In fact, when people push back on the idea of creating a corporate blog or writing an e-book, I always suggest making some simple and short video interviews with a Flip as an easy way to create valuable content that helps get the word out right away. Hey, did I mention that this is easy?

Some companies have even started experimenting with providing Flip video cameras to employees and even customers. For example, Sven Patrick

---

[1] www.theflip.com/

[2] www.youtube.com/watch?v=jgTZPwqsN64

Larsen, chief marketing officer for Bogota, Columbia-based digital agency Zemoga,[3] told me that he gives custom-designed Flip video cameras to all of his employees and customers. Zemoga decorates the custom cameras with what Larsen calls a "Z Portrait." "The customized Flips started as a cool employee and client gift, but they've quickly become an essential tool for all Zemoga team members," Larsen says. "We've used them at work (to capture client meetings, discovery sessions, and interaction tests), home, and play, and our clients and team members have spread their experiences (and the Zemoga brand) across the Web. It's a terrific example of empowering clients, giving up control of the brand message, and seeing it spread like wildfire as a result!"

Getting Started With Video

Whether they're new to the game or have been offering Web video for years, organizations get their video content onto the computer screens (and video iPods) of buyers in several different ways:

- *Posting to video-sharing sites:* YouTube[4] is the most popular video-sharing site on the Web, although there are others, such as Vimeo.[5] Organizations post video content on YouTube and send people a link to the content (or hope that it goes viral). You can also embed a YouTube video into your site, your blog, or even your news release. Creating a simple video is easy—all you need is a YouTube account and a digital video camera (in case you don't have your Flip yet, note that your mobile phone may have video capability). There are all sorts of enhancements and editing techniques you can use to make the video more professional. An example of compelling video contributed by a company and available on YouTube is the Smirnoff "teapartay" video,[6] which features old-money New Englanders rapping. It reminds me of people I went to college with, so I've watched it a bunch of times. IBM has experimented with "mockumentaries," including a hysterical six-part series

---

[3] http://frombogotawithlove.com/
[4] www.youtube.com/
[5] www.vimeo.com/
[6] www.youtube.com/watch?v=4y4-5Zouvjs

called "The Art of the Sale," which is like a cross between *The Office* and a sales training video. And the viral components of these corporate videos clearly work, because here I am sharing them with you.[7]

- *Developing an online video channel:* Companies that take online video programming seriously develop their own channel, often with a unique URL. Examples include Weber Grills' Weber Nation web site,[8] which features videos of grilling classes.

- *Attempting stealth insertions to YouTube:* Some companies try to sneak corporate-sponsored video onto YouTube in a way that makes it seem like it was consumer-generated. The YouTube community is remarkably skilled at ratting out inauthentic video, so this approach is fraught with danger.

- *Vlogging:* Short for "video blogging," this term refers to video content embedded in a blog. The text part of the blog adds context to each video and aids with search engine marketing.

- *Vodcasting:* A vodcast is like a podcast but with video—a video series tied to a syndication component with iTunes and RSS feeds. For example, BMW[9] offers a weekly vodcast series of two-to-three-minute videos about what's going on at BMW. The company uses the vodcasts to publicize the cool things it's doing around the world.

- *Inviting your customer communities to submit video:* This technique is how some companies, including Mentos and Tourism Queensland (which we learned about in Chapter 6) try to generate viral marketing interest. These companies sponsor contests where customers submit short videos. The best are usually showcased on the company site, and the winners often get prizes. In some cases, the winning videos are also played on TV as "real" commercials.

For much more detailed information about video, check out *Get Seen: Online Video Secrets to Building Your Business* by Steve Garfield.

Owen Mack,[10] co-founder and head of strategy and development for coBRANDiT, a company that does social media video production, is a pioneer

---

[7] www.youtube.com/watch?v=MSqXKp-00hM

[8] www.webernation.com/

[9] www.bmw-web.tv/en/channel/new

[10] http://cobrandit.com/

in using video for marketing and PR purposes. From the early days of online video, Mack has helped companies like Puma and Pabst Brewing create video strategies. "Video is an extension of the blogging ethos," Mack says. "Do you have an interesting story to tell? If you don't, can you develop something? You need to see what people are saying about you already and know how you can mesh with that. Transparency and openness are required. Done properly, video is very compelling."

Knifing the Competition . . . and It's All Caught on Video

Mack has taken his interest and expertise in online video to help create video content to market products for a kitchen retail store his family owns in Boston. Called KitchenArts,[11] it's basically a hardware store for cooks. "We have a staff of only four people, but we launched a vlog," he says. "We shoot quick-and-dirty video about the things that we sell, like how to use kitchen knives. We use a $300 camera, and then we link to our eBay store where people can buy—this is the low-cost, grassroots way to do video."

Mack's use of video for KitchenArts has allowed the small company to present information in a way that the big players don't. "Our competition is places like Williams-Sonoma," he says. "I can't compete with them by doing a better web site. But I can do a better job with video. I can transmit the ethos and show the personality and demonstrate knowledge of our products on the Web. It's basically home video, but we show how to use things and demonstrate products, so we compete with the big guys. It's also cheap. The eBay store and blog software combined is only about $50 a month."

KitchenArts has nearly 100 different products for sale online, each with a short video demonstration segment. "It's not making barrel-loads of money, but the sales we make from video as a percentage of my extremely low costs represent terrific margins."

Mack sees video as an important component in an effective marketing mix. "For brands big and small, it's just about putting out interesting and engaging information about your story," he says. "Anybody can do it. The bigger companies can build brand communities to excite brand loyalists and advocates. In this way, video extends the two-way dialog of the blog."

---

[11] http://cobrandit.com/kitchenarts/

Podcasting 101

A podcast is a piece of audio content tied to a subscription component so people can receive regular updates. The simplest way to think of podcasting is that it's like a radio show except that you listen to each episode at your convenience by downloading it either to your computer or to a mobile device like an iPod. The equipment you need to start podcasting will range in cost from a few hundred dollars at the low end to a bit over a thousand dollars for professional-level sound. Plus, you'll probably want to host your audio files on an external server requiring a monthly fee.

How do you get started? "I've found that the most important thing is show preparation," says John J. Wall, producer and co-host of Marketing Over Coffee,[12] a twenty-minute news, talk, and entertainment show covering both new and classic marketing. "Unless you are real comfortable talking extemporaneously, you will want to have a script laid out ahead of time. It just sounds more polished when you do." I don't have my own podcast, but as a frequent guest on radio shows and podcasts, I agree with Wall—the best shows I participate in are those where the interviewer knows the material and keeps things focused.

Beginning with developing a script, following are the steps and technical issues involved with producing a podcast. To really learn the ins and outs before you start your own podcast, you might want to check out one of the detailed books on the subject, such as *Podcasting for Dummies*, 2nd edition, by Tee Morris and Evo Terra.

- *Show preparation* includes gathering ideas for the show and creating a script. Think about your buyer personas and what you can discuss that interests them. If you plan to interview guests, make sure you know how to pronounce their names (don't laugh, this is a frequent mistake) and you have their titles, affiliations, and other information correct. It's common practice to plug a guest's business, so know ahead of time what URL or product you will mention.
- *Recording when you are near your computer* is done with a microphone (many options to choose from) that delivers the audio into your

---

[12] www.marketingovercoffee.com/

computer. You'll need podcasting software such as StudioRack[13] as an interface to create and publish your podcast.

- *Mobile recording gear* is required if you are going to do the roving-reporter thing and interview people at events or perhaps your employees around the world. Mobile recording gear is made by several companies including Marantz.[14]
- *Phone interviews* require a way to record both sides of a conversation. A good way to go is to use Skype[15] through your computer and then record on a digital recorder (again, try Marantz).
- *Editing your audio files* is optional; you can always just upload the files as you recorded them. If you choose to clean them up, you can edit at the micro-scale (removing *um*, *uh*, and other audible pauses) or at the macro-scale (e.g., removing the last five minutes of an interview). Many podcasters edit segments that they recorded at different times, putting them together to create a show. Audacity[16] and Apple's GarageBand[17] are two software packages that include many of the audio capabilities of a professional radio station and make editing simple.
- *Postproduction editing* sometimes includes running a noise-reduction program (to get rid of that annoying air-conditioner noise in the background) and sound compression (to even out the volume of sections that have been recorded at different times and places). The Levelator[18] is a free application that can be used for both purposes.
- *Tagging the audio* is an important step that some people overlook or perform without taking due care. This step involves adding text-based information about the audio to make it easier for people to find. This information is what appears in the search engines and audio distribution sites such as iTunes. Your tags also display on listeners' iPod displays, so don't ignore or gloss over this step.
- *Hosting and distribution* are necessary to ensure that people can easily obtain your podcasts. Services such as Liberated Syndication[19] host the

---

[13] http://studiorack.com/

[14] www.d-mpro.com/users/folder.asp?FolderID=1823

[15] www.skype.com/

[16] http://audacity.sourceforge.net/

[17] www.apple.com/ilife/garageband/

[18] www.conversationsnetwork.org/levelator

[19] https://www.libsyn.com/

(sometimes very large) audio files and syndicate them to the distribution networks such as iTunes.

- *Promotion* is essential to make sure that people find out about your podcasts. If you do interview shows (which are an easy way to get started and provide excellent content), make sure that you provide links to the show to all of the guests. Many people will help you promote a show that they have been featured on. You will also want to network with other podcasters in your space, because very short on-air plugs cross-promoting other podcasts are common and a good way for people to build audiences. Don't forget to put links to your podcast on your web site, in your email signature, and on your offline materials including business cards and brochures. Also, send out a news release alerting people to important shows (see Chapter 17).

- *A companion blog* is a key component used by nearly all pod-casters to discuss the content of each show. An important reason for having a companion blog is that its text will be indexed by the search engines, driving more people to sign up for the podcast feed. A blog also allows the show's host to write a few paragraphs about the content of that particular show and to provide links to the blogs and web sites of guests who will be appearing (so people can get a sense of a show's content prior to listening). Most organizations that use podcasting as a marketing tool also use the podcast blog as a place to move people into the sales process by providing links to the company site or to demonstrations or trial offers.

"You can be up and running with your new podcast in less than a month," says Wall. "The principles are all quite simple, but it takes a bit of time to figure out the various hardware and software elements. But the community is very helpful. Make sure you let other podcasters know that you have a new show, because we often reference each other with quick on-air plugs."

My Audio Is Your Podcast

The Student Loan Network[20] is an online student loan company that's been around since 1998. The company is a significant lender, with $150 million to $200 million in loans produced each year. The Student Loan Network site

---

[20] www.studentloannetwork.com/

excels as an online guide to student loans and financial aid, and it reaches students and parents directly with financial aid advice and student loan services. Particularly interesting is the company's *Financial Aid Podcast*,[21] a six-days-per-week podcast available on iTunes and other podcast distribution and subscription services.

"We're always looking for a competitive edge online," says Christopher S. Penn, chief evangelist for The Student Loan Network and host of *Financial Aid Podcast*. His show helps students (and some parents, too) make college more affordable by discussing topics such as credit cards, international student issues, private student loans, and scholarships. But Penn also produces episodes dealing with other aspects of finance that interest young people. The podcast was the first and is by far the most popular show about financial aid for college-bound students. "So much of modern American society revolves around money in one way or another, and the more I learn about it, the more I see, the more I understand," Penn says on the bio page of his podcast's companion blog. "Money, economics, all that stuff is so important, so vital to understand, and it's what really drives me to crank out a podcast every single day. Each day, another piece gets added to the puzzle, and I know a little bit more about how to make the world work for me—and for my listeners."

"The audience for *Financial Aid Podcast* is primarily people who are looking to get into college, are currently in college, or have just graduated," Penn says. "The nice thing about the college aid demographic is that they all have iPods, which is ideal for the podcast as a marketing tool." Because Penn understands his buyer personas—young people—he can speak to them in an authentic, resonant way. Penn knows that for his demographic, a podcast is perfect, because so many people are already listening to audio and have iTunes accounts.

"Podcasting is great marketing because, like blogging, it is a human voice," Penn says. "Most podcasts don't have a PR stamp on them, so the shows come across as being human. The reason why this is interesting is that there is a big marketing shift going on right now. The older, traditional advertising model, like 1950s TV, is that we publish and you consume. However, today's marketing model is that we publish and you respond. It provides me real feedback from real people, and I have conversations. I can be interactive."

---

[21] www.financialaidpodcast.com/

Penn sees a clear link between marketing and customer service at companies. He suggests that customer service needs to be real and authentic and have a human voice, just like great marketing. "There is no such thing as 'on message' anymore," Penn says. "[Customer service] is no longer about spin, but instead becoming a part of the conversation. Now I think that companies that do not make the jump to blogging and podcasting and interacting with customers look like dinosaurs. Some industries are tailor-made for this, but they do not get it. For example, I would think that real estate agents could do a great job with video podcasts, but it is very rare. If you have a customer services department, you need to be doing this kind of marketing."

Penn has conducted research about his audience and has adapted his show accordingly. "Podcasting is time-shifted," he says. "You can take it with you and listen to it at any time. My shows are all 18 to 24 minutes, because 24 minutes is the average commute, and the average American's attention span is 18 minutes." Penn also has an interesting perspective on competition. He says that he competes with every other podcaster, because listeners have only 24 hours in a day.

Penn has learned that the best way to drive his listeners into The Student Loan Network sales process is to mention URLs on his show. But he is quick to point out that the show is not a sales pitch. "The podcast is not an immediate business generator. We are real and authentic. We want to help people. We want to be beneficial to people," he says. However, based on promotions the company has run on the podcast and other social media properties like ScholarshipPoints.com, Penn estimates that $75 million of loans are generated directly from the podcast and social media. "It's way beyond beer money," he says.

Who would have thought that a podcast would help to sell tens of millions of dollars in student loans? What Penn clearly realized was that members of his buyer persona, young people, are active podcast listeners. Penn's decision to start the *Financial Aid Podcast* has certainly paid off; are you missing out on a similar opportunity?

Audio and video content on the Web is still new for marketers and communicators. But the potential to deliver information to buyers in fresh and unique ways is greater when you use a new medium. And while your competition is still trying to figure out "that blogging thing," you can leverage your existing blog into the new worlds of audio and video and leave the competition way behind.

17

How to Use News Releases to Reach Buyers Directly

As the fascinating case studies from Chapter 7 show, the Web has changed the rules for news releases. Buyers now read your news releases on Google, Yahoo!, and other search engines, on vertical market portals, and with RSS readers. Thus, smart marketing and PR professionals craft news releases to reach buyers directly, propelling books to number-one spots on bestseller lists, driving more Web traffic, securing more donations, and selling more products. Again, this is not to suggest that mainstream media and media relations programs are no longer important. In most markets, mainstream media and the trade press remain vital. But your primary audience is no longer just a handful of journalists. Your audience is millions of people with Internet connections and access to search engines and RSS readers. So, how do you get started with a direct-to-buyer news release program? Let's start by recalling the New Rules of News Releases from Chapter 7:

- Don't just send news releases when big news is happening; find good reasons to send them all the time.
- Instead of just targeting a handful of journalists, create news releases that appeal directly to your buyers.
- Write releases that are replete with keyword-rich copy.
- Include offers that compel consumers to respond to your release in some way.
- Place links in releases to deliver potential customers to landing pages on your web site.

- Optimize news release delivery for searching and browsing.
- Add social media tags for Technorati, DIGG, and del.icio.us so your release will be found.
- Drive people into the sales process with news releases.

In this chapter, we'll use these rules to develop a news release strategy.

Developing Your News Release Strategy

The most important thing to think about as you begin a news release program is, once again, the need to write for your buyers. You should consider what you learned through the buyer persona research part of your marketing and PR plan (described in Chapter 10) and develop an editorial calendar for news releases based on what buyers need to know. Implementing a news release strategy to reach buyers directly is like publishing an online news service— you are providing your buyers with information that they need in order to find your organization online and then learn more about you.

Part of thinking like a publisher is remembering the critical importance of content. "Everything is content-driven in public relations," says Brian Hennigan, marketing communications manager for dbaDIRECT,[1] a data infrastructure management company. "I like using news releases to reach the market and my potential customers.

With news releases, for a hundred bucks you can talk to the world." Hennigan supplements his news releases with longer and more detailed white papers to get dbaDIRECT ideas into the market. "I write the news releases like news stories," he says. "We look at the needs of the market and entrepreneurial trends as interesting, and we write to these trends."

As you make this fundamental change in how you do news releases, you will probably find yourself wondering, at first, what to write about. The rule of thumb is: Big news is great, but don't wait. Write about pretty much anything that your organization is doing.

- Have a new take on an old problem? Write a release.
- Serve a unique marketplace? Write a release.
- Have interesting information to share? Write a release.
- CEO speaking at a conference? Write a release.

---

[1] www.dbadirect.com/

- Win an award? Write a release.
- Add a product feature? Write a release.
- Win a new customer? Write a release.
- Publish a white paper? Write a release.
- Get out of bed this morning? Okay, maybe not . . . but now you're thinking the right way!

Publishing News Releases through a Distribution Service

The best way to publish news releases so they are seen by your buyers is to simultaneously post a release to your own web site and send it to one of the news release wires. The benefit of using a news release distribution service is that your release will be sent to tne online news services, including Yahoo!, Google, Bing, and many others. Many news release distribution services reach trade and industry web sites as well. In fact, you can often reach hundreds of web sites with a single news release. The significant benefit of this approach is that your release will be indexed by the news search engines and vertical market sites, and then when somebody does a search for a word or phrase contained in your release, *presto*, that potential customer finds you. As an added bonus, people who have requested alerts about your industry from sites that index news releases will get an alert that something important—your news release—is available.

There are a number of options for wire distribution of news releases. I've included some of the U.S. news release distribution services here. Similar services exist in other countries, such as CanadaNewsWire[2] serving the Canadian market. Take a look at the various services and compare them yourself.

A Selection of the Larger U.S. News Release Distribution Services

- Business Wire: www.businesswire.com
- GlobeNewswire: www.globenewswire.com
- Marketwire: www.marketwire.com
- PrimeNewswire: www.primenewswire.com
- PR Newswire: www.prnewswire.com
- PRWeb: www.prweb.com

---

[2] www.newswire.ca/

In order to get your news releases to appear on the online news services, including Google News, you just have to purchase a basic news release coverage area offered by a news release distribution service. Coverage is based on geographical distribution of your release to reporters. Because I am located in the Boston area, the cheapest distribution with some services for me is the Boston region. The services also have many value-added options for you to consider, such as national distribution. But what is important to know is that most news release distribution services include distribution to online media such as Google News in *any geographical distribution*. So, as you make your choice, remember that when your purpose for sending news releases is to reach buyers via search engines and vertical sites, maximizing the newsroom and geographical reach offered by a service is less important than ensuring that your releases are included on major online news sites.

Reaching Even More Interested Buyers with RSS Feeds

Many news release distribution services also offer RSS (Really Simple Syndication) feeds of their news releases, which they make available to other sites, blogs, journalists, and individuals. This means that each time you publish a news release with the service, the news release is seen by thousands of people who have subscribed to the RSS content feeds in your market category (as offered by the distribution service). So if you tag your release as being important for the automotive industry, your news release will be delivered to anyone (or any site) that has subscribed to the news release distribution service's automotive RSS feed. And online news services such as Google News have RSS feed capability, too, allowing people to receive feeds based on keywords and phrases. Each time your release includes a word or phrase of importance to someone who has saved it as part of their alerts, a link to your news releases will appear via email or RSS feed in near real time in the future.

Simultaneously Publishing Your News Releases to Your Web Site

Post your news releases to an appropriate and readily findable section of your web site. Many organizations have a media room or press section of their web site, which is ideal (see Chapter 18 for details on how to create your online media room). You should keep the news release live for as long as the content is appropriate, perhaps for years. This is very important because most of the online news sites do not maintain archives of news for more than a few months. If potential customers look for the content of your news release the week after it is distributed via a service, they will certainly find it on Google News and the others. But they won't find it if they do the search next year unless the release is on your own site as a permanent link so that it is indexed by Google.

The Importance of Links in Your News Releases

Particularly because your releases may be delivered by feeds or on news services and various sites other than your own, creating links from your news releases to content on your web site is very important. These links, which might point to a specific offer or to a landing page with more information, allow your buyers to move from the news release to specific content on your web site that will then drive them into the sales process, as we saw in the previous chapter.

However, there is another enormous benefit to including links in news releases. Each time your news release is posted on another site, such as an online news site, the inbound link from the online news site to your web site helps to increase the search engine ranking of your site, because the search engines use inbound links as one of the important criteria for their page-ranking algorithms. So when your news release has a link to your site and it is indexed somewhere on the Web, you actually increase the ranking of the pages on your site! Said another way, when your news release appears on a web site somewhere and there is a link in your news release that points to a URL on your site, the search engines will increase the rankings of the page where the URL is pointing. Sending a news release that includes links increases your own web site's search engine rankings.

Focus on the Keywords and Phrases Your Buyers Use

As I've suggested before, one thing successful publishers do that Web marketers should emulate is to understand the audience first and then set about to satisfy their informational needs. A great way to start thinking like a publisher and to create news releases that drive action is to focus on your customers' problems and then create and deliver news releases accordingly. Use the words and phrases that your buyers use. Think about how the people you want to reach are searching, and develop news release content that includes those words and phrases. You can get the information you need to do so by thinking back to your buyer personas. Don't be egotistical and write only about your organization. What are your buyers' problems? What do they want to know? What words and phrases do they use to describe these problems? I know, I've said this already several times—that's because it is very important.

CruiseCompete.com,[3] cited by *Kiplinger* as one of the 25 Best Travel Sites, helps people secure quotes for cruises from multiple travel agencies, based on the dates and ports specified. CruiseCompete.com is a great example of a company that uses news releases to reach people based on the phrases that their buyers are searching with. For example, during the lead-up to the holiday season, the company issued a news release via Market Wire with the headline "Cruise Lines Set Sail With Hot Holiday Vacation Prices." Importantly, part of an early sentence in the release, " . . . some seven-night vacations can be booked for well under $1,000 per person, including Thanksgiving cruises, Christmas cruises and New Year's cruises," included three critical phrases. Not only did this release's mention of "Thanksgiving cruises," "Christmas cruises," and "New Year's cruises" generate traffic from users searching on these common phrases, it also helped guide searchers into the sales cycle; each of the three phrases in the news release was hyperlinked to a purpose-built landing page on the CruiseCompete.com site that displayed the holiday cruise deals. Anyone who clicked on the "Christmas cruises" link was taken directly to deals for Christmas cruises.[4]

What makes this case so exciting is that at the time I was writing this, the CruiseCompete.com holiday cruise news release was at the top of the Google News search results for the phrases "Thanksgiving cruises," "Christmas cruises," and "New Year's cruises." More importantly, the bump that the links in the news release gave to the three landing pages helped those pages reach the top of the Google Web search results lists. For example, the

---

[3] www.cruisecompete.com/

[4] www.cruisecompete.com/specials/holiday/christmas_cruises/1

CruiseCompete.com landing page for the phrase "Christmas cruise" was ranked in the fourth position among 5,830,000 other hits on Google.

"We know that people have thought about traveling for the holidays," says Heidi M. Allison-Shane,[5] a consultant working with CruiseCompete.com. "We use the news releases to communicate with consumers that now is the time to book, because there are dynamite prices and they will sell out." Allison-Shane makes sure that CruiseCompete includes the ideal phrases in each news release and that each release has appropriate links to the site. This strategy makes reaching potential customers a matter of "simply understanding what people are likely to be searching on and then linking them to the correct page on the site where we have the content that's relevant," she says. "We try to be useful with the right content and to be focused on what's relevant for our consumers and to provide the links that they need. This stuff is not difficult."

The CruiseCompete.com news release program produces results by increasing the Google rankings for the site. But the news releases also reach buyers directly as those buyers search on relevant phrases. "Each time we send a targeted news release, we see a spike in the Web traffic on the site," Allison-Shane says.

As you craft your own phrases to use in your news releases, don't get trapped by your own jargon; think, speak, and write like your customers do. Though you may have a well-developed lexicon for your products and services, these words don't necessarily mean much to your potential customers. As you write news releases (or any other form of Web content), focus on the words and phrases that your buyers use. As a search engine marketing tool, news releases are only as valuable as the keywords and phrases that are contained in them.

Include Appropriate Social Media Tags

Many (but not all) news release distribution services provide a way to include social media tags to make the news releases easy to find on services like Technorati, DIGG, and del.icio.us. Use them! Social media tags make your releases much easier to find. For example, the Technorati search engine, which many people turn to for the latest blog posts from around the world in

---

[5] www.allisonandtaylor.com/

categories that interest them, also include news release content. So if I check out the "Marketing" category on Technorati (which I frequently do), I will see not only the latest blog posts that are tagged "Marketing" by the blogger but also any news releases that are tagged "Marketing" by the organization that issued the release. The key is that in an online world, you must do everything you can to ensure that your news releases are displayed and retrievable in as many relevant places as possible.

To make it easy to remember all the various tags and other features (such as associated photos and audio feeds) of a well-executed news release, Todd Defren, principal at SHIFT Communications, created a social media news release template.[6] "All news release content will ultimately wind up on the Web," he says. "So why not put it out in such a way that makes it accessible to anybody who can use that content? Both traditional and new-media journalists are used to working in a hyperlinked environment and are used to people providing context through social bookmarking sites such as del.icio.us and buttons to add to DIGG. The template makes it easy to remember to do all of those things." Defren's template is an excellent tool to use as you develop your news releases because it helps you get the most out of all the available features that can make the release more useful and easier to find.

If It's Important Enough to Tell the Media, Tell Your Clients and Prospects, Too!

Many companies devote extensive resources to their PR and media relations programs. Often, the results of these efforts are buried in a difficult-to-find news section of the company web site. Consider rewriting your news releases in an easy-to-read paragraph or two and make it a section of your email newsletter for clients and prospects. Or establish RSS feeds to deliver your news to anyone who's interested. And don't forget your employees—if they know about your news, they can be your greatest evangelists.

One of the most cost-effective ways to reach buyers is to look for ways to leverage the work you're already doing by repurposing content for other audiences. Too often, organizations spend tons of money on, say, a PR program that targets a handful of journalists but fails to communicate the same

---

[6] www.pr-squared.com

information to other constituents. Or a company's advertising program designed to generate new sales may drive people to a web site that doesn't match the message of the ads, resulting in lost interest. Sadly, the failure to integrate sales, marketing, and communications—both online and offline—will always result in lost opportunities. Happily, the Web makes it a relatively simple task to integrate your news release program into your larger online strategy.

Here's one more thing that you may never have considered: Having a regular editorial calendar that includes a series of news releases also means your company is busy. When people go to your online media room and find a lack of news releases, they often assume that you are not moving forward or that you have nothing to contribute to the industry. In the new world of marketing, consistent, high-quality news release content brands a company or a nonprofit as a busy market player, an active expert in the industry, and a trusted resource to turn to.

18

The Online Media Room: Your Front Door for Much More Than the Media

The online media room (sometimes called a press room or press page) is the part of your organization's web site that you create specifically for the media. In some organizations this page is simply a list of news releases with contact information for the organization's PR person. But many companies and nonprofits have elaborate online media rooms with a great deal of information available in many different formats: audio, video, photos, news releases, background information, financial data, and much more. A close cousin to the online media room is the online Investor Relations room that many public companies maintain; however, I don't cover IR sites in this book.

Before I give you ideas on how to create a valuable online media room of your own, I want you to consider something that is vitally important: All kinds of people visit your online media room, not just journalists. Stop and really let that soak in for a moment. Your buyers are snooping around your organization by visiting the media pages on your web site. Your current customers, partners, investors, suppliers, and employees all visit those pages. Why is that? Based on casual research I've done (I often speak about visitor statistics with employees who are responsible for their organizations' online media rooms), I'm convinced that when people want to know what's *current* about an organization, they go to an online media room.

Visitors expect that the main pages of a web site are basically static (i.e., they are not updated often), but they also expect that the news releases and media-targeted pages on a site will reveal the very latest about a company. For many companies, the news release section is one of the most frequently visited parts of the web site. Check out your own web site statistics; you may be amazed at how many visitors are already reading your news releases and other media pages online.

So I want you to do something that many traditional PR people think is nuts. I want you to design your online media room for your *buyers*. By building a media room that targets buyers, you will not only enhance those pages as a powerful marketing tool, you will also *make a better media site for journalists*. I've reviewed hundreds of online media rooms, and the best ones are built with buyers in mind. This approach may sound a bit radical, but believe me, it works.

Your Online Media Room as (Free) Search Engine Optimization

When news releases are posted on your site, search engine crawlers will find the content, index it, and rank it based on words, phrases, and other factors. Because news release pages update more often than any other part of a typical organization's web site, search engine algorithms (tuned to pay attention to pages that update frequently) tend to rank news release pages among the highest on your site, driving traffic there first.

"There's no question that a well organized media room often has higher search results and drives more traffic because of the way the search engines work," says Dee Rambeau, founder and managing partner of The Fuel Team, a provider of online tools for professional business communicators. "A news release dynamically builds out a new set of content in your online media room, with each news release generating its own indexable page, which the search engines all capture. Google and the other search engines love fresh content that relates back to similar content on the other pages of the site. Aggressive companies take advantage of this by sending news releases frequently to get high rankings from the search engines. Frequency has a great deal to do with search engine rankings—if you do 10 news releases, that's great; 20 is better, and 100 is better still."

When an explosion at the Imperial Sugar Company (ISC) sugar refinery at Port Wentworth (near Savannah, GA) occurred in February 2008, fires burned for nearly two weeks. It was the mainstream media's dream story: death and fire affecting a big corporation. Unfortunately for ISC, when journalists writing their stories turned to the search engines for information about the company, many outdated reports and information appeared on the first pages of Google and the other search engines.

When the crisis subsided, executives at ISC hired David E. Henderson and the team at The News Group Net LLC[1] to create a brand-new, content-rich ISC Newsroom.[2] "The ISC Newsroom positions the Imperial Sugar Company as an authoritative voice in the sugar industry, in the U.S., Mexico, and elsewhere," says Henderson, an Emmy-Award-winning former CBS News correspondent and veteran communications strategist. "It is a one-stop shop for the best thinking and views on sugar and all of the issues and market forces that surround it."

Henderson and his team chose to present a steady flow of legitimate news stories (not just press releases) as well as high-quality news images shot by former AP and *People* photographer Ed Lallo.[3] "While most corporate online newsrooms are dusty and static press release archives, ISC Newsroom is always fresh, not only with stories about the company but about the industry, customers, and the communities in which the company does business," Henderson says.

According to Henderson, the main goal of the ISC Newsroom is to be clearly heard and stand out in all of the right ways. "We're expressing the ISC corporate voice above the noise of the marketplace, where often people much less qualified—but far more vocal—pump out their opinions into mainstream and social media. The sheer speed, volume, and rapid dissemination of information—right or wrong—can inundate communications and sway public opinion," he says. Of course, when a company like ISC creates information in a newsroom and updates it frequently, the valuable content is indexed by the search engines and will gravitate into the top positions.

Best Practices for Online Media Rooms

An online media room is an important part of any organization's web site and a critical aspect of an effective media relations strategy. When done well, an online media room will turn journalists who are just browsing into interested

---

[1] www.thenewsgroup.net/
[2] www.iscnewsroom.com/
[3] www.lallophoto.com/

writers who will highlight your organization positively in their stories. And more importantly, an online media room can move your buyers into and through the sales process, resulting in more business for your organization and contributing to meeting your organization's *real goals* of revenue and customer retention. I've noticed as I've checked out hundreds of online media rooms that most fail to deliver compelling content. Sure, they may look pretty, but often the design and graphics, not the content that journalists (and your buyers) require, are in the forefront. The following sections give you useful tips that will help your online media room work as effectively as some of the best ones I've seen.

You Control the Content

One important consideration that many marketing and PR people overlook when considering the benefits of an online media room is that *you control the content*, not your IT department, Webmaster, or anyone else. The best practice idea here is for *you* to design your online media room as a tool to reach buyers and journalists, and you don't need to take into consideration the rules for posting content that the rest of the organization's site may require. If you build this part of your site using a specialized online media room content-management application such as the one offered by The Fuel Team[4] or the MediaRoom[5] product from PR Newswire, you will control a corner of your organization's web site that you can update whenever you like using simple tools, and you won't need to request help from anyone in other departments or locations. So start with your needs and the needs of your buyers and journalists, not the needs of those who own the other parts of your organization's web site.

Start with a Needs Analysis

When designing a new online media room (or planning an extensive re-design), start with a needs analysis. Before you just jump right into site aesthetics and the organization of news releases, take time to analyze how the

---

[4] www.thefuelteam.com/
[5] www.mediaroom.com/

site fits into your larger marketing, PR, and media relations strategy. Consider the buyer persona profiles you built as part of your marketing and PR plan. Talk with friendly journalists so you can understand what they need. Who are the potential users of the online media room and what content will be valuable to them? When you have collected some information, build buyers' and journalists' needs into your online media room. As you work toward starting your design, try to think a bit more like a publisher and less like a marketing and PR person. A publisher carefully identifies and defines target audiences and then develops the content required to meet the needs of each distinct demographic. Graphical elements, colors, fonts, and other visual manifestations of the site are also important but should take a back seat during the content-needs analysis process.

Optimize Your News Releases for Searching and for Browsing

The best online media rooms are built with the understanding that some people need to search for content and others are browsing. Many people already know what they are looking for—the latest release, perhaps, or the name of the CEO. They need answers to specific questions, and organizations must therefore optimize content so that it can be found, perhaps by including a search engine. The second way that people use content is to be told something that they do not already know and therefore couldn't think to ask. This is why browsability is also important; it allows users to stumble across useful information they didn't even know they were looking for. While many Web-savvy marketers understand the importance of search-engine optimization, they often forget that sites must be designed for browsing, too. Failing to do so is particularly unfortunate because the high traffic on news release pages comes partly from the many people who browse these pages as they conduct research.

You should deploy a navigational design in a way that provides valuable information visitors might not have thought to ask for. Consider including multiple browsing techniques. For instance, you can create different links to targeted releases for different buyer personas (maybe by vertical market or some other demographic factor appropriate to your organization). You might also organize the same releases by product (because some members of the media may be covering just one of your products in a review or story), by geography, or by market served. Most organizations simply list news releases in reverse-chronological order (the newest release is at the top of the page, and ones from last year are hidden away somewhere). While this is fine for the main news release page, you need to have additional navigation links so people can browse the releases. Don't forget that people may also need to print out news releases, so consider providing printer-friendly formats (e.g., PDF format as well as HTML).

Create Background Information That Helps Journalists Write Stories

You should publish a set of background materials about your organization, sometimes called an online media kit or press kit, in an easy-to-find place in your online media room. This kit should contain a lot of information, basically anything you think journalists might need in order to write about you and your products or services. Company history and timeline, executive biographies, investor profiles, board of advisors' or board of directors' bios, product and service information, information about analysts who cover your company, and links to recent media coverage will help your media kit save journalists time and tedious effort. Make this content easy to find and to browse with appropriate navigational links. I think a set of information organized around customers and how they use products and services offered by the company is another key component of an online media room, and I rarely see it. Case studies in the customers' own words are particularly useful, not only for journalists but also for buyers. Remember, the easier you make a journalist's job, the more likely she is to write about your organization, particularly when she is on a tight deadline. I recall researching a feature story I was writing for *EContent* magazine called "On Message: The Market for Marketing-Specific Content Management." In the article I was looking at companies and products that help marketers to organize information, and I knew the top players in the field and interviewed company executives for the article. But to round out the piece, I needed to include some newer niche companies in the space. How did I choose the companies that made it in? You guessed it—the ones that made my job easiest by having an effective online media room that helped me to instantly understand the company and its products.

Include Multimedia Content

Innovative communicators make use of nontext content, such as photos, charts, graphs, audio feeds, and video clips, to inform site visitors and the media. Include executive photos, logo images, product photos, and other content that is ready (and preapproved) to be published or linked to by journalists. You should offer audio and video clips (such as parts of executive speeches or product demonstrations), photos, and logos in such a way that journalists can use them in their written stories as well as on TV and radio shows. Again, you will find that many people besides journalists will access this, so include appropriate content for your buyer personas as well as for the media.

For an excellent example of the use of video, check out how Neighborhood America[6] integrated video into the company's online media room.

Include Detailed Product Specs and Other Valuable Data

Communicators who use online media rooms to offer valuable content are more likely to score the positive story. However, organizations often shy away from posting much of their best content because they deem it proprietary. On many sites, even information like detailed product specifications and price lists are available only through a direct connection with a PR contact or a lengthy registration form with approval mechanisms. Yet this is exactly the sort of content that, if freely available, would help convince journalists to write a story. All communicators and marketing professionals working at corporations, government agencies, or nonprofits struggle to decide what content is appropriate to post on their organizations' sites. However, with well-meaning executives who worry about corporate image, legal departments with a reflexive tendency to say "no," and salespeople who think it is easier to sell when they're the sole source of knowledge, it might be difficult to gain the necessary approvals to post proprietary content. But there is no doubt that the more valuable your media room's content looks to reporters and buyers, the more attractive your company will look to them as well.

---

[6] www.neighborhoodamerica.com/mediaroom

If Appropriate, Go Global

The Web has made reaching the world far easier, so when it is appropriate, the effort to create and offer local content to customers worldwide can help an organization better serve both local and global journalists. Many organizations, particularly those headquartered in the United States, make the mistake of including site content that reflects (and therefore has value for) only the home market. Basic approaches to get your site up to global standards might include offering case studies from customers in various countries or spec sheets describing products with local country standards (such as metric measurements or local regulatory compliance). Sometimes the little things make a difference. For example, don't forget that the rest of the world uses standard A4 paper instead of the U.S. letter size, so having fact sheets and other materials that print properly on both formats is useful to users outside the United States. Providing content in local languages can also help show the global aspect of your business, though this need not mean a wholesale translation of your entire online media room. A simple Web landing page with basic information in the local language, a few news releases, a case study or two, and appropriate local contact information will often suffice.

Provide Content for All Levels of Media Understanding

To be effective, communicators at many organizations specifically design media room content that supports journalists' level of knowledge of your organization. Some journalists may never have written about your company before; they need the basics spelled out in easy-to-understand language. In other cases, a reporter or analyst may have been covering the company for years, enjoy personal relationships with the executives, and know a great deal about what's going on with you, your competitors, and your market. You need content for this person, too; she may want to compare your offerings, and she therefore needs detailed company information, lists of features and benefits, and stories about your customers. Of course, all reporters need easy navigation directly to content so they get what they need quickly. In my experience, the vast majority of online media rooms are little more than online brochures with a bunch of news releases. Don't let the opportunities that the Web offers pass your online media room by. Help journalists along the path to their keyboards by offering content directly linked to their various levels of understanding.

List Executive Appearances, Conferences, and Tradeshow Participation

One of the best ways to positively influence journalists is to visit with them in person. Many journalists attend tradeshows, conferences, and other events on a regular basis and use that time to meet with representatives of companies that they may consider writing about. The best way to get your organization on journalists' calendars is to make certain that they know where your executives will be appearing. List all appropriate public speaking appearances, tradeshow and conference participation, and other events in a separate calendar section in your online media room. Make certain to list all appropriate future events, and remember to include any international events. Keep the older listings up for at least a few months after the events to show that you are in demand as experts in your field, but be sure to keep the list up to date. Don't forget that even this information is not just for the media. Even if they do not attend industry events, your buyers will see that your company is active and that your executives are in demand as speakers and presenters; this adds to your corporate credibility and your image as an industry leader.

Include Calls to Action for Journalists

It is a great idea to include special offers for the media. Perhaps the simplest thing to offer is an executive interview. But why not include a trial or demonstration offer of some kind, where journalists get to test out your offerings, attend your events, or in some way experience what your organization does? You can even create a landing page specifically for journalists with a registration form and special offers. Include this link within news releases and other pages in the online media room to drive interested journalists to the landing page.

Embrace Bloggers as You Do Traditional Journalists

Bloggers who cover your company visit your online media room. Encourage them by responding to inquiries quickly, by including bloggers in your news release distribution email list, and by granting them interviews with executives upon request. The fact is that bloggers are influential, and they want to be treated with the same respect as traditional journalists. It's to your advantage to do so.

Avoid Jargon, Acronyms, and Industry-Speak

I review more than a hundred news releases in an average week. Some releases are sent directly to me from companies that want me to write about them in a magazine article, an upcoming book, or my blog, and others I find by checking out online media rooms. I visit many online media rooms in an average week and read the other content available as well as news releases. Unfortunately, most online media rooms are chock full of jargon, three-letter acronyms that I don't understand, and other egocentric nonsense. I'm interested in what companies are up to, but I'm just too busy to decipher gobbledygook. I normally give a news release 10 seconds to catch my attention, but the surest way to get me to delete a release in frustration is to write in a way that I just can't understand. If your mother doesn't understand your news, a journalist probably won't, either.

An Online Media Room to Reach Journalists, Customers, Bloggers, and Employees

"As we were looking for solutions to reach the media, one of the frustrations we had was getting timely information onto our corporate web site," says Clay Owen, senior director of media relations at Cingular Wireless. "We used to have a process that went through the Information Technology department, and they would say 'Okay, we will get it up onto the site a week from Thursday.' But I used to be a producer at CNN, and I'm used to instantaneous news. So it was frustrating that I couldn't get the news releases up right away."

Owen implemented an online media room primarily to put control of media content into his own hands so that he could get news releases up onto the site right away. "What we've tried to do is have a lot of information," he says. "The media is looking for more than the news release. They want images, both high-resolution and Web versions, and they want fact sheets, so we've put a lot of time into our online press kit. Journalists are looking for value-add on a corporate media site, and it needs to be much more than just a news release. We also focus on optimizing our pages for keywords and phrases so that Google and the other search engines can find the information."

As Owen launched the Cingular Wireless online media room, he found that the bloggers who cover the wireless and gadget space make heavy use of the content. "You have to hit the bloggers several different ways because it is a crowded marketplace for ideas," he says. "So we send bloggers our news releases and encourage them to make use of the online media room."

The Cingular Wireless online media room was severely tested during the 2005 hurricane season; Cingular serves customers in hard-hit areas such as New Orleans and Florida. "It was a real eye-opener for us because we didn't realize the power of getting a lot of news up onto the site really quickly," Owen says. "It was the first series of storms of that severity in the Internet age. Even though we were updating the pages every few hours, we just couldn't get information out quickly enough. I drew from my experience at CNN. As more and more journalists have access to the Internet, it is up to us to get information to them in a timely manner. We have to 'feed the beast,' and there's no way to do that without an online media room that I can post to directly. Going through the Information Technology department wouldn't have worked."

To make it easy for all kinds of people, not just journalists, to get updates, Owen created a new URL that pointed to specific pages in the Cingular online media room. "We built out a section for consumers by working with our Customer Services people that included a Frequently Asked Questions section and toll-free numbers for customers," he says. "We answered questions like 'What if I can't pay my bill this month?' We found that the media room was also a vehicle for communications with our employees who were in the disaster area. It was an extraordinary time and extraordinary measures were needed, and we were very pleased with the responses."

Based on his site statistics, the Cingular Wireless online media room clearly serves more people than just journalists. "We know that a large number of consumers find their way to the media room, because the online media room had 18,000 page views at its peak on September 5, 2005," he says. "And our average was 10,000 page views per day in the month of September 2005 compared to a baseline of about 2,000 page views per day in August 2005, before the storms."

As the Cingular Wireless example shows, it is important for all companies to be prepared to communicate during emergency situations. While the highest traffic to the Cingular Wireless online media room in recent years was during the 2005 hurricane season, the numbers they got during this period helped Owen to see a trend that was already happening: that consumers *do* think to use online media rooms when they need information.

Really Simple Marketing: The Importance of RSS Feeds in Your Online Media Room

To provide alternative content routes, many organizations use digital delivery methods, including email newsletters for journalists and bloggers and RSS feeds, as part of their online media rooms; this pushes content directly to the media and other interested people. Smart organizations are using RSS (Really Simple Syndication) to easily update prospects, customers, investors, and the media, but too few organizations are using this simple marketing technique for sharing valuable information.

RSS feeds can (and should) be added to most parts of your web site. But because they are essentially subscription mechanisms to regularly updated content, many organizations have the RSS subscription page as part of the online media room and use it as a primary way to deliver news release content. Companies such as Microsoft, IBM, and Intel syndicate information via RSS feeds to reach specific external audiences such as the media, Wall Street analysts, customers, partners, distributors, and resellers. For example, Intel[7] offers a suite of feeds that includes Intel Products, Intel Press Room, Intel Investor Relations, Software at Intel, Networking and Communications, Intel Reseller Center, and IT@Intel. It also offers country-specific RSS feeds from Brazil, China, France, Germany, Italy, Japan, Russia, and others. How cool is it that interested people subscribe to just-right corporate information from Intel in the same way that they subscribe to media feeds from major newspaper and magazine sites and those of independent bloggers? This is just another example of how the main currency of online marketing is excellent content delivered in the way that people demand.

The online media room is a place where many people congregate, not just journalists. It is one place on your organization's web site that *you can control*, without interference, approval processes, and IT support, so it presents a terrific opportunity for marketing and PR people to get content out into the marketplace. On the Web, success equals content. And one of the easiest ways to get content into the market is via an online media room with RSS feeds.

---

[7] www.intel.com/intel/rss.htm

19

The New Rules for Reaching the Media

As the Web has made communicating with reporters and editors extremely easy, breaking through using the online methods everyone else uses has become increasingly difficult. These days, you can find the email addresses of reporters in seconds, either through commercial services that sell subscriptions to their databases of thousands of journalists or simply by using a search engine. Unfortunately, way too many PR people are spamming journalists with unsolicited and unrelenting commercial messages in the form of news releases and untargeted broadcast pitches. I hate to say it, but among the many journalists I speak with, the PR profession has become synonymous with spammers. For years, PR people have been shotgun-blasting news releases and blind pitches to hundreds (or even thousands) of journalists at a time—without giving any thought to what each reporter actually covers—just because the media databases the PR people subscribe to make it so darn simple to do.

> Barraging large groups of journalists with indiscriminate PR materials is not a good strategy to get reporters and editors to pay attention to you.

Nontargeted, Broadcast Pitches Are Spam

As I've said, I get dozens of news releases, pitches, and announcements from PR agency staffers and corporate communications people every week. Like all journalists, my email address is available in many places: in the articles I write, on my blog, in my books, and at the *EContent* magazine web site (I'm a contributing editor). That easy availability means that my address has also been added to various databases and lists of journalists. Unfortunately, my email address also gets added (without my permission) to many press lists that PR agencies and companies compile and maintain; whenever they have a new announcement, no matter what the subject, I'm part of the broadcast message. *Ugh.* The PR spam approach simply doesn't work. Worse, it brands your organization as one of the "bad guys."

Okay, that's the depressing news. The good news is that there are effective "new rules" approaches that work very well to get your messages into the hands (and onto the screens) of reporters so they will be more likely to write about you. Don't forget that reporters are always looking for interesting companies, products, and ideas to write about. They want to find you. If you have great content on your web site and your online media room, *reporters will find you* via search engines.

Try to think about reaching journalists with ways that aren't just one-way spam. Pay attention to what individual reporters write about by reading their stories (and, better yet, their blogs) and write specific and targeted pitches crafted especially for them. Or start a real relationship with reporters by commenting on their blogs or sending them information that is not just a blatant pitch for your company. Become part of their network of sources, rather than simply a shill for one company's message. If you or someone in your organization writes a blog in the space that a reporter covers, let him know about it, because what you blog about may become prime fodder for the reporter's future stories. Don't forget to pitch bloggers. Not only does a mention in a widely read blog reach your buyers, reporters and editors read these blogs for story ideas and to understand early market trends.

The New Rules of Media Relations

The Web has changed the rules. If you're still following the traditional PR techniques, I'm sure you're finding that they are ineffective. To be much more successful, consider and use The New Rules of Media Relations:

- Nontargeted, broadcast pitches are spam.
- News releases sent to reporters in subject areas they do not cover are spam.
- Reporters who don't know you yet are looking for organizations like yours and products like yours—make sure they will find you on sites such as Google and Technorati.
- If you blog, reporters who cover the space will find you.
- Pitch bloggers, because being covered in important blogs will get you noticed by mainstream media.
- When was the last news release you sent? Make sure your organization is "busy."
- Journalists want a great online media room.
- Include video and photos in your online media room.
- Some (but not all) reporters love RSS feeds.
- Personal relationships with reporters are important.
- Don't tell journalists what your product does. Tell them how you solve customer problems.
- Does the reporter have a blog? Read it. Comment on it. Track back to it (send a message whenever you blog on a subject that the reporter blogged about first).
- Before you pitch, read (or listen to or watch) the publication (or radio program or TV show) you'll be pitching to.
- Once you know what a reporter is interested in, send her an individualized pitch crafted especially for her needs.

Blogs and Media Relations

Getting your organization visible on blogs is an increasingly important way not only to reach your buyers, but also to reach the mainstream media that cover your industry, because reporters and editors read blogs for story ideas. Treat influential bloggers exactly as you treat influential reporters—read their stuff and send them specifically targeted information that might be useful to them. Offer them interviews with your executives and demonstrations or samples of your products. Offer to take them to lunch.

"For a company or product that sells into a niche, you'll never get noticed by editors at major publications like the *Wall Street Journal*, but you will get niche bloggers to be interested in you," says Larry Schwartz, president of

Newstex,[1] a company that syndicates blogs for distribution to millions of people in corporations, financial institutions, and government agencies. "For example, if you are in the consumer technology business, getting your product mentioned in Gizmodo[2] and getting a link back to your site from Gizmodo are probably more important than even a mention in the *Wall Street Journal*. Increasingly, the way for people to find out about products is through blogs, and you often get a link to your web site, too. It used to be that the moment of truth was when somebody went to the store to find your product. Now the moment of truth is a link to your site from a blog."

Pitching influential bloggers as you would pitch mainstream media is an important way to get noticed in the crowded marketplace of ideas. But even more effective is having your own blog so that bloggers and reporters find you. "Blogging gives me a place in the media community to stand out," says John Blossom, president of Shore Communications Inc.,[3] a research and analysis company. Blossom has been blogging since March 2003 and writes about enterprise publishing and media markets. "In ways that I didn't expect, my blog has allowed me to become a bit of a media personality. I've been picked up by some big bloggers, and that makes me aware that blogging is a terrific way to get exposure, because the rate of pickup and amplification is remarkable. The press reads my blog and reaches out to me for quotes. Sometimes I'm quoted in the media by a reporter who doesn't even speak with me. For example, a reporter from the *Financial Times* recently picked up a quote and used it in a story—based on my blog alone."

Launching Ideas with the U.S. Air Force

The web sites of the United States Air Force are chock-full of photos, video, and articles written by Air Force Public Affairs officers, all serving to provide the media with information they need to craft a story. These officers don't sit around all day writing press releases and pitching the media with story ideas. Rather, they publish information themselves, information that generates interest from reporters.

---

[1] www.newstex.com/
[2] www.gizmodo.com/
[3] www.shore.com/

"Instead of pushing things out, people are finding us and our information," says Captain Nathan Broshear, director of public affairs at 12th Air Force (Air Forces Southern), the Air Force component to U.S. Southern Command and based at Davis-Monthan Air Force Base in Tucson, Ariz. Broshear is no stranger to working with mainstream media representatives, having previously managed hundreds of Iraq and Afghanistan-based reporters in that high-pressure war zone environment.

"People are finding our web sites to be valuable. For example, many reporters are currently interested in the Predator, Global Hawk, and Reaper systems, our unmanned aerial vehicles. And when they see the pages on our site about Predator and Reaper, then they know whom to contact."

For example, Technical Sergeant Eric Petosky, who works with Broshear in Public Affairs, wrote a story called "Global Hawk flying environmental mapping missions in Latin America, Caribbean,"[4] which he posted on the site with photos.[5] When a reporter becomes interested in a system like the Global Hawk, he or she can find the information on the site. "The Air Force is a big organization, and if a reporter goes to the Pentagon, it is hard to find the right person. We write stories so reporters can envision what their angle might look like." And together with the stories, photos, and videos is the necessary contact information for getting in touch with the appropriate Air Force Public Affairs staff member.

The published information about unmanned aerial systems proved valuable when *60 Minutes*, the weekly CBS television magazine, became interested in the story. Broshear teamed with Captain Brooke Brander, chief of public affairs at Creech Air Force Base in Nevada (where the pilots of the unmanned systems are based), to help lay the groundwork for the story. They worked with *60 Minutes* producers for more than five months. *Drones: America's New Air Force* aired on *60 Minutes* on May 10, 2009, with Lara Logan reporting on the increasing use of drones in the battlefield.

Another success story from Broshear's use of online content to help reporters involves Operation New Horizons in Guyana. Operation New Horizons is part of an Air Force program to build infrastructure, partnerships, and relationships in other countries. "The Air Force is building a school and a clinic while providing free medical care for about 100,000 people," Broshear says.

---

[4] www.12af.acc.af.mil/news/story.asp?id=123147613
[5] www.12af.acc.af.mil/photos/index.asp

"We partner with nongovernmental organizations to make certain the local school, clinics, and doctors have what they need to continue providing services even after U.S. military members depart."

To get the story out to both the local community in Guyana and people back in the United States, Broshear works with those on the ground to create content reporters can draw from to craft their stories—without the need for constant contact from public affairs staff. "We post photos onto Flickr[6] and have a Facebook page[7] and a blog[8] written by people on the ground. And what's interesting is that the blogs get three times more traffic than our main pages. The newspapers in the local communities are pulling photographs from the sites. After we introduce the projects and key military personalities to the local media the first time through a press release or visit to the construction sites, we don't need to do anything, because the media are pulling information from the blog that we created."

As you know if you've read this far, the importance of creating valuable content (photos, video, news stories) and posting it on your site is the theme of this book. When you create that content, you reach people who are looking for what you have to offer. Broshear reminds us how sometimes those people are members of the mainstream media and great content can serve as the catalyst to getting the coverage your organization desires. "Here in U.S. Air Force Public Affairs, we're not launching missiles," he says. "We're launching ideas." And those ideas lead to major stories in top-tier media.

How to Pitch the Media

As marketers know, having your company, product, or executive appear in an appropriate publication is great marketing. That's why billions of dollars are spent on PR each year (though much of it's wasted, I'm afraid). When your organization appears in a story, not only do you reach the publication's audience directly, you also can point your prospects to the piece later, using reprints or Web links. Media coverage means legitimacy. As I've said, broadcast spamming of the media doesn't work. But sometimes you really want to target a specific publication (your hometown paper, perhaps). So, what should you do?

---

[6] www.flickr.com/photos/newhorizonsguyana/
[7] www.facebook.com/pages/New-Horizons-Guyana/47224824949
[8] http://newhorizonsguyana.blogspot.com/

- *Target one reporter at a time.* Taking the time to read a publication and then crafting a unique pitch to a particular journalist can work wonders. Mention a specific article he wrote and then explain why your company or product would be interesting for the journalist to look at. Make certain to target the subject line of the email to help ensure that it gets opened. Recently I got a perfectly positioned pitch crafted especially for me from a company that provides a Web-based sales-lead qualification and management system. The PR person had read my blog and knew what I was interested in, so I emailed back within minutes to set up an interview with the company's CEO.

- *Help the journalist to understand the big picture.* Often it's difficult to understand how some widget or service or organization actually fits into a wider trend. You make a journalist's job much easier if you describe the big picture of why your particular product or service is interesting. Often this helps you get mentioned in the reporter's future articles or columns about trends in your space.

- *Explain how customers use your product or work with your organization.* Reporters hear hundreds of pitches from company spokespeople about how products work. But it's much more useful to hear about a product in action from someone who actually uses it. If you can set up interviews with customers or provide written case studies of your products or services, it will be much easier for journalists to write about your company.

- *Don't send email attachments unless asked.* These days, it is a rare journalist indeed who opens an unexpected email attachment, even from a recognized company. Yet many PR people still distribute news releases as email attachments. Don't do it. Send plain-text emails instead. If you're asked for other information, you can follow up with attachments, but be sure to clearly reference in the email what you're sending and why, so the journalist will remember asking for it.

- *Follow up promptly with potential contacts.* Recently I agreed to interview a senior executive at a large company. An eager PR person set it up, and we agreed on date and time. But I never got the promised follow-up information via email, which was supposed to include the telephone number to reach the executive. Needless to say, the interview didn't happen. Make certain you follow up as promised.

- *Don't forget, it's a two-way street—journalists need you to pitch them!* The bottom line is that reporters want to know what you have to say. It is unfortunate that the spam problem in PR is as big as it is, because it makes journalists' jobs more difficult.

As an illustration of this last point, a company executive I met at a conference made a comment on a new trend that gave me a brilliant idea for my column. I was delighted, because it made my life easier. Thinking of column subjects is hard work, and I need all the help I can get. The executive's company fit in perfectly with the column idea, and I'll use his product as the example of the trend he told me about. Without the conversation, the column would never have been written—but a straight product pitch wouldn't have worked. We reporters need smart ideas to do our job. Please.

"The single most effective thing PR people do is read what I write and send me personalized, smart pitches for stories that I am actually likely to write," says Peter J. Howe, a business reporter for the *Boston Globe*.[9] Howe has been at the *Globe* for 20 years and spent the last 7 years covering telecommunications, the Internet, energy, and, most recently, airline companies. Howe prefers to be pitched by email, with a subject line that helps him to know it's not spam. "'PR pitch for *Boston Globe* Reporter Peter Howe' is actually a very effective way to get my attention. If you're getting literally four or five hundred emails a day like I am, cute subject lines aren't going to work and in fact will likely appear to be spam."

Howe's biggest beef with how PR people operate is that so many have no idea what he writes about before they send him a pitch. "If you simply put 'Boston Globe Peter Howe' into a Google.com/news search and read the first ten things that pop up, you would have done more work than 98 percent of the PR people who pitch me," he says. "It's maddening how many people in PR have absolutely no sense of the difference between what the *Boston Globe* covers and what, say, *Network World* or *RCR Wireless News* or the *Nitwitville Weekly News* covers. And I don't mean to sound like a whining diva; the bigger issue is that if you're not figuring out what I cover and how before you pitch me, you are really wasting your own time."

Howe also encourages people to try to think big. "If you have a small thing to pitch, pitch it. But try to also think of the bigger story that it can fit into a page-one or a Sunday section front story," he says. "That could even wind up meaning your company is mentioned alongside three or four of your

---

[9] http://boston.com/

competitors, but wouldn't you rather be mentioned in a page-one story than in a 120-word news brief?"

There is no doubt that mainstream media are still vital as a channel for your buyers to learn about your products. Besides all the people who will see your company, product, or executive's name, a mention in a major publication lends you legitimacy. Reporters have a job to do, and they need the help that PR people can provide to them. But the rules have changed. To get noticed, you need to be smart about how you tell your story on the Web—and about how you tell your story to journalists.

20 Search Engine Marketing

Search engine marketing is remarkable because, unlike almost every other form of marketing, it does not rely on the interruption technique. Think again for a moment about what I've called "old-rules" marketing and its interruption-based advertising techniques. As I've discussed in previous chapters, the old rules required you to interrupt TV viewers and hope they weren't already flipping to another channel; or to interrupt people as they sorted through the mail and hope your message wouldn't go into the junk-mail pile; or to interrupt magazine readers and hope they would pause at your stinky pull-out perfume sample. These days, ads are everywhere—on signs along the highway, on the sides of supermarket carts, in elevators. These interruptions are not only annoying for consumers (and harmful to a brand if overdone); they are also increasingly ineffective.

Now think about how you use search engines. Unlike nontargeted, interruption-based advertising, the information that appears in search engines after you've typed in a phrase is content you actually want to see. You're actually *looking* for it. This should be a marketer's dream-come-true.

Here's something very important to consider: *This entire book is about search engine marketing.* Please pause to reflect on that. If you followed the New Rules of Marketing and PR as outlined in these pages, you will have built a fantastic search engine marketing program! You started with your buyer personas, then you built content especially for these buyers—content that talks about the problems they face in the words and phrases they actually use. Then you delivered the content in the online forms they prefer (podcasts, blogs, e-books, web sites, and so on). This terrific content designed especially for your buyers will be indexed by the search engines and . . . that's it. You already have a terrific search engine marketing program!

But even a great program can benefit from focused enhancements, so in this chapter we'll talk about how to further develop and improve your search engine marketing strategies. Let's start with a few basic definitions:

- *Search engine marketing* means using search engines to reach your buyers directly. Search engines include general search engines such as Google and Yahoo! as well as vertical market search engines that are specific to your industry or to the people you are trying to reach.
- *Search engine optimization (SEO)* is the art and science of ensuring that the words and phrases on your site, blog, and other online content are found by the search engines and that, once found, your site is given the highest ranking possible in the *natural search results* (i.e., what the search engine algorithm deems important for the phrase entered).
- *Search engine advertising* is when a marketer *pays* to have advertising appear in search engines when a user types in a particular phrase that the marketer has "purchased." Usually this advertising comes in the form of small text ads appearing next to the natural search results for a particular search term. Google AdWords[1] and Yahoo! Search Marketing[2] are the two large search engine advertising programs. Marketers bid to have their ads appear based on keywords and phrases, competing against others who want the same phrases. Your ad will appear somewhere in the list of ads for that phrase based on a formula used by the search engine that takes into account two main factors: how much you are willing to bid (in dollars and cents) for each person who clicks the ad, plus your click-through rate (the number of people who click your ad divided by the number of people who see it in the search results).

Making the First Page On Google

Colin Warwick, signal integrity product manager in the Design & Simulation Software division of Agilent Technologies, is responsible for marketing

---

[1] https://adwords.google.com/

[2] http://searchmarketing.yahoo.com/

software to help engineers overcome limitations in high-speed digital connections. As he was working on marketing plans, he came to the realization that traditional business-to-business marketing techniques like trade shows are expensive and increasingly ineffective. He also came to understand the importance of search engines for his business. "Everyone understands Google," he says. "Everybody can instantly see when you enter a phrase into Google if your competitors come up and you don't or vice versa."

The most important search term for Warwick's products is "signal integrity," and Agilent product information was coming up on the fifth page of results—clearly not ideal. So Warwick set out to make Agilent appear at the top of the search results by creating a blog focused on signal integrity.[3] Everything, from the name and URL of the blog to the excellent content, was designed to appeal to the buyer personas interested in this topic and to drive solid search engine rankings. "There are only 50,000 signal integrity engineers in the entire world, and our average sale is about $10,000 with a six-month sales cycle," Warwick says. "While the competitors show their brochures, we have a valuable blog. It helps a great deal to have such valuable information, both for search engine results and in the selling process."

Warwick says that executives at Agilent were very supportive of his starting the blog, but there were some guidelines that he had to work within. "The company said I could blog but that the IT department would not support it," he says. "So I needed to create the blog outside of the company domain. I was required to follow some very commonsense rules: don't mention the competition, link to the Agilent terms of service and privacy policy, and include a copyright notice. It has been a very good experience. Companies need to trust that employees will do the right thing and let people blog."

The results have been very encouraging. "Many customers say that they like the blog, and our salespeople tell prospects about it," Warwick says. "Having a blog allows me to be spontaneous. For example, I can put diagrams up very quickly and let people know valuable information. If we needed to put content on the corporate site, it would take three days. With the blog I can get into a conversation in just five minutes."

So what about the search results? On Google, Warwick's blog is now on the first page of results for the phrase "Signal Integrity" (at the number four position

---

[3] http://signal-integrity-tips.com/

when I checked). "Prior to starting the blog, the company products page was ranked number 44 on Google," Warwick says. "That's a huge improvement."

But there are many added benefits to blogging that took Warwick by surprise. "Trade magazine journalists read the blog, and they include links to it in their blogrolls," he says. "And I am making great Web connections. For example, I asked Paul Rako, an important journalist at *EDN* [a news and information source for Electronics Design Engineers], to moderate a panel for me, and he did because he knows me from the blog."

Search Engine Optimization

In my experience, people often misunderstand search engine marketing because there are a slew of SEO firms that make it all seem so darned complicated. To add to the problem, many (but certainly not all) SEO firms are a bit on the shady side, promising stellar results from simply manipulating keywords on your site. Perhaps you've seen the spam email messages of some of these snake-oil salesmen (I've received hundreds of unsolicited email messages with headlines like: "Top Search Engine Rankings Guaranteed!"). While many search engine marketing firms are completely reputable and add tremendous value to marketing programs, I am convinced that the single best thing you can do to improve your search engine marketing is to focus on building great content for your buyers. Search engine marketing should not be mysterious and is certainly not trickery.

However, the many intricacies and nuances that can make good search engine marketing great are beyond the scope of this small chapter. Many excellent resources can help you learn even more about the complexities of search engine marketing and especially search engine algorithm factors such as the URL you use, placement of certain words within your content, tags, metadata, inbound links, and other details. These resources also add to our discussion in Chapter 10 of how to identify appropriate keywords and phrases. A great place to start understanding search engine optimization is Search Engine Watch,[4] where you will find resources and active forums to explore. I also recommend a book called *Search Engine Marketing, Inc.* by Mike Moran and Bill Hunt. To learn more about search engine advertising,

---

[4] http://searchenginewatch.com/

start with the tutorials and Frequently Asked Questions pages of the Google AdWords and Yahoo! Search Marketing sites.

The Long Tail of Search

Perhaps you've already tried search engine marketing. Many marketers have. In my experience working with many organizations, I've learned that search engine marketing programs often fail because the marketers optimize on general keywords and phrases that do not produce sufficiently targeted results. For example, someone in the travel business might be tempted to optimize on words like *travel* and *vacation*. I just entered "travel" into Google and got 124 million hits. It is virtually impossible to get to the top of the heap with a generic word or phrase like "travel," and even if you did, that's not usually how people search. *It is ineffective to try to reach buyers with broad, general search terms.*

You have a choice when you create search engine marketing programs. One method is to optimize on and advertise with a small number of words and phrases that are widely targeted, in order to try to generate huge numbers of clicks. Think of this approach as an oceangoing drag fishing boat with huge nets used to harvest one species of fish. Sure, you capture thousands of fish at a time, but you throw away all that are not the species you're after, and it is a very expensive undertaking.

True success comes from driving buyers directly to the actual content they are looking for. Several years ago I wanted to take my family on vacation to Costa Rica, so I went to Google and typed in "Costa Rica Adventure Travel." I checked out a bunch of sites at the top of the search results (both the natural search results and the advertisements) and chose one that appealed to me. After exchanging several emails to design an itinerary, I booked a trip for several thousand dollars, and a few months later I was checking out howler monkeys in the rainforest. This is how people *really* search (for what they are looking for on the Web, not for howler monkeys). If you're in the Costa Rican adventure travel business, don't waste resources optimizing for the generic term "travel." Instead, run search engine marketing programs for phrases like "Costa Rica ecotourism," "Costa Rica rainforest tour," and so on.

The best approach is to create separate search engine marketing programs for dozens, hundreds, or even tens of thousands of *specific* search terms that people might actually search on. Think of this approach as rigging thousands of individual baited hooks on a long line and exposing them at precisely the right time to catch the species of fish you want. You won't catch a fish on each and every hook. But with so many properly baited hooks, you will certainly catch lots of the fish you are fishing for.

Carve Out Your Own Search Engine Real Estate

One rarely discussed but very important aspect of search engine marketing is choosing product and company names so that they will be easy to find on the Web via search engines. When you consider the name of a new company, product, book, rock band, or other entity that people want to find on the Web, you typically go through a process of thinking up ideas, getting a sense of whether these names sound right, and then perhaps seeing if you can copyright or trademark the ideas. I would suggest adding one more vital step: You should run a Web search to see if anything comes up for your proposed name; I urge you to drop the name idea if there are lots of similarly named competitors—even if the competition for the name is in a different industry. Your marketing goal should be that when someone enters the name of your book or band or product, the searcher immediately reaches information about it. For example, before I agree to a book title, I make certain those names are not being used in any other way on the Web. It was important for me to "own" my titles on the search engines; searching on *Eyeball Wars*, *Cashing in with Content*, *The New Rules of Marketing and PR*, and *World Wide Rave* brings up only my books plus reviews, articles, or discussions about them.

Many people ask me why I use my middle name in my professional endeavors, and I've had people accuse me of being pretentious. Maybe I am a *bit* pretentious, but that's not why I use my middle name—Meerman. The reason is simple: There are so many other David Scotts out there. One David Scott walked on the moon as commander of Apollo 15. Another is a six-time Iron Man Triathlon Champion. Yet another is a U.S. Congressman from Georgia's 13th district. Good company, all, but for clarity and search engine optimization purposes, I chose to be unique among my fellow David Scotts by becoming David Meerman Scott.

The lesson here is that if you want to be found on the Web, you need a unique identity for yourself, your product, and your company to stand out from the crowd and rise to prominence on search engines. As you are thinking of names to use for marketing, test them out on the search engines first and try to carve out something that you alone can own.

Web Landing Pages to Drive Action

Although I won't try to cover all the details of search engine marketing, I definitely want to touch on one of the most common mistakes made by search engine marketers. Most people focus a great deal of time on keyword and phrase selection (that's a good thing!), and they also do a good job of ensuring that their organization ranks highly for those phrases by optimizing the site and/or purchasing search engine advertising. But most organizations are terrible at building a landing page—the place people go after they click on a search hit.

Think back to our last example. As I was planning my Costa Rican vacation, many of the sites that were ranked highly for the phrase I entered were a kind of bait and switch. I thought I would be getting targeted information about Costa Rican travel and was instead taken to a generic landing page from a big travel agency, an airline, or a hotel chain. No, thanks, I'm not interested. I wanted information on Costa Rica, not an airline or hotel chain, and so I clicked away in a second. Because I wanted information about Costa Rican adventure travel, I chose the landing page that had the best information, one from an outfit called Costa Rica Expeditions.[5] This means that you're likely to need dozens or hundreds of landing pages in order to implement a great search engine marketing program.

> You need to build landing pages that have specific content to enlighten and inform the people who just clicked over to your site from the search engine.

Marketing with Web landing pages is one of the easiest and most cost-effective ways to get a message read by a target market, and it's a terrific tool for moving buyers through the sales cycle. A landing page is simply a place to

---

[5] www.costaricaexpeditions.com/

publish a targeted message for a particular demographic that you're trying to market to, and they are used not only in search engine marketing but other Web marketing programs as well. For example, landing pages are ideal for describing special offers mentioned on your web site or calls to action referenced in another content page (such as a blog or e-book). Landing pages also work well for telling an organization's story to a particular target market, promoting a new product offering, or providing more information to people who link from your news releases. Marketing programs such as search engine optimization are—to borrow an idea from the classic sales cycle definition—designed to attract the prospect's attention. The landing page is where you take the next step; once you've got your audience's attention, you must generate and develop customer interest and conviction, so that your sales team gets a warm lead ready to be worked to a closed sale, or so you can point people to an e-commerce page where they can buy your product right away.

Effective landing page copy is written from, you guessed it, the buyers' perspective, not yours. Landing pages should provide additional information to searchers, information based on the offer or keyword they just clicked on. Many successful organizations have hundreds of landing pages, each optimized for a particular set of related search engine marketing terms.

Don't make the mistake so many organizations do by investing tons of money into a search engine advertising program (buying keywords) and then sending all the traffic to their homepage. Because the homepage needs to serve many audiences, there can never be enough information there for each search term. Instead, keep the following landing page guidelines in mind:

- *Make the landing page copy short and the graphics simple:* The landing page is a place to deliver a simple message and drive your prospect to respond to your offer. Don't try to do too much.
- *Create the page with your company's look, feel, and tone:* A landing page is an extension of your company's branding, so it must adopt the same voice, tone, and style as the rest of your site.
- *Write from the prospect's point of view:* Think carefully of who will be visiting the landing page, and write copy for that demographic. You want visitors to feel that the page speaks to their problems and that you have a solution for them.
- *A landing page is communications, not advertising:* Landing pages are where you communicate valuable information. Advertising gets people

to click to your landing page, but once a prospect is there, the landing page should focus on communicating the value of your offering to the buyer.

- *Provide a quote from a happy customer:* A simple testimonial on a landing page works brilliantly to show people that others are happy with your product. A sentence or two with the customer's name (and affiliation if appropriate) is all you need.

- *Make the landing page a self-contained unit:* The goal of a landing page is to get prospects to respond to your offer so you can sell to them. If you lose traffic from your landing page, you may never get that response. Thus, it is sometimes better to make your landing page a unique place on the Web and *not* provide links to your main web site.

- *Make the call to action clear and easy to respond to:* Make certain you provide a clear response mechanism for those people who want to go further. Make it easy to sign up or express interest or buy something.

- *Use multiple calls to action:* You never know what offer will appeal to a specific person, so consider using more than one. In the business-to-business world, you might offer a white paper, a free trial, an ROI calculator, and a price quote all on the same landing page.

- *Ask only for necessary information:* Don't use a sign-up form that requires your prospects to enter lots of data—people will abandon the form. Ask for the absolute minimum you can get away with—name and email address only, if you can, or perhaps even just email. Requiring any additional information will reduce your response rates.

- *Don't forget to follow up!:* Okay, you've got a great landing page with an effective call to action, and the leads are coming in. That's great! Don't drop the ball now. Make certain to follow up each response as quickly as possible.

Search Engine Marketing in a Fragmented Business

The market that Scala, Inc.[6] serves is so fragmented, people can't even agree on what the product category is called: Digital Signage, Digital In-Store Merchandising, Electronic Display Networks, Electronic Billboards, or any of a

---

[6] www.scala.com/

dozen other names are used. And to make the marketing challenge even more difficult, potential customers in this market don't congregate at any one tradeshow, magazine, or Web portal. And that's just the way Gerard Bucas, president and CEO of Scala, Inc., likes it because he uses search engine marketing to his advantage to reach buyers. "We pioneered the digital signage industry," he says. "Our services are used for retail, corporate communications, factory floor, and many other diverse business applications." Because Scala serves so many buyers in diverse market segments, there is no clear decision maker. In retail it's the marketing department. In corporate communications for internal purposes it is often the CEO or the HR department. And the company serves many verticals such as cruise lines, casinos, and more. "Since we can't possibly advertise in so many different places to reach these people, we rely on a great web site with a strong focus on search engine marketing."

Bucas says it is critical to use the same terminology as his target market and to include industry terms that lead to an appropriate Scala page. "We continuously monitor the top 30 to 40 search terms that people look for when they search for us on the Net," he says. "When we find new terms, we write content that incorporates those terms, and as the term becomes more important, we expand on the content."

For Bucas, effective search engine marketing means understanding his buyers and creating compelling content using important keywords and phrases and then getting each one indexed by the search engines. "For example, *digital signage* is one of our search terms," he says. "We want to be at the top of the results. But we also care about similar phrases such as *digital sign* and *digital signs*. Each of the terms gives different results. It's amazing to me."

The Scala site includes detailed product content, client case studies, and information on how digital signage is used in different industries. "Regular news releases and case studies are all intended to bring search engines to us," he says. "With case studies and news releases, we're getting some phrases into the market that we don't often use, which cause some long tail results with the search engines."

Scala has a lead-generation system using search engines to drive buyers to landing pages where traffic converts into leads that are funneled into the company's reseller channel. In this system, the company gathers names through offers (such as a free demo DVD[7]) on each landing page. "Our

---

[7] www.scala.com/demodvd/

resellers love us because we're constantly pumping them with new leads," Bucas says. "We effectively help to generate business for them, so they become very loyal to us. Our partners see the value of the lead generation." According to Bucas, the lead system, which manages more than 4,000 open sales leads at any one time, automates communication at particular points in the sales process by sending email to prospects.

The success Scala enjoys shows how a well-executed content strategy on the Web will deliver buyers to landing pages who are actually looking for a product. "We are growing very rapidly," Bucas says. "And a large percentage of the business comes from Web leads—certainly more than 50 percent of our business comes from the Web."

If you're planning on implementing the ideas in this book, you will, by definition, be doing search engine marketing. You will understand your buyers and create great, indexable Web content especially for them. The best search engine marketing comes from paying attention to and understanding your buyers, not from manipulating or tricking them. Still, once you've executed a great content strategy, adding effective landing pages and focusing on the long tail of search terms will give you an even more powerful marketing asset that will generate results for months and years to come.

21 Make It Happen

Thanks for hanging in there with me and for reading this far! When I speak to audiences and run seminars on the New Rules of Marketing and PR, this is the point at which many people are stimulated to get out there and make it happen. They want to start a blog right away or shoot a video for YouTube or generate some news releases or begin buyer persona research in preparation for writing a marketing and PR plan that will guide them to create a content-rich web site. If that describes you, great!

But in the audiences of my seminars and speeches there is always another group of people who tend to feel a bit overwhelmed. There is just too much information, they say, or too many new and unfamiliar ideas. If you are in this category, you might be thinking that the people profiled in the book were able to figure out things that are just too complex and time-consuming for you to tackle, especially given your already hectic schedule. Hey, we all have stuff on our plates, and for most of us, implementing the ideas in the book will represent an addition to our workload. But here's one of the greatest things about the *New Rules of Marketing and PR*: You can implement these ideas in bits and pieces! In fact, I don't expect anybody to implement *all* the ideas here. I don't do *that* many of them myself (okay, I admitted it—don't tell). Yes, I have a blog, and it is very important to me. I'm on Twitter and I create some original videos. But I don't have a podcast, and I'm not on MySpace or LinkedIn. I just do what I can and what works for me. And so should you.

Unlike a linear, offline marketing campaign where you must take a methodical, step-by-step approach leading up to a big "release day," the Web is

. . . well, it's a *web*. You can add to the Web at any time because it is iterative, not linear. Think about the last print advertisement you or others in your organization did. Everything had to be perfect, requiring thorough proofreading, tons of approvals from your colleagues (or your spouse), lengthy consultation with a bunch of third parties such as advertising agencies and printers, and—above all—lots of money. Your neck was on the line if there was a screw-up, so you obsessed over the details. Contrast that with a Web content initiative that you can implement quickly, get people to check out live, and make changes to on the fly. It really is much less stressful to create an online program. If you create a Web page that doesn't work for you, you can just delete it. You can't do that with a print ad or direct-mail campaign. So I would urge you to think about how you might *selectively* experiment with the ideas in these pages rather than fret about coordinating them all and trying to get everything right on the first go.

Many organizations I've worked with have found that an excellent approach is first to do some buyer persona research. By reading the publications that your buyers read, perhaps attending a Webinar that they attend, reading a few of the blogs in the space, and maybe interviewing a few buyers, you can narrow down the book's large list of techniques to determine the most appropriate Web-based marketing and PR initiatives for you and work on them first.

Others have found that the best way to get started is to add a few pages of targeted thought leadership content for an important buyer personas to an existing web site (perhaps with links from the homepage). What's great about this approach is that you don't have to redesign your site; all you are doing is *adding* some valuable content to what you already have. That's easy, right?

Still another first step might be to read the blogs in your market and begin to comment on them in order to coax your blogging voice out of its shell. Once you feel comfortable, you can take the plunge by creating your own blog. But the good news is that you don't need to show the world right away—you can password protect it and share it with only a few colleagues at first. Then, with some feedback you can tweak your approach and finally remove the password protection, and you're off. The important thing is to just get out there. Remember, on the Web, you are what you publish.

Getting the Help You Need (and Rejecting What You Don't)

As you develop a strategy to get started implementing the new rules of marketing and PR, you may find occasions to call on others for help. Many people tell me that they occasionally need the services of an agency to provide them with some extra people to help execute a big project. But I constantly hear that they have difficulty finding people skilled in using the ideas that we've been discussing in this book. Still others report that well-meaning colleagues and meddlesome bosses have an annoying tendency to look over shoulders and second-guess them as they start a blog, get going on Twitter, or begin filming YouTube videos. Add to that mix the fact that, in many larger organizations, the legal department tends to muck things up with nitpicky rules about what can and cannot be said. If these sound like some of the problems that you're encountering, fear not! Here are some things you can do to get the help you need, while rejecting what you don't.

The One Question to Ask a Prospective Agency

An increasingly large cadre of self-proclaimed new marketing "gurus" claim to be really good at generating attention using the new rules of marketing and PR. In addition, I've noticed that in the past several years, established agencies of all kinds are adding departments devoted to social media. Traditional advertising agencies that have focused on television commercials for decades all of a sudden claim to be experts on blogging. Public relations agencies skilled in relating to the media somehow become instant experts in Facebook and Twitter. So how do you navigate all these potential partners if you really do need some help implementing the ideas in this book?

Many people ask me if I can recommend an agency that understands social media or to help them evaluate agencies that claim to be good at this kind of work. My answer to the challenge of finding good people is simple: Ask the prospective agency to show you its social media presence. Ask about such things as blogs, Twitter feeds, YouTube videos, e-books, web sites, Facebook profiles, and any other stuff they have. Make it an open-ended question. This is not to say that an agency needs to be active in every medium, but if they are worthy of taking your money to advise you on the use of these tools, then they should certainly be out there using them. My theory is that if an agency can't blog or tweet or create interesting content for themselves with any success, then they're going to come up short for clients as well. The answers can be fascinating! All of a sudden many of these self-styled experts clam up and don't say much. This vetting tool eliminates 95 percent of agencies who just plain stink at understanding social media.

When Lawyers Get in the Way

At many larger organizations, the legal department is heavily involved in all marketing and communications initiatives, frequently requiring every blog post and press release to be vetted by a lawyer. In some extremes, corporate legal eagles even forbid employees from starting a blog or participating on Twitter and Facebook at work. I've found that the restrictions come down to two factors: *ignorance of social media* and *a lack of trust in employees*.

Since legal people don't usually understand social media themselves (and don't use them for business in their jobs), they naturally respond by just slapping on controls. After all, their job is to reduce risks within a company, so it's temptingly simple to just say "no." This is especially true in companies that mistrust their employees. However, if a company trusts its employees and understands that social media can be a powerful way to do business, then it is the lawyers' job to create an environment where you can do what you know is right.

My recommendation is to work with your managers and your organization's legal team (and perhaps the human resources department as well) to create guidelines that you can operate under. Your company's guidelines should include advice about how to communicate in any medium, including face-to-face conversations, presentations at events, email, social media, online forums and chat rooms, and other forms of communication. Rather than putting restrictions on social media (that is, the technology), it's better to focus on guiding the way people behave. The corporate guidelines should include statements that employees can't reveal company secrets, can't use inside information to trade stock or influence prices, and must be transparent and provide their real name and affiliation when communicating. You might take a look at how IBM, a company on the forefront of embracing employee use of social media, has handled this issue. IBM has developed a set of social computing guidelines[1] for employees' use of blogs, wikis, social networks, virtual worlds, and social media. You may have to take the lead on creating the guidelines at your organization, but the effort will be worth it.

Bring a Journalist onto Your Team

A remarkable convergence is upon us right now, creating a perfect opportunity for you to hire someone with the skills that you need. Sadly, many mainstream media outlets are reducing their pools of staff journalists. Newspapers, magazines, radio, and television outlets face tough economic challenges and, unfortunately, that means that many talented reporters and editors have been (or will be) laid off. I've had a chance to speak with several dozen journalists recently, and many are downcast about career prospects.

At the same time, people like you in many different organizations—corporations, nonprofits, government agencies, and educational institutions—finally understand the value of the ideas we've explored in this book. One of the best ways to create great Web content is to actually hire a journalist, either full-time or part-time, to create it. Journalists, both print and broadcast, are great at understanding an audience and creating content that buyers want to consume—it's the bread and butter of their skill set. I'm not talking about PR and media relations here. This isn't about hiring a journalist to write press releases and try to get his or her former colleagues to write or broadcast about you. Instead, I'm talking about having journalists create stories just as they are doing now—but for a corporation, a government agency, a nonprofit, or an educational institution instead of a media outlet.

Editors are in demand by companies that create terrific online media rooms, like the one over at Cisco Systems.[2] What better background than journalism could there be for the person running your online media efforts? Is running the Cisco newsroom really that much different than running a newspaper site? For much smaller organizations, maybe it makes sense to hire a freelance print journalist to help you with that e-book. Again, what better way to create valuable information than to hire someone who has done it for years? Sure, Web marketing represents a dramatically different job

---

[1] www.ibm.com/blogs/zz/en/guidelines.html

[2] http://newsroom.cisco.com/dlls/index.html

description from, say, beat reporter. Yet times (including the *New York Times*) are changing. And that gives smart marketers an amazing opportunity to hire people with the skills we need.

Managing Your Colleagues and Bosses

If I may be so bold as to boil down into one word thousands of conversations I've had over the past 10 years, as well as my five years' worth of blogging and the entire contents of this book, it would be this: *attention*. Entrepreneurs, CEOs, and business owners want people to pay attention to their company. Marketers, PR pros, advertisers, and salespeople are on the payroll to generate attention. Hopefully this book opened your eyes to a new approach to this classic problem.

I've identified four main ways to generate attention in today's marketing landscape. We've discussed them throughout these pages, so this list is not really new, but seeing them all collected together will give us some fresh perspective for dealing with people who might be skeptical or meddlesome.

1. *You can buy attention with advertising* such as television commercials, magazine and newspaper ads, the Yellow Pages, billboards, trade show floor space, direct mail lists, and the like.
2. *You can get attention from the editorial gatekeepers* at radio and TV stations, magazines, newspapers, and trade journals.
3. *You can have a team of salespeople generate attention one person at a time* by knocking on doors, calling people on the telephone, sending personal emails, or waiting for individuals to walk into your showroom.
4. *You can earn attention online by using the ideas in this book*, creating something interesting and publishing it online for free: a YouTube video, blog, research report, series of photos, Twitter stream, e-book, Facebook fan page, or other piece of Web content.

In order to understand the motivations of your colleagues and bosses as they offer advice and give you unwanted criticism, I recommend that you know and understand these four means of generating attention. And you should understand the point of view of the person you are talking to about attention, especially when their inevitable pushback about earning it in new ways surfaces.

You see, most organizations have a corporate culture centered around one of these approaches. For examples, P&G primarily generates attention through advertising, Apple via PR, EMC via sales, and Zappos via the new rules of marketing & PR. Often the defining organizational culture springs from the founder or CEO's strong point of view. So if the CEO came up through the sales track, all attention problems are likely to become sales problems. Chances are that your colleagues and bosses did not come up via the social media track, nor have they likely read this book. The point is, you'll have to *convince* your boss to invest in social media, because it's likely he or she doesn't consider it the most important way of gaining attention. Most organizations overspend on advertising and sales and underinvest in social media, but nearly all organizations should be doing some combination of each. If you can help your bosses and colleagues understand this trend, they'll probably lighten up a little.

Great for Any Organization

There's no doubt that your organization will benefit from your getting out there and creating Web content in whatever form you're most comfortable with. But I'm also convinced that no matter who you are or what you do, your professional and personal life will improve, too. If you are an innovator using the ideas in this book, it may lead to greater recognition in the office. And if you're like many bloggers and podcasters I know, you will derive a therapeutic benefit as well. It's fun to blog and tweet and it makes you feel good to get your ideas out into the world.

If you're like me, you will prefer to write rather than create audio or video content. But I know plenty of people who hate to write and have created terrific photo, video, and audio content to reach buyers. And it works for all kinds of organizations: corporations, nonprofits, rock bands, and politicians. People often say to me: "But I'm just a _____ [fill in the blank with *pastor, painter, lawyer, consultant, sales representative, auto dealer, real estate agent*], why should I blog or create a podcast?" My answer is that you'll not only reach your buyers directly with targeted content, you'll have fun, too—Web content is for everyone, not just big companies.

In fact, one of my all-time favorite examples of success with the *New Rules of Marketing and PR* comes from an unlikely marketer: the pastor of a church in Washington, D.C. But his isn't a typical church, because he doesn't actually have a church building. Instead he uses video technology, blogs, podcasts, and the Web to tell stories and build a spiritual community both on- and offline.

"The church should be using technology to reach people; that's what Gutenberg did in the fifteenth century with the printing press," says Mark Batterson, lead pastor of National Community Church (also known as TheaterChurch.com), a multisite church in the Washington, D.C., metropolitan area that conducts five services per week in three nontraditional locations. "Most churches have a church building, but we feel that a building can be an obstacle to some people, so we do church in theaters and have built the largest coffee house in the Washington, D.C., area."

What distinguishes National Community Church is Batterson's approach of embracing technology and Web marketing and applying it to church. The TheaterChurch.com site[3] includes a content-rich web site, podcasts of the weekly services, a motivational Webcast series, video, an email newsletter, Batterson's extremely popular Evotional blog[4] (tagline: "Spirit Fuel"), and Twitter feed.[5] "The greatest message deserves the greatest marketing," Batterson says. "I am challenged that Madison Avenue and Hollywood are so smart at delivering messages. But I believe that we need to be just as smart about how we deliver our messages."

Attendance at National Community Church exceeds 1,000 adults in an average weekend; 70 percent of them are single people in their twenties. "I think we attract twenty-somethings because our personality as a church lends itself to twenty-somethings," Batterson says. "Our two key values are authenticity and creativity. That plays itself out in the way we do church. I think that church should be the most creative place on the planet. The Medieval church had stained glass to tell the gospel story to the churchgoers, who were mostly illiterate. We use the movie studio to tell the story to people. We use video to add color and to add flavor to what we do. If Jesus had video in his day, it wouldn't surprise me if he made short films."

Batterson's focus on the web site, podcasts, and online video (as well as video at the services) means that National Community Church staff members have some unique job titles, including "media pastor," "digital pastor," and

[3] http://theaterchurch.com/
[4] www.evotional.com/
[5] http://twitter.com/MarkBatterson

"buzz coordinator." "We want to use technology for really good purposes," Batterson says. "Our web site and my blog are our front door to National Community Church. The site is a virtual location in a sense. We have a lot more people who listen to the podcast and watch the Webcast than who go to the services, so it is a great test drive for people. They can get a sense of the church before they arrive physically."

Batterson has gained online fame well beyond the Washington, D.C., area—his blog is followed by tens of thousands of readers all over the world, and the podcast is one of the fastest growing church podcasts in America. He also wrote a book that was released in October 2006, called *In a Pit with a Lion on a Snowy Day: How to Survive and Thrive When Opportunity Roars.* "Blogging cuts six degrees of separation into three," he says. "I write knowing that my audience is another pastor in Australia, a housewife in Indiana, my friends, and people in Washington, D.C. Marketing through my blog is powerful. For example, last week I did a blog post about my book and asked my blogging friends to also post about it. We went up to number 44 on the Amazon best-seller list, and Amazon sold out of the book that day. They just ordered another thousand copies."

Batterson's enthusiasm for how churches can use the Web has caught the attention of thousands of other church leaders who follow his blog. "The two most powerful forms of marketing are word of mouth and what I call word of mouse. A guy named John Wesley, who founded the Methodist church, traveled 250,000 miles on horseback and preached something like 40,000 sermons. With one click of the mouse, I preach that many sermons with my podcast—that's word of mouse. It is about leveraging the unique vehicles on the Web. The message has not changed, but the medium has changed. We need to continually find new vehicles to get the messages out."

Now It's Your Turn

Isn't the power of Web content and the *New Rules of Marketing and PR* something? Here's a guy who's a church leader *without* a church building, and through innovative use of a blog, a podcast, and some video, he has become a leader in his field. He's got a bestselling book and tens of thousands of devoted online followers. Whether you're religious or not, you've got to be impressed with Batterson's business savvy and with the way the new rules have helped him reach his buyers.

You can do it, too. It doesn't matter what line of work you're in or what group of buyers you're trying to reach. You can harness the power of the Web to reach your target audience directly.

If you're like many of my readers, my consulting clients, and the people who attend my seminars, you have colleagues who will argue with you about the new rules. They will say that the old rules still apply. They will tell you that you need to spend big bucks on advertising. They will tell you that the only way to do PR is to get the media to write about you. By now you know that they are wrong. If I haven't convinced you myself, surely the 50 or so innovative people profiled in these pages must have. Go on. Be like the people you met in this book—get out there and make it happen!

Acknowledgments for the Second Edition

First, a disclosure: Because I do advisory work, run seminars, and do paid speaking gigs in the world that I write about, there are inevitable conflicts. I have friends in some of the organizations that I discuss in this book, as well as on my blog and on the speaking circuit, and I have run seminars or advised several of the companies mentioned in the book.

I would like to offer my special thanks and gratitude to Robert Scoble, co-author of *Naked Conversations*, for writing the terrific Foreword to this book.

At John Wiley & Sons, my publisher Matt Holt and my editor Shannon Vargo have steered me through the publishing business with wit and wisdom. We've now done three books together and more are on the way. Also at Wiley, thanks to Kim Dayman, Beth Zipko, Cynthia Shannon, Peter Knapp, Deborah Schindlar, and Lori Sayde-Mehrtens for their help and support.

Kyle Matthew Oliver read every word of each draft of this book, and his sound advice and practical suggestions made it much better.

I would also like to thank the thousands of bloggers who added to the conversations around the *New Rules of Marketing and PR* by writing on their blogs, or by leaving intelligent and useful comments on my blog.

And especially, thank you to my wife Yukari and daughter Allison for supporting my work and understanding when I am under deadline or away from home speaking in some far-flung part of the world.

Index

About the Author

David Meerman Scott is a marketing strategist, keynote speaker, and seminar leader. The programs he has developed have won numerous awards and are responsible for selling over $1 billion in products and services worldwide.

For most of his career, Scott worked in the online news business. He was vice president of marketing at NewsEdge Corporation and held executive positions in an electronic information division of Knight-Ridder, at the time one of the world's largest newspaper companies. He's also held senior management positions at an e-commerce company, been a clerk on a Wall Street bond-trading desk, worked in sales at an economic consultancy, and acted in Japanese television commercials.

Today he spends his time evangelizing the new rules of marketing and PR by delivering keynote speeches to groups all over the world and teaching full-day workshops for companies, nonprofits, and government clients. His keynotes and seminars enlighten and inspire audiences through a combination of education, entertainment, and motivation. He has presented at hundreds of conferences and events in more than 20 countries on four continents.

A graduate of Kenyon College, Scott has lived in New York, Tokyo, Boston, and Hong Kong.

Check out his blog at www.WebInkNow.com or follow him on Twitter @dmscott.

Preview
World Wide Rave

Creating Triggers That Get Millions of People to Spread Your Ideas and Share Your Stories

A World Wide Rave!

What the heck is that?

A World Wide Rave is when people around the world are talking about you, your company, and your products. It's when communities eagerly link to your stuff on the Web. It's when online buzz drives buyers to your virtual doorstep. It's when tons of fans visit your Web site and your blog because they genuinely want to be there.

Rules of the Rave:

- Nobody cares about your products (except you).
- No coercion required.
- Lose control.
- Put down roots.
- Point the world to your (virtual) doorstep.

You can trigger a World Wide Rave: Just create something valuable that people want to share and make it easy for them to do so.

What happens when people can't stop talking online about you, your company, and your products? A World Wide Rave is born that can propel a brand or company to seemingly instant fame and fortune. How do you create one? By learning the secret to getting links, YouTube, Facebook, and blog buzz to drive eager buyers to your virtual doorstep. For free.

In *World Wide Rave*, David Meerman Scott, author of the award-winning hit book *The New Rules of Marketing and PR*, reveals the most exciting and powerful ways to build a giant audience from scratch.

The following is an excerpt from *World Wide Rave* by David Meerman Scott, from John Wiley & Sons.

Imagine you're the head of marketing at a theme park, and you're charged with announcing a major new attraction. What would you do? Well, the old rules of marketing suggest that you pull out your wallet. You'd probably spend millions to buy your way into people's minds, interrupting them with TV spots, billboards by the side of the highway, and other creative Madison Avenue advertising techniques. You'd also hire a big PR agency, who would beg the media to write about your attraction. The traditional PR approach requires a self-congratulatory press release replete with company muckety-mucks claiming that the new attraction will bring about world peace by bringing families closer together.

That's not what Cindy Gordon, vice president of New Media and Marketing Partnerships at Universal Orlando Resort, did when she launched The Wizarding World of Harry Potter. Other large entertainment companies would have spent millions of dollars to interrupt everyone in the country with old-rules approaches: Super Bowl TV ads, blimps, direct mail, and magazine ads. Instead, Gordon told just seven people about the new attraction.

And those seven people told tens of thousands.

Then mainstream media listened to those tens of thousands and wrote about the news in their newspaper and magazine articles, in TV and radio reports, and in blog posts. Gordon estimates that 350 million people around the world heard the news that Universal Orlando Resort was creating The Wizarding World of Harry Potter theme park.

All by telling just seven people.

When $7 = 350,000,000$

Recognizing that millions of fans around the world are passionate about all things Harry Potter, Gordon knew she could rely on a world wide rave to spread her story. After all, Harry is a global phenomenon. The series of books by author J.K. Rowling has been translated into 65 languages and has sold more than 325 million copies in more than 200 territories around the world. The films, produced by Warner Bros. Pictures, have grossed $3.5 billion world wide at the box office.

Gordon and her counterpart at Warner Bros. chose to launch The Wizarding World of Harry Potter by first telling the exciting news to a very small group of rabid fans. Seven people at the top Harry Potter fan sites, such as Mugglenet,[1] were hand-selected by Gordon's team, with Warner Bros. and Rowling herself providing input about the choices. These seven (affectionately referred to by Gordon's team as "the AP of the HP world") were invited to participate in a top-secret webcast held at midnight on May 31, 2007.

The webcast was hosted by Scott Trowbridge, vice president of Universal Creative, and featured Stuart Craig, the academy award-winning production designer for all the Harry Potter films. In the webcast, live from the "Dumbledore's Office" set at Leavesden Studios, Craig discussed how his team of 20 designers is bringing together The Wizarding World of Harry Potter theme park.

"If we hadn't gone to fans first, there could have been a backlash," Gordon says. She imagined the disappointment dedicated Harry Potter fans might feel if they learned about Universal Orlando's plans in, say, the *New York Times* rather than an insider fan site.

Soon after the webcast, the team sent an e-announcement to their in-house, opt-in email list of park guests so they could hear the news directly too. Team members also sent the e-announcement to friends and family. During the secret webcast, a Web micro-site[2] went live to provide a place for bloggers and the media to link to for information on the theme park, which is slated to open in late 2009 or early 2010. Visitors to the site learned that the park will feature immersive rides and interactive attractions, as well as experiential shops and restaurants that will enable guests to sample fare from the wizarding world's best known establishments.

Because Gordon's team launched The Wizarding World of Harry Potter through social media—putting fans first—they were able to run the entire promotion in-house, with a very small marketing budget (covering the

[1] www.mugglenet.com/app/category/show/76

[2] www.universalorlando.com/harrypotter/

webcast infrastructure and the micro-site production) and a tiny development team. They did not hire an agency, and they did no widespread outbound media relations, no marketing stunts, no CEO conference call, and no expensive advertising.

Of course, not all companies have Harry Potter on their team. But Gordon still accomplished a remarkable feat with an approach that most large organizations would not have taken. She told just seven people, and the power of the world wide rave she created led to 350 million people hearing the news.

Marketing Advice from Cindy Gordon, Vice President of New Media and Marketing Partnerships, Universal Orlando Resort

"Nimble companies are using the Web in ways that they could never do before. New media has created a new marketing environment where the old rules of marketing no longer apply. When you have a passionate fan base for your brand, the Internet is especially vital for going viral. Communicating to a small but powerful group of fans first online to enlist their support is a smart way to ensure positive coverage in the mainstream press. The power of the Internet makes it easier for people to fall in love with you faster. But beware—it also makes it easier for them to fall out of love with you faster. It's a double-edged sword. Listen constantly to what's being said about you. Social media technologies do not make a brand viral; they merely allow consumers to tell others about good brands. The main thing is to be different and relevant with your brand. And when you have that, the sheer power of the Internet can accelerate your brand. Traditional media takes weeks to build brand awareness and months to build preference. The Internet can make your brand famous literally overnight."

A Formula for Success

One of the coolest things about the Web is that when an idea takes off, it can propel a brand or company to seemingly instant fame and fortune. *For free.* Whatever you call it—viral, buzz, word-of-mouse, or word-of-blog— having other people tell your story, creating a *world wide rave* drives action. One person sends it to another, then that person sends it to yet another, and on and on.

The challenge for marketers is to harness the amazing power of the world wide rave. I hope this book helps you learn about other people's success so you can apply some of their ideas and lessons in your own efforts.

As you will learn, the formula for success includes a combination of some great—and free—Web content (a video, blog entry, interactive tool, or e-book) that provides valuable information (or is groundbreaking or amazing or hilarious or involves a celebrity), plus a network of people to light the fire and links that make your content very easy to share.

The *World Wide Rave* Empowers You

You and I are incredibly lucky.

For decades, the only way to spread our ideas was to buy expensive advertising or beg the media to write (or broadcast) about our products and services. But now our organizations have a tremendous opportunity to publish great content online—content that people *want* to know about and that they are *eager to share* with their friends, family, and colleagues.

The *World Wide Rave* is the single most empowering tool available to marketers today. I wrote this book so you can take advantage of the power of spreading ideas too. In it, I share ideas that will help you create your own idea spreading strategies and campaigns. These are the "new rules" I've used to create marketing programs that have sold more than a billion dollars' worth of products and services world wide.

I hope the following don't sound too self-promotional, but I am absolutely blown away by how well the world wide rave works, and I just want to share a few comments about how it's helped me:

- If you had Googled my full name, David Meerman Scott, a few years ago, you would have gotten zero hits. Now there are nearly 100,000 references, all talking about me and my ideas—and all the result of people sharing my ideas online.
- My first e-book, *The New Rules of PR: How to Create a Press Release Strategy for Reaching Buyers Directly*,[3] has been downloaded more than 250,000 times since it was released in early 2006, and it has led directly

---

[3] www.DavidMeermanScott.com/documents/New_Rules_of_PR.pdf

to hundreds of thousands of dollars in speaking engagements in the past couple of years.

- I spent almost no money promoting *The New Rules of Marketing and PR* when it came out in hardcover. Because of a world wide rave from more than 500 bloggers all over the planet who wrote about the book on their blogs, it sold nearly 30,000 copies in six months, making it the number one bestselling PR and Web marketing book in the world. As of this writing, the book is being translated into 19 languages.

- The power of a world wide rave—people sharing my ideas—led directly to members of the mainstream media finding me without me pitching them. I've had a front page quote in the *Wall Street Journal*, appeared on MSNBC and Fox, and had my ideas written about in magazines such as *BusinessWeek*, *Entrepreneur*, and *Publishers Weekly*, as well as many newspapers, radio shows, podcasts, and Webinars. *And the reporters and editors found me!*

Imagine how much I would have had to pay to get an equivalent number of people to pay attention via advertising and other old-rules approaches! Millions of dollars, perhaps.

That's the power of the world wide rave, and that's what I am excited to share with you in this book.

Success comes from self-publishing Web content that people want to share. It's not about gimmicks. It's not about paying an agency to interrupt others. It's about harnessing the world wide rave, the most empowering form of marketing there is.

Cindy Gordon of Universal Orlando Resort launched The Wizarding World of Harry Potter by publishing a micro-site and a webcast.

That's it. Using an idea spreading strategy, Gordon reached 350,000,000 people with two pieces of internally created Web content.

You can achieve similar success, and I'll show you how.

The rest of *World Wide Rave* contains more fascinating examples of success in which I'll introduce you to smart marketers and let them tell you, in their own words, what they did to succeed. And throughout, I'll provide specific advice on how you can launch your own YouTube videos, e-books, and other techniques that unleash the amazing power of the world wide rave to spread your ideas for free!

Preview
The New Rules of
Social Media book series

David Meerman Scott is editing a series of social media books for John Wiley & Sons.

The New Rules of Social Media series features books that expand on the ideas of Scott's bestseller, *The New Rules of Marketing & PR*, providing valuable insights and detail on the different aspects of social media marketing.

Each book in David Meerman Scott's *The New Rules of Social Media* series is written by social media experts addressing a topic within their realm of expertise. While some titles, like *Inbound Marketing: Get Found Using Google, Social Media, and Blogs*, cover broad topics, others are more specific, for example, *Get Seen: Online Video Secrets to Building Your Business*.

No matter what the business need relating to social media, *The New Rules of Social Media Series* offers an unprecedented resource.

Inbound Marketing: Get Found Using Google, Social Media, and Blogs

Brian Halligan and Dharmesh Shah

Stop pushing your message *out* and start pulling your customers *in*.

Traditional "outbound marketing" methods like cold-calling, email blasts, advertising, and direct mail are increasingly less effective. People are getting better at blocking these interruptions out using Caller ID, spam protection, TiVo, and so on. People are now increasingly turning to Google, social media, and blogs to find products and services. *Inbound Marketing* helps you take advantage of this change by showing you how to get found by customers online.

Inbound Marketing is a how-to guide to getting found via Google, the blogosphere, and social media sites.

- Improve your rankings in Google to get more traffic.
- Build and promote a blog for your business.
- Grow and nurture a community in Facebook, LinkedIn, Twitter, and so forth.
- Measure what matters and do more of what works online.

The rules of marketing have changed, and your business can benefit from this change. *Inbound Marketing* shows you how to get found by more prospects already looking for what you have to sell.

Get Seen: Online Video Secrets to Building Your Business

Steve Garfield

The era of online video has arrived—make it work for your business.

In 2008, the world of online video exploded. Hollywood got into the game, professional actors and writers joined in, and independent producers looked to find their niche. Now, companies are wide awake to the opportunities for product and brand promotion as well as customer engagement. So how do you want to fit into the new online video universe?

The must-have guide, *Get Seen* by Steve Garfield, the "Paul Revere of video blogging," offers a quick and complete toolkit to get you up to speed on the latest that online video and related media have to offer:

- Examines success stories of companies using online video
- Presents a series of plans and tools businesses can follow as they expand onto the social web

- Provides clear direction on how to record, edit, and export videos, where to post them, how to build a community around their content, and how to increase views by going viral

If you're ready to take full advantage of online video's many benefits, *Get Seen* is the one resource you need.

Social Media Metrics: How to Measure and Optimize Your Marketing Investment

Jim Sterne

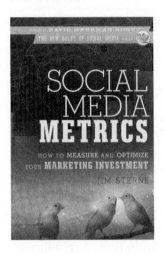

Whether you are selling online, through a direct sales force, or via distribution channels, what customers are saying about you online is now more important than your advertising. Social media is no longer a curiosity on the horizon but a significant part of your marketing mix.

A shift in philosophy, a modification in strategy, and brand new metrics are the keys to marketing success in this interconnected world. While other books explain why social media is critical and how to go about participating, this book focuses on measuring the success of your social media marketing efforts.

Success metrics in business are based on business goals where fame does not always equate to fortune. Having more Twitter followers or Facebook friends than the competition might not result in value. Read this book to determine which social media efforts are working for you, where to allocate more social media resources, and how to convince those who are afraid of "new things" that social media is a valuable business tool and not just a toy for the overly-wired.

Knowing what works and what doesn't is terrific, but only in a constant and unchanging world. *Social Media Metrics* is loaded with specific examples of specific metrics you can use to guide your social media marketing efforts as new means of communication.

Have David Meerman Scott Speak at Your Next Event!

David Meerman Scott is available for keynote presentations and full-day seminars. He is a frequent speaker at trade shows, conferences, and company events around the world.

Scott knows that sitting through a boring or off-topic speech is utterly painful. So he keeps things a bit edgy and uses stories and humor to make his points. But whenever he is in front of a group, be it six or six hundred, he provides valuable and actionable information about the new rules of marketing and PR, online thought leadership, and reaching buyers directly with Web content.

Satisfied audiences include: Cisco, HP, Microsoft, Ford Motor Company, Jackson Healthcare, Century 21, The New York Islanders, NASDAQ Stock Market, the Government of Ontario, McKesson, U.S. Air Force, U.S. Department of Defense, SAP, Digital River, Hill & Knowlton, Hanley Wood, Dow Jones, Business Marketing Association, National Investor Relations Institute, Milken Institute Global Conference, America Credit Union Conference, Self Storage Association, TS2, Giant Screen Theater Association, Realtors® Conference, and many, many more . . .

All of Scott's presentations are a combination of three things: education, entertainment, and motivation.

Visit www.DavidMeermanScott.com for more information.